TORCHWOOD

STATION ZERO

Titan
COMICS

TORCHWOOD: STATION ZERO

ISBN: 9781785856815

Published by Titan Comics, a division of Titan Publishing
Group, Ltd., 144 Southwark Street, London SE1 OUP.
Torchwood is a BBC Worldwide Production for the
BBC. Executive Producers: Russell T. Davies, Julie
Gardner, and Jane Tranter. Original series created by
Russell T. Davies, and developed and produced by BBC
Cymru Wales. BBC, 'TORCHWOOD' and the Torchwood
word marks, logos and devices are trademarks of the
British Broadcasting Corporation and are used under
license. BBC logo © BBC 1996. All rights reserved.
The Ice Maiden and its designated crewmembers are
© John Barrowman and Carole E. Barrowman 2012,
as originated in the Torchwood novel 'The Exodus
Code.' With the exception of artwork used for review
purposes, no portion of this book may be reproduced
or transmitted in any form or by any means, without
the express permission of the publisher Titan Comics
or the BBC. Printed in China. Titan Comics does not
read or accept unsolicited TORCHWOOD submissions
or ideas, stories, or artwork.

Front cover art: Claudia Caranfa
Back cover art: Kelly Yates

10 9 8 7 6 5 4 3 2 1

A CIP catalogue record for this title is available from
the British Library.

First published August 2017

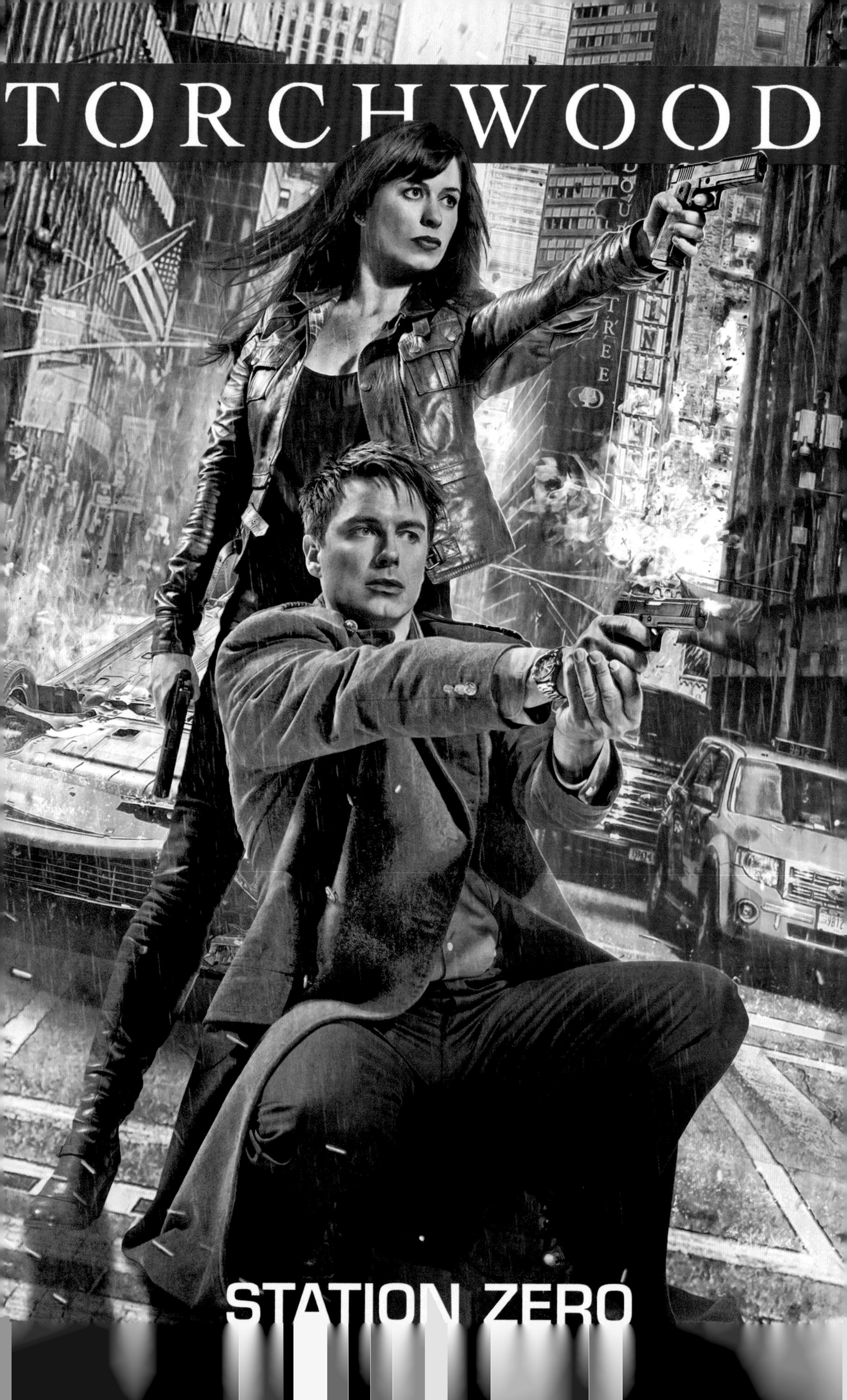
TORCHWOOD
STATION ZERO

SCRIPT
JOHN BARROWMAN &
CAROLE BARROWMAN

ART
NEIL EDWARDS

COLORISTS
NICOLA RIGHI, ALBERTO BUGIU,
ROD FERNANDES, DIJJO LIMA

LETTERERS
RICHARD STARKINGS AND COMICRAFT'S
JIMMY BETANCOURT

EDITOR
NEIL D. EDWARDS

TITAN COMICS

SENIOR EDITOR Martin Eden **SENIOR PRODUCTION CONTROLLER** Jackie Flook
PRODUCTION CONTROLLER Peter James **PRODUCTION SUPERVISOR** Maria Pearson
PRODUCTION ASSISTANT Natalie Bolger **ART DIRECTOR** Oz Browne **HEAD OF RIGHTS**
Jenny Boyce **PUBLISHING MANAGER** Darryl Tothill **PUBLISHING DIRECTOR** Chris Teather
OPERATIONS DIRECTOR Leigh Baulch **EXECUTIVE DIRECTOR** Vivian Cheung **PUBLISHER**
Nick Landau

www.titan-comics.com

For information on Rights, contact
Jenny Boyce at **Jenny.Boyce@titanemail.com**
Follow us on **Twitter: @comicstitan**
Become a fan on Facebook:
facebook.com/comicstitan

TITAN

BBC

TORCHWOOD

FOREWORD

EVERYTHING'S CHANGING. AGAIN.

For Captain Jack, Gwen, and the crew of the *Ice Maiden*, the conspiracy they're uncovering above the earth and below the Arctic will have far-reaching consequences. In fact, what happens in this story's conclusion will rock Torchwood's core. It's an outcome that puts a crazy complicated spin on Jack and Gwen's relationship (we've always thought *Torchwood* was, in part, a love story), and 'Station Zero''s outcome is one we imagined from the start.

Wait! No flipping to the final panels. Take your time. Travel first to the future to learn about Captains Jack and John's past at the Time Agency. Meet Docilis, a svelte and handsome flying alien with whom both Captains may have been, let's say, friendly. On the way to a final confrontation with the Navigators (and the gob-smacking conclusion), relish the blockbuster action that Neil Edwards' artistry brings to life. Savor the humor and the rapport among the characters, and, finally, discover the identity of our story's snarky narrator.

Along the way, we pay homage to one of our favorite lesser-known alien species in the *Doctor Who* universe – the Vervoids – and we give our usual nods and winks to *Torchwood*'s rich mythology.

Thanks for travelling with us on this adventure. Now, turn the page.

Cheers,

John and Carole

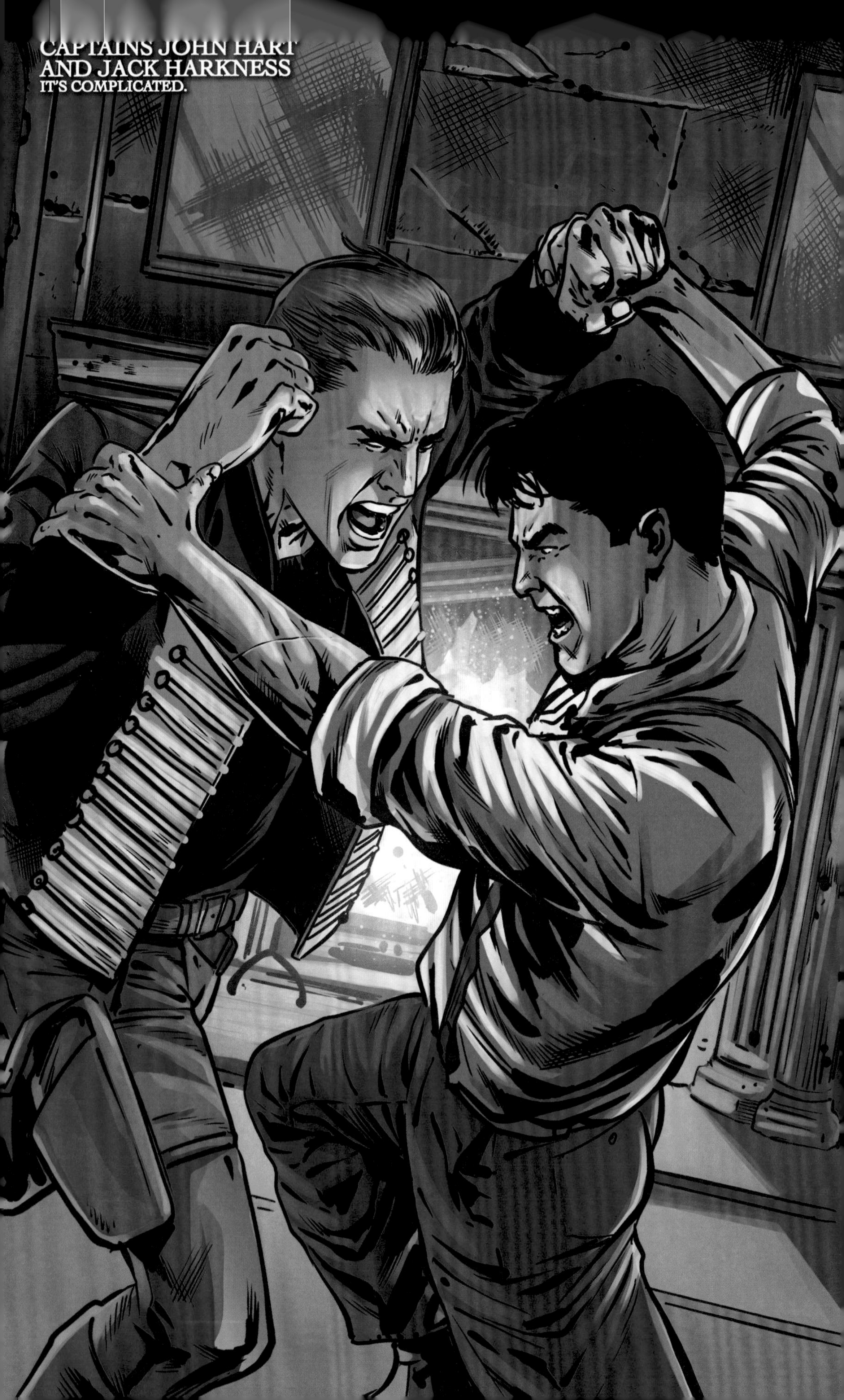
CAPTAINS JOHN HART
AND JACK HARKNESS
IT'S COMPLICATED.

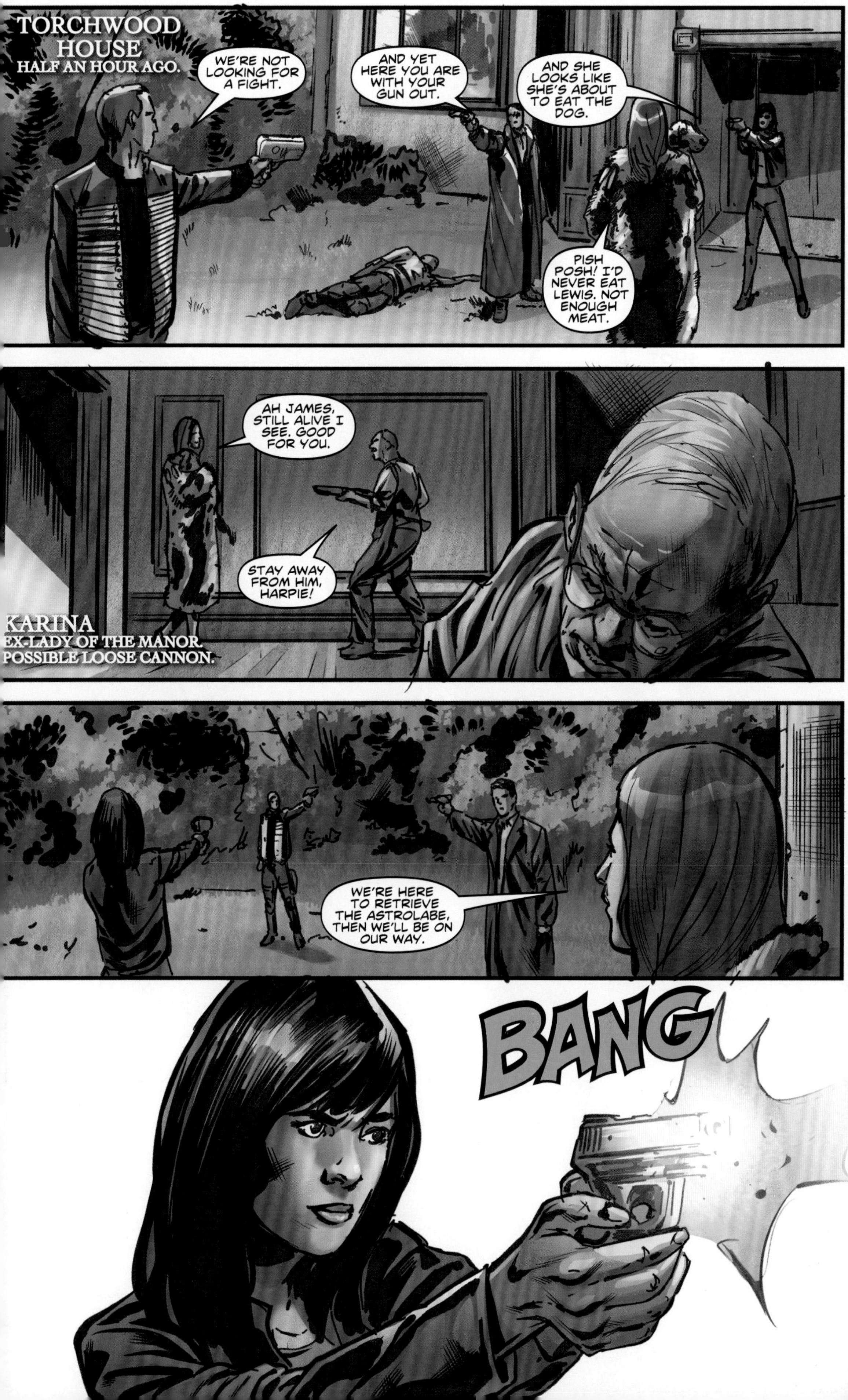
TORCHWOOD HOUSE
HALF AN HOUR AGO.
WE'RE NOT LOOKING FOR A FIGHT.
AND YET HERE YOU ARE WITH YOUR GUN OUT.
AND SHE LOOKS LIKE SHE'S ABOUT TO EAT THE DOG.
PISH POSH! I'D NEVER EAT LEWIS. NOT ENOUGH MEAT.
AH JAMES, STILL ALIVE I SEE. GOOD FOR YOU.
STAY AWAY FROM HIM, HARPIE!
KARINA
EX-LADY OF THE MANOR.
POSSIBLE LOOSE CANNON.
WE'RE HERE TO RETRIEVE THE ASTROLABE, THEN WE'LL BE ON OUR WAY.
BANG

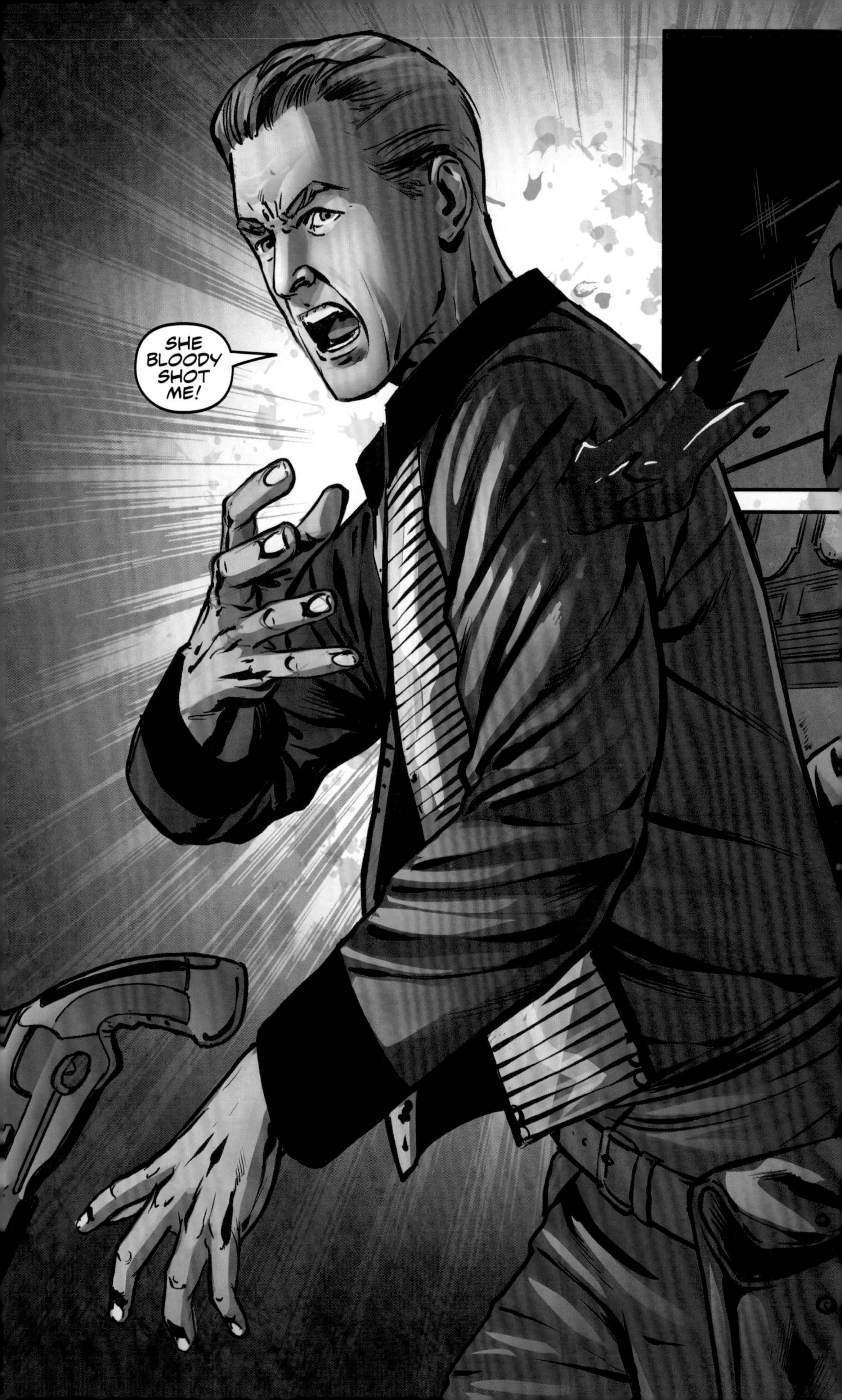
SHE BLOODY SHOT ME!

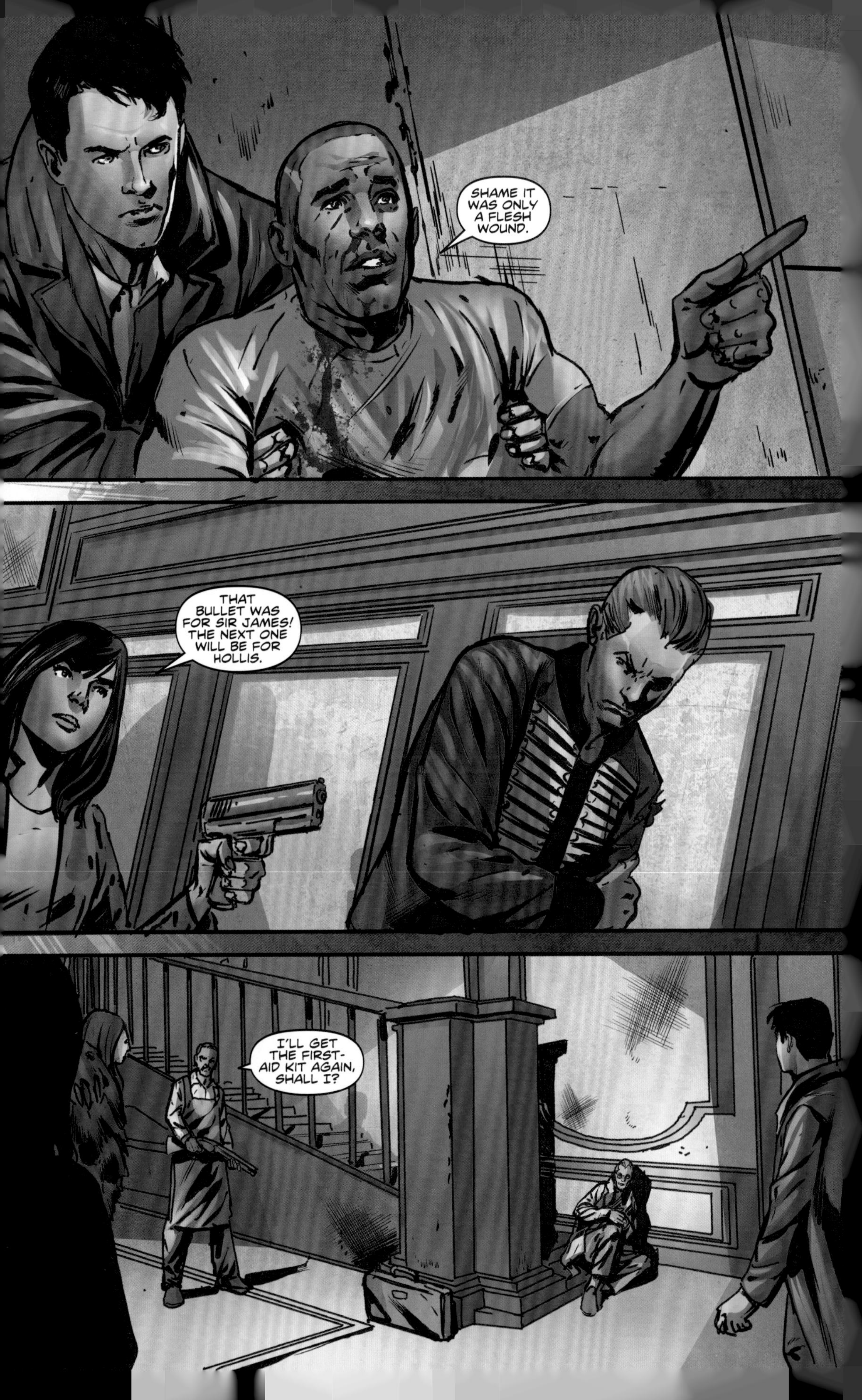
SHAME IT WAS ONLY A FLESH WOUND.
THAT BULLET WAS FOR SIR JAMES! THE NEXT ONE WILL BE FOR HOLLIS.
I'LL GET THE FIRST-AID KIT AGAIN, SHALL I?

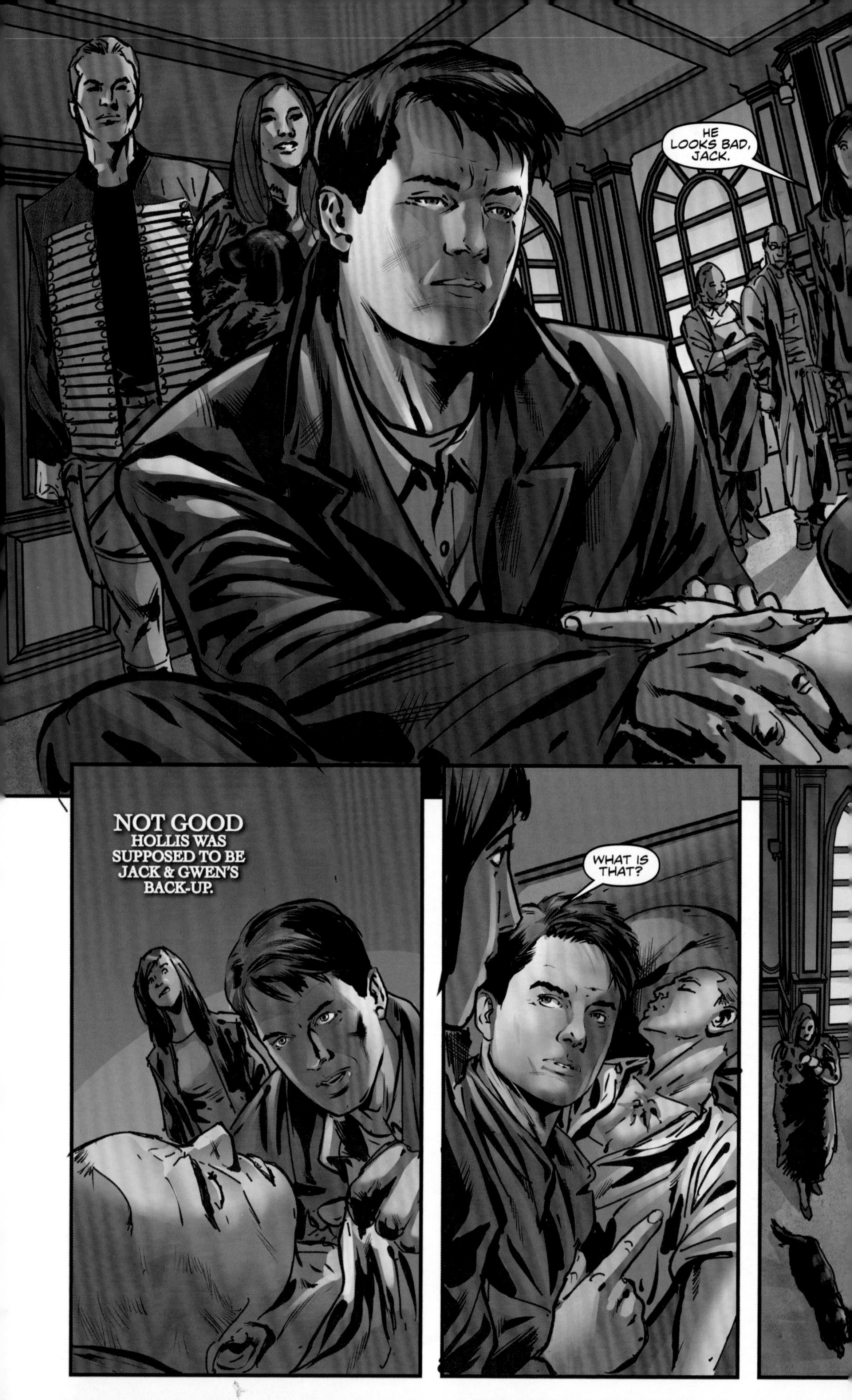
HE LOOKS BAD, JACK.
NOT GOOD
HOLLIS WAS SUPPOSED TO BE JACK & GWEN'S BACK-UP.
WHAT IS THAT?

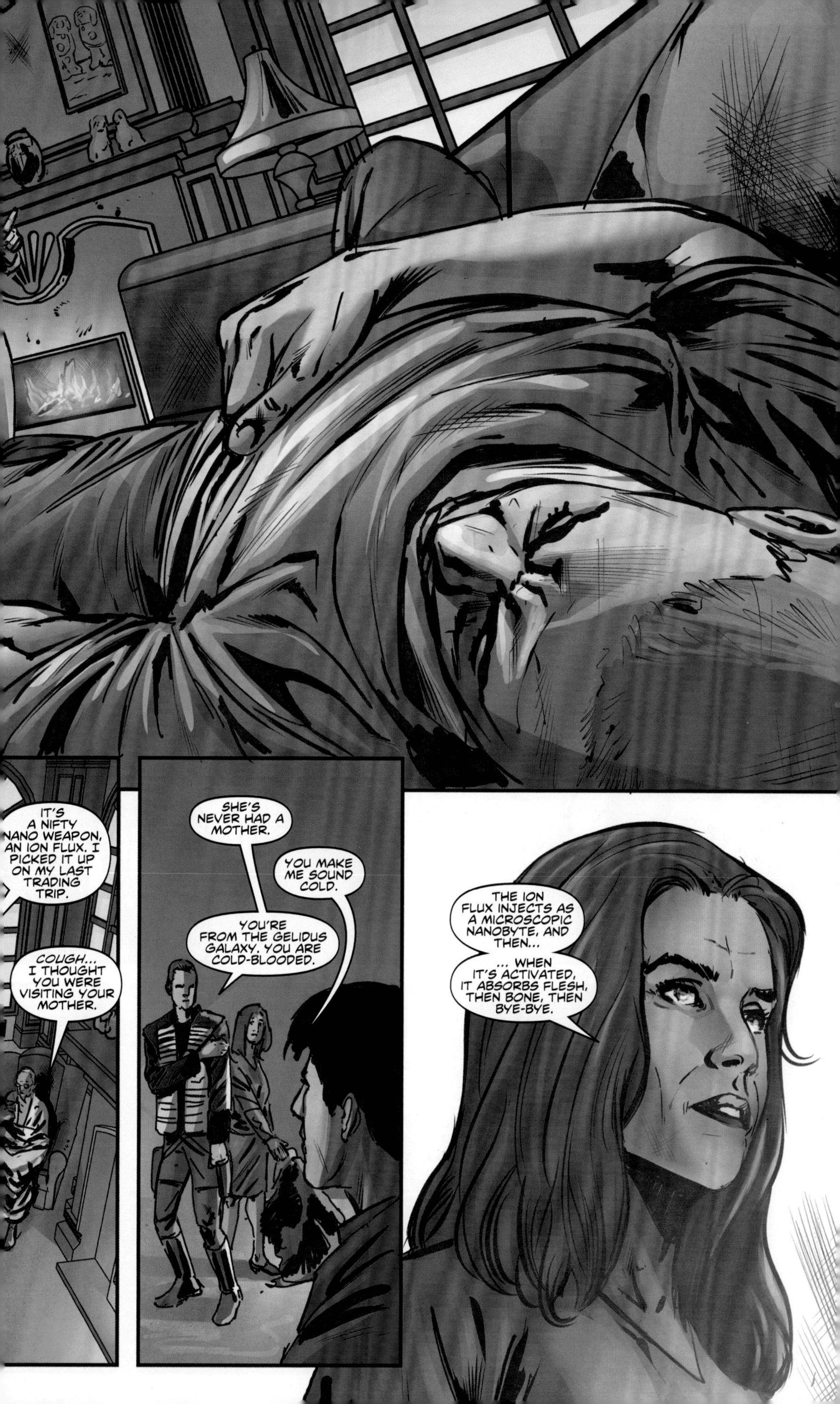
IT'S A NIFTY NANO WEAPON, AN ION FLUX. I PICKED IT UP ON MY LAST TRADING TRIP.
COUGH... I THOUGHT YOU WERE VISITING YOUR MOTHER.
SHE'S NEVER HAD A MOTHER.
YOU MAKE ME SOUND COLD.
YOU'RE FROM THE GELIDUS GALAXY. YOU ARE COLD-BLOODED.
THE ION FLUX INJECTS AS A MICROSCOPIC NANOBYTE, AND THEN...
... WHEN IT'S ACTIVATED, IT ABSORBS FLESH, THEN BONE, THEN BYE-BYE.

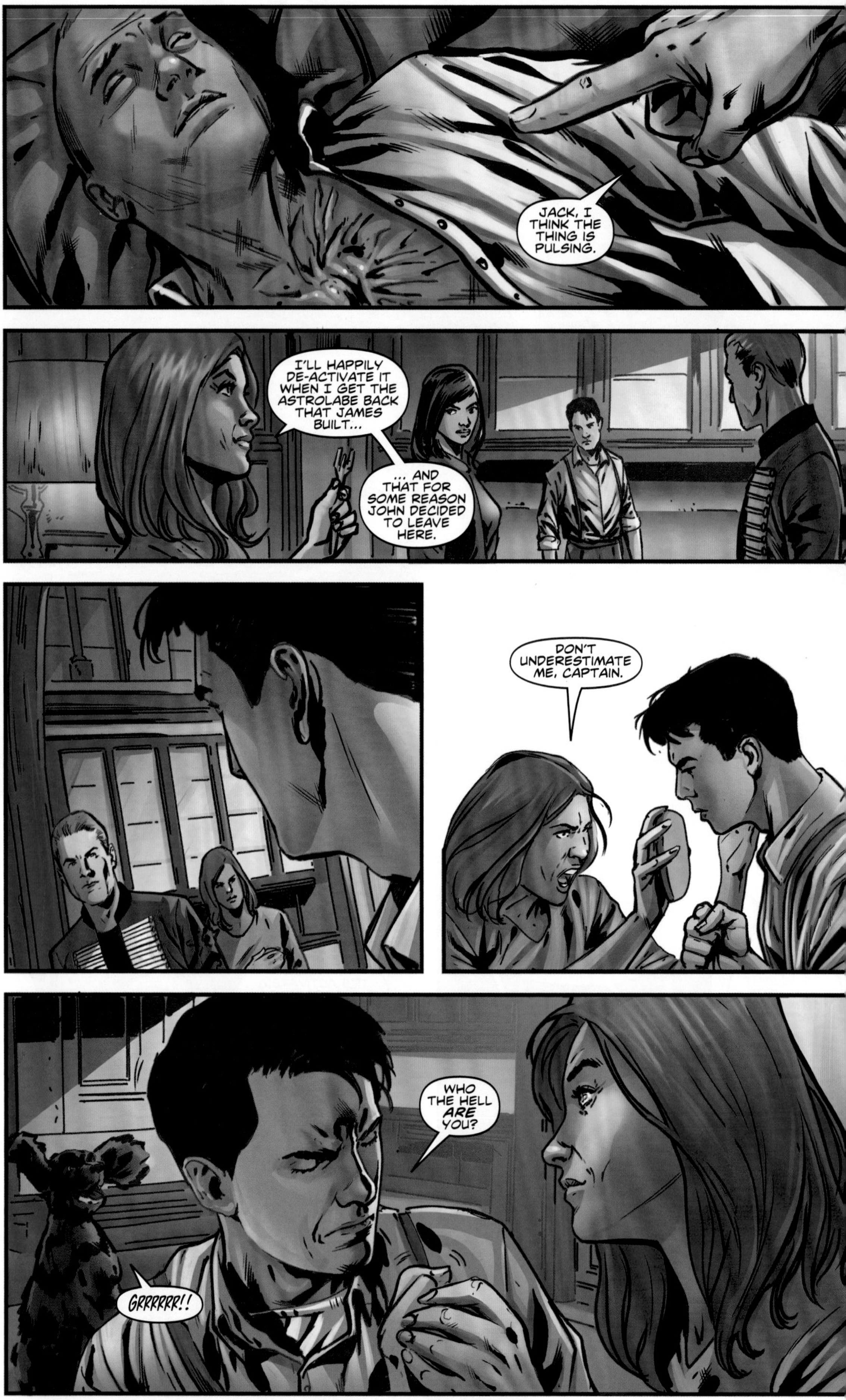

JACK, I THINK THE THING IS PULSING.
I'LL HAPPILY DE-ACTIVATE IT WHEN I GET THE ASTROLABE BACK THAT JAMES BUILT...
... AND THAT FOR SOME REASON JOHN DECIDED TO LEAVE HERE.
DON'T UNDERESTIMATE ME, CAPTAIN.
WHO THE HELL ARE YOU?
GRRRRRR!!

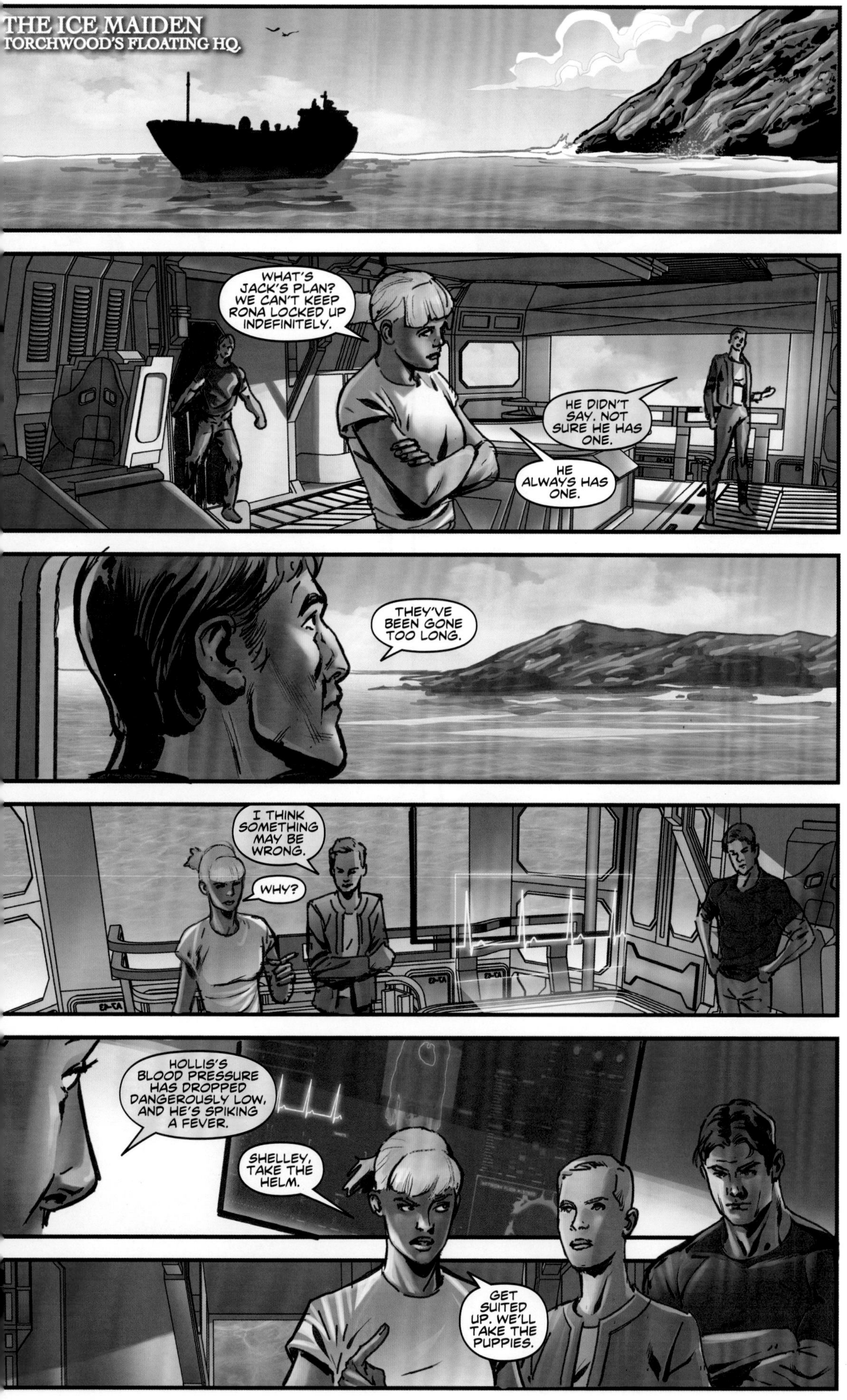
THE ICE MAIDEN
TORCHWOOD'S FLOATING HQ.
WHAT'S JACK'S PLAN? WE CAN'T KEEP RONA LOCKED UP INDEFINITELY.
HE DIDN'T SAY. NOT SURE HE HAS ONE.
HE ALWAYS HAS ONE.
THEY'VE BEEN GONE TOO LONG.
I THINK SOMETHING MAY BE WRONG.
WHY?
HOLLIS'S BLOOD PRESSURE HAS DROPPED DANGEROUSLY LOW, AND HE'S SPIKING A FEVER.
SHELLEY, TAKE THE HELM.
GET SUITED UP. WE'LL TAKE THE PUPPIES.

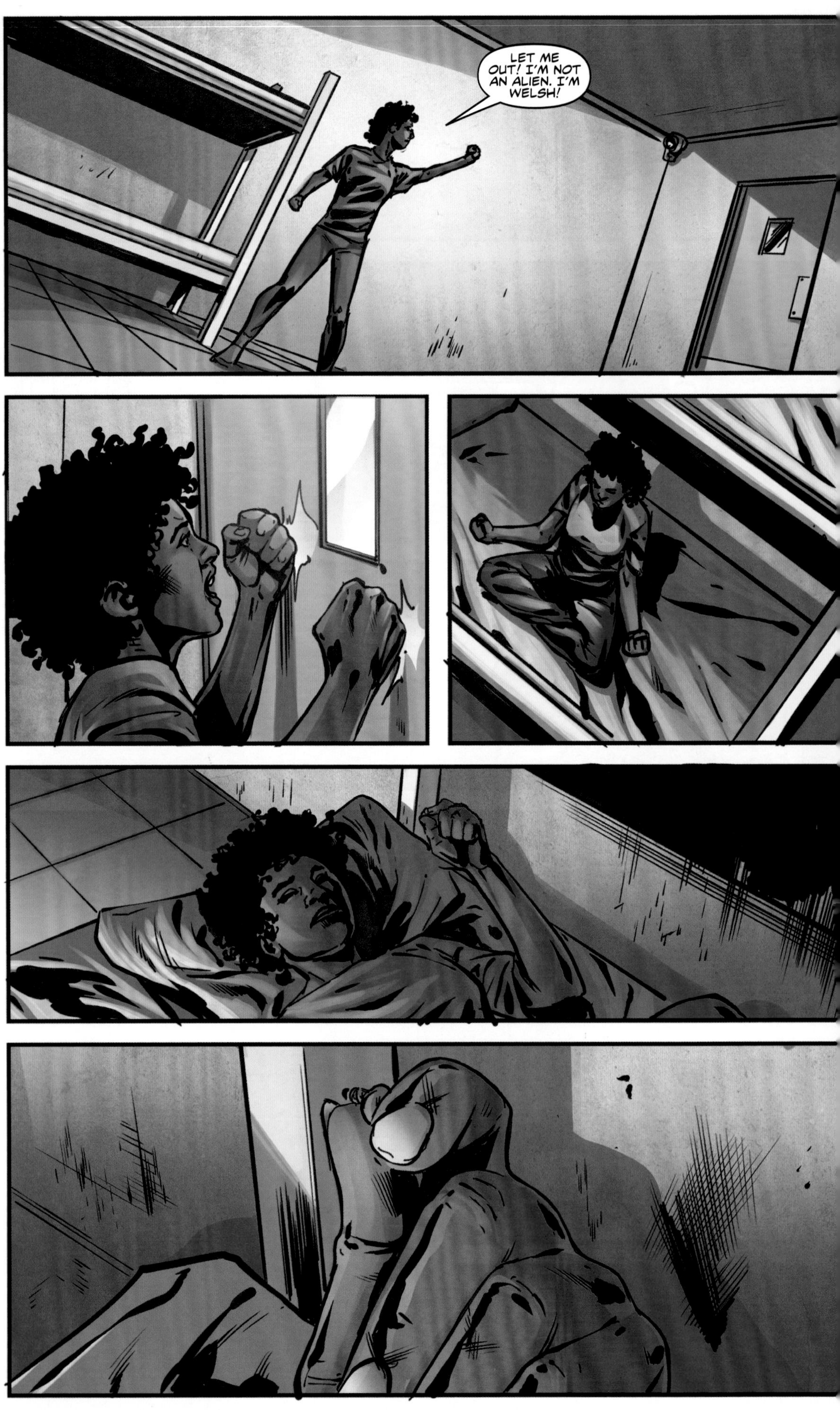
LET ME OUT! I'M NOT AN ALIEN. I'M WELSH!

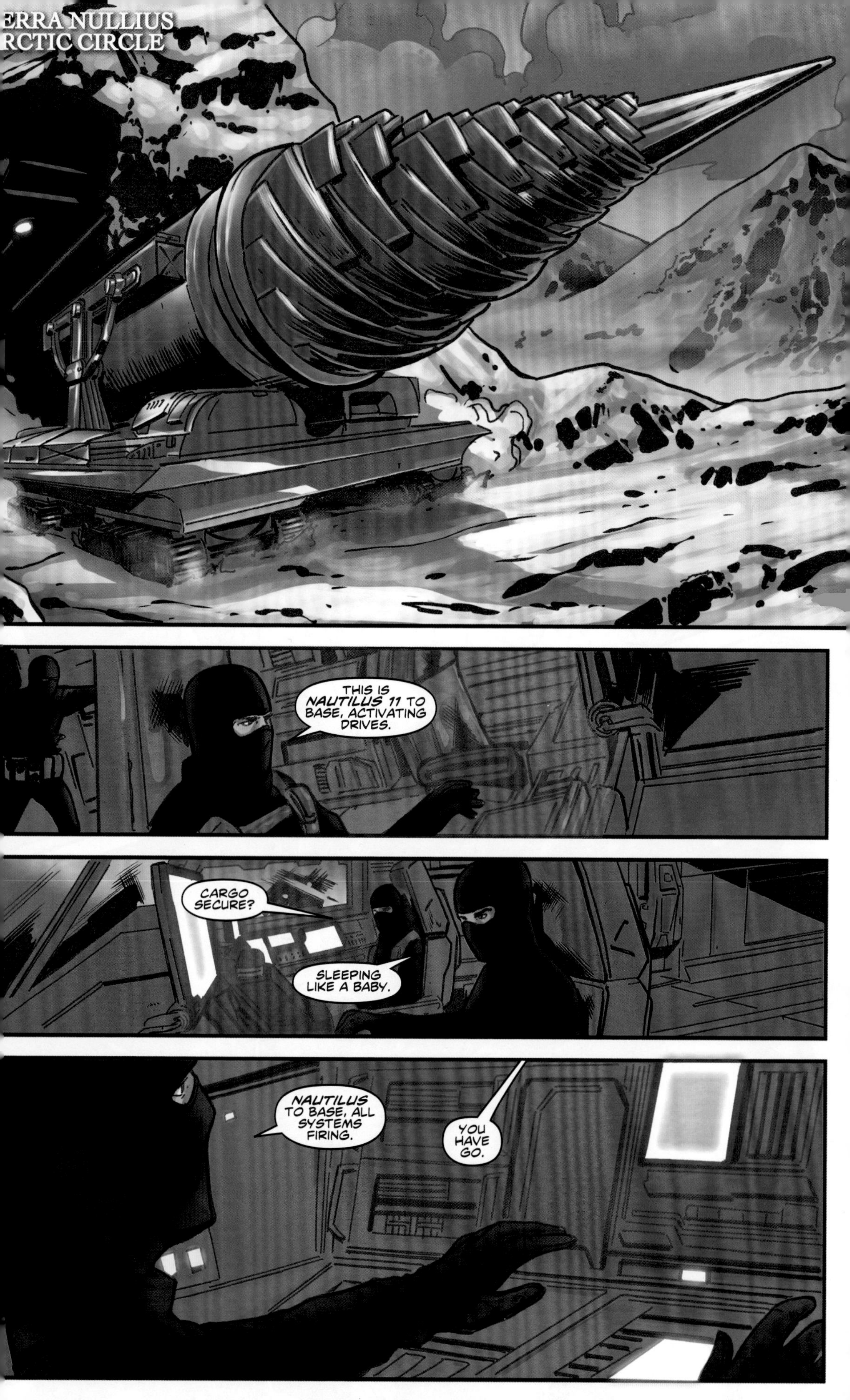
ERRA NULLIUS
RCTIC CIRCLE
THIS IS NAUTILUS 11 TO BASE, ACTIVATING DRIVES.
CARGO SECURE?
SLEEPING LIKE A BABY.
NAUTILUS TO BASE, ALL SYSTEMS FIRING.
YOU HAVE GO.

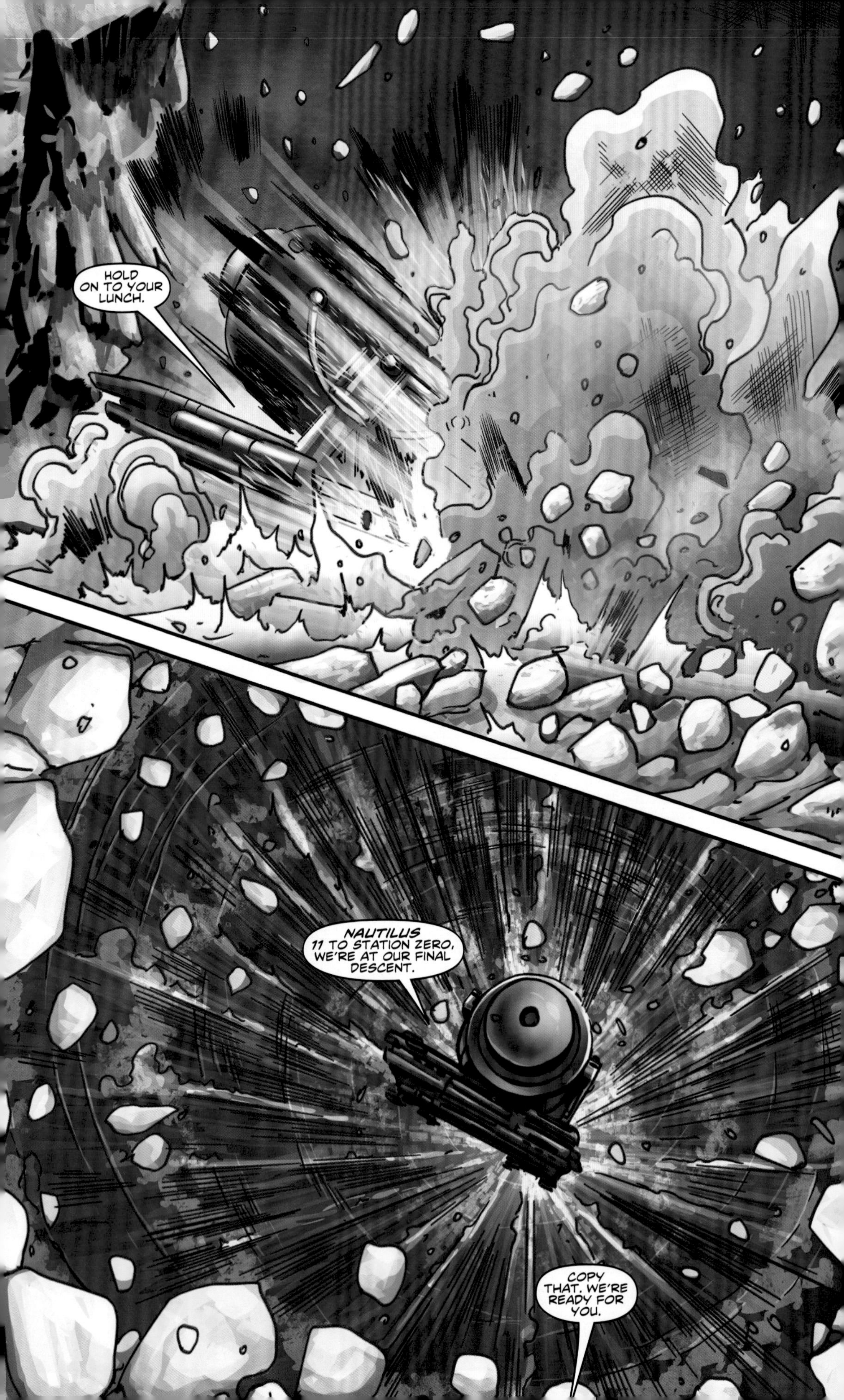
HOLD ON TO YOUR LUNCH.
NAUTILUS 11 TO STATION ZERO, WE'RE AT OUR FINAL DESCENT.
COPY THAT. WE'RE READY FOR YOU.

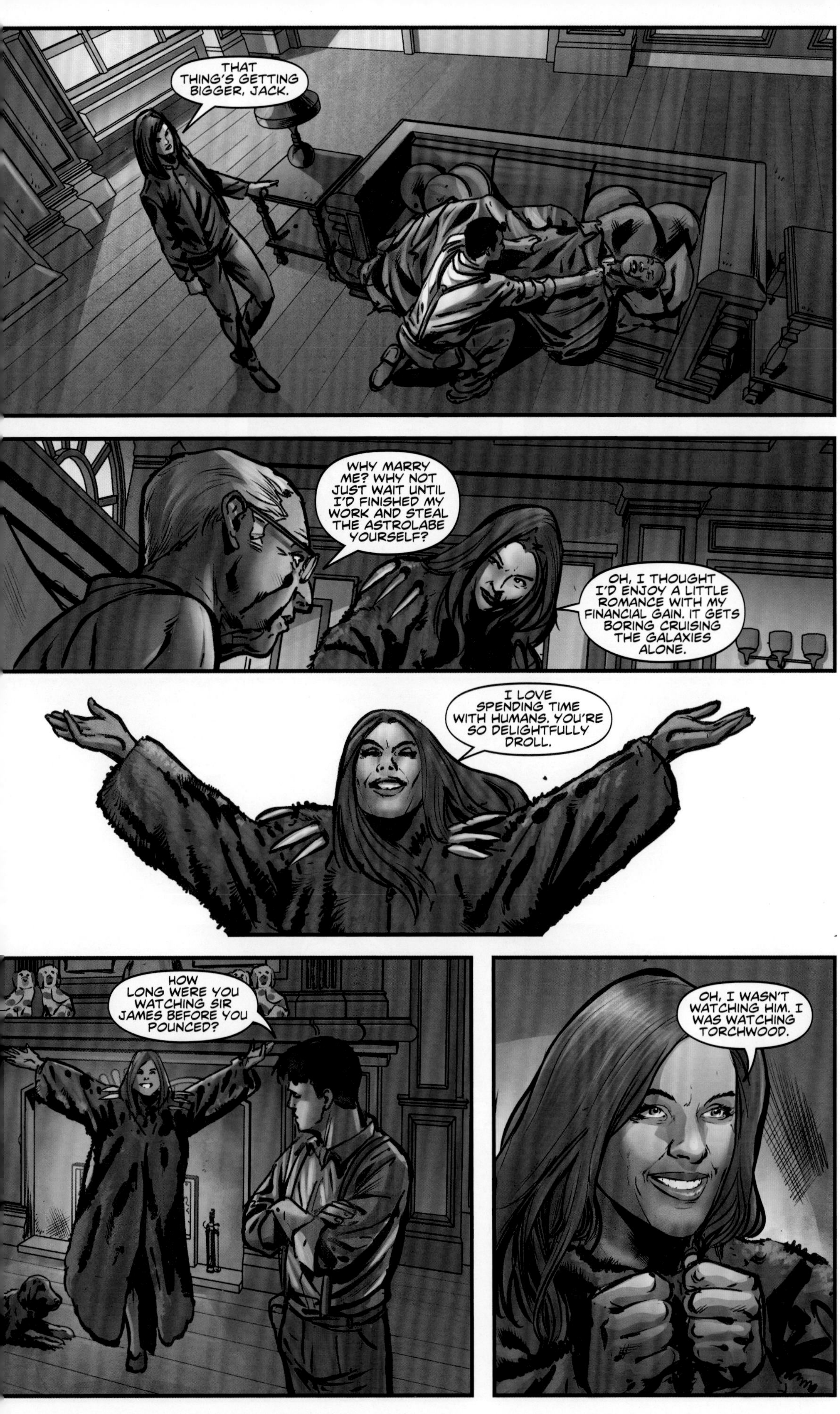
THAT THING'S GETTING BIGGER, JACK.
WHY MARRY ME? WHY NOT JUST WAIT UNTIL I'D FINISHED MY WORK AND STEAL THE ASTROLABE YOURSELF?
OH, I THOUGHT I'D ENJOY A LITTLE ROMANCE WITH MY FINANCIAL GAIN. IT GETS BORING CRUISING THE GALAXIES ALONE.
I LOVE SPENDING TIME WITH HUMANS. YOU'RE SO DELIGHTFULLY DROLL.
HOW LONG WERE YOU WATCHING SIR JAMES BEFORE YOU POUNCED?
OH, I WASN'T WATCHING HIM. I WAS WATCHING TORCHWOOD.

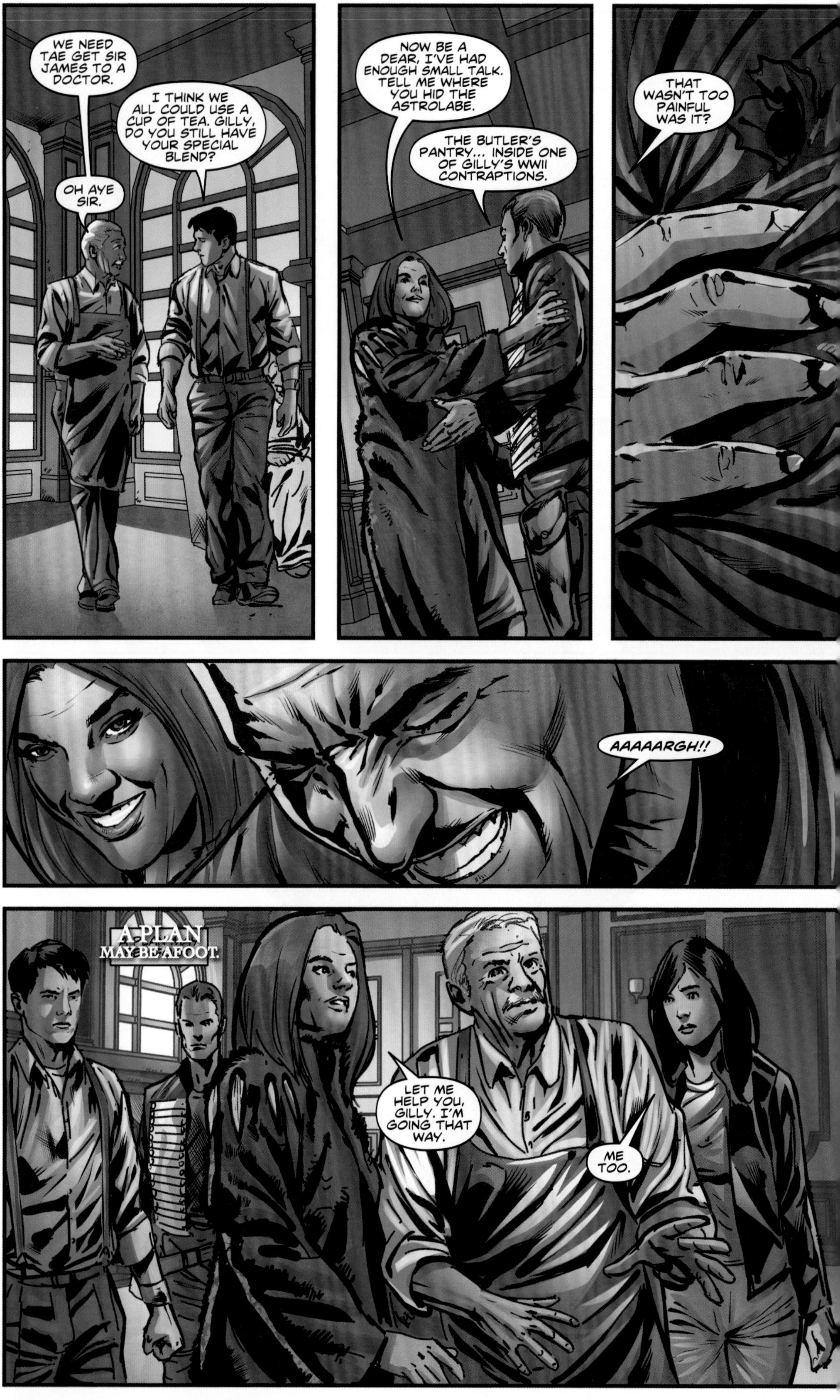
WE NEED TAE GET SIR JAMES TO A DOCTOR.
I THINK WE ALL COULD USE A CUP OF TEA. GILLY, DO YOU STILL HAVE YOUR SPECIAL BLEND?
OH AYE SIR.
NOW BE A DEAR, I'VE HAD ENOUGH SMALL TALK. TELL ME WHERE YOU HID THE ASTROLABE.
THE BUTLER'S PANTRY... INSIDE ONE OF GILLY'S WWII CONTRAPTIONS.
THAT WASN'T TOO PAINFUL WAS IT?
AAAAARGH!!
A PLAN MAY BE AFOOT.
LET ME HELP YOU, GILLY. I'M GOING THAT WAY.
ME TOO.

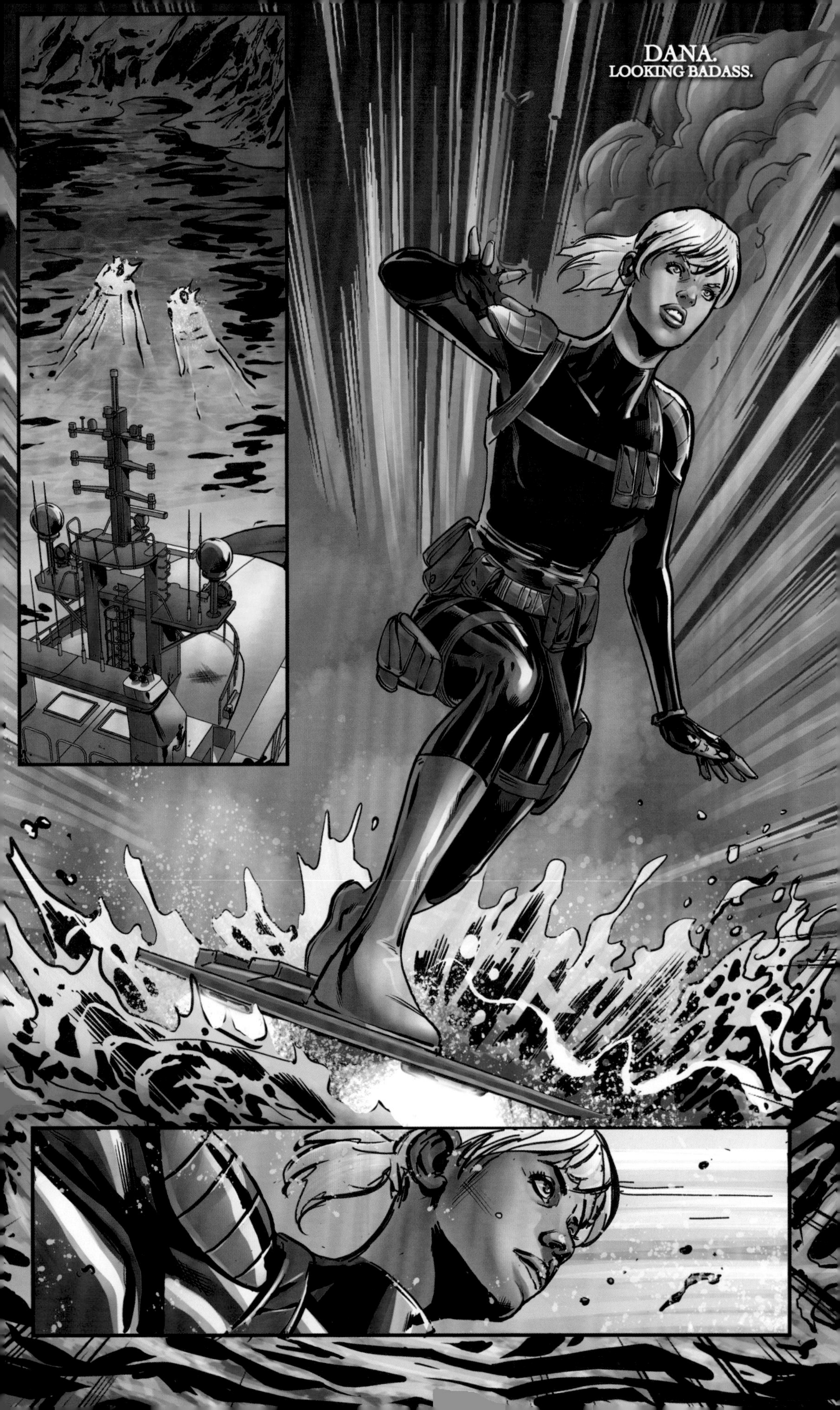
DANA.
LOOKING BADASS.

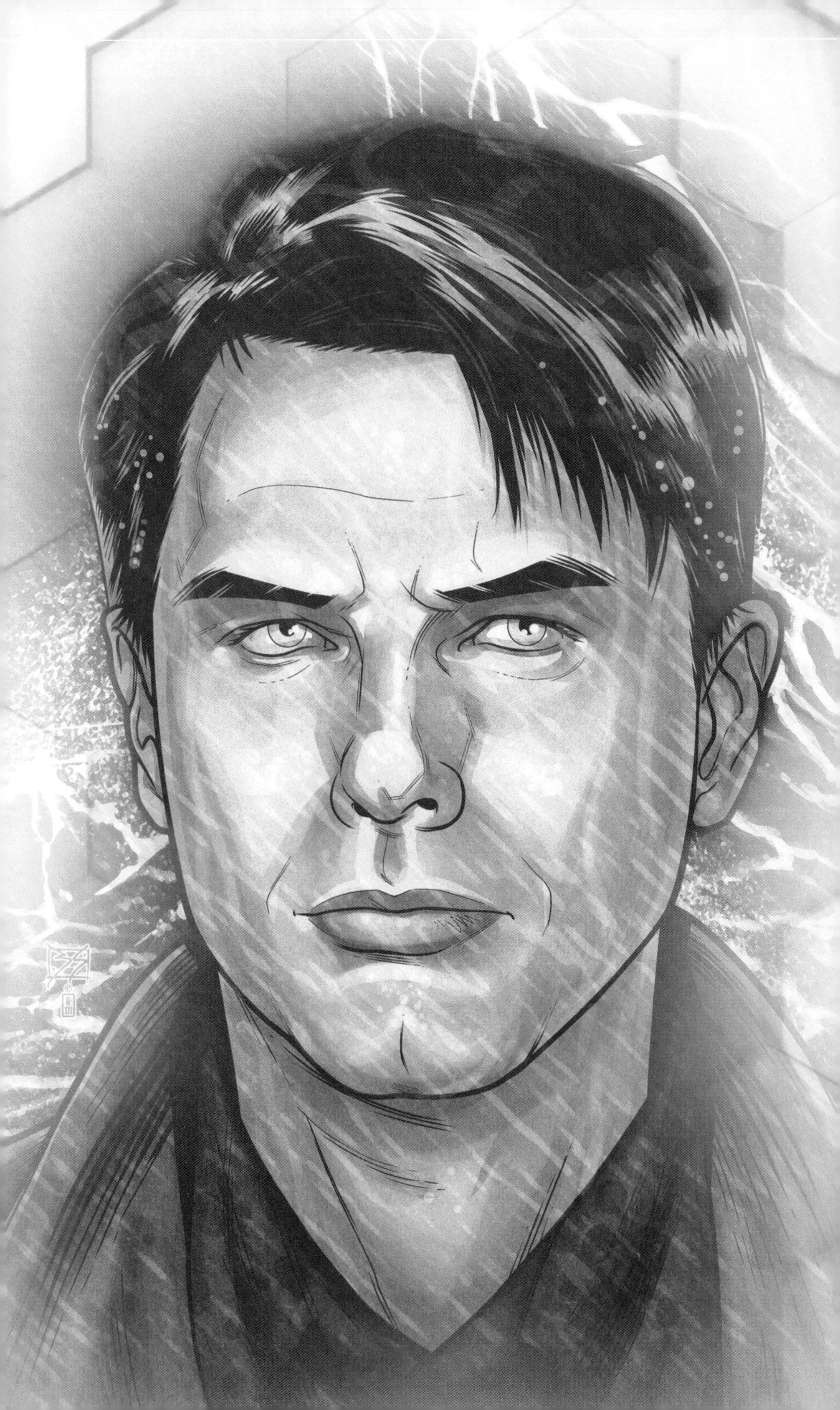

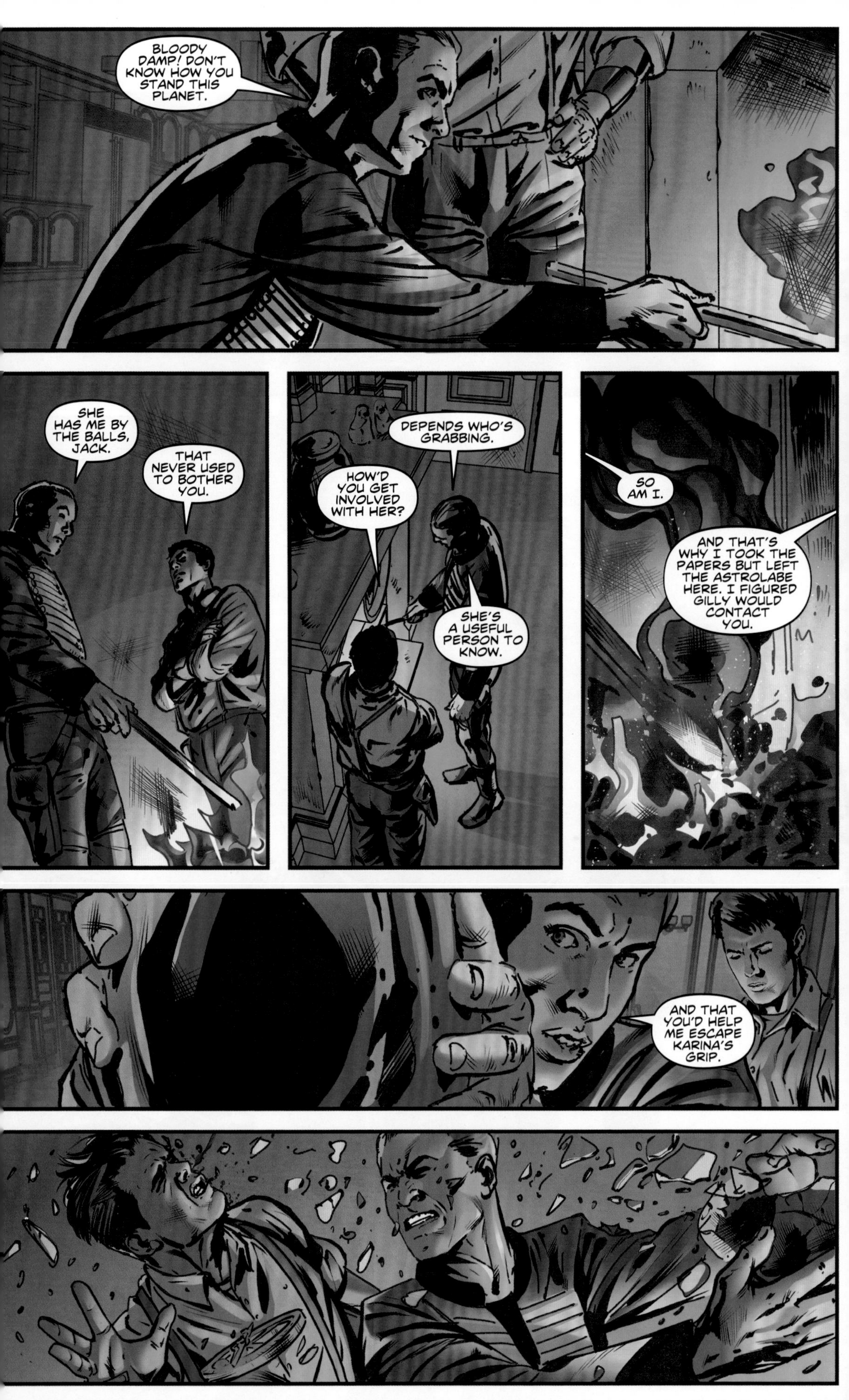
BLOODY DAMP! DON'T KNOW HOW YOU STAND THIS PLANET.
SHE HAS ME BY THE BALLS, JACK.
THAT NEVER USED TO BOTHER YOU.
DEPENDS WHO'S GRABBING.
HOW'D YOU GET INVOLVED WITH HER?
SHE'S A USEFUL PERSON TO KNOW.
SO AM I.
AND THAT'S WHY I TOOK THE PAPERS BUT LEFT THE ASTROLABE HERE. I FIGURED GILLY WOULD CONTACT YOU.
AND THAT YOU'D HELP ME ESCAPE KARINA'S GRIP.

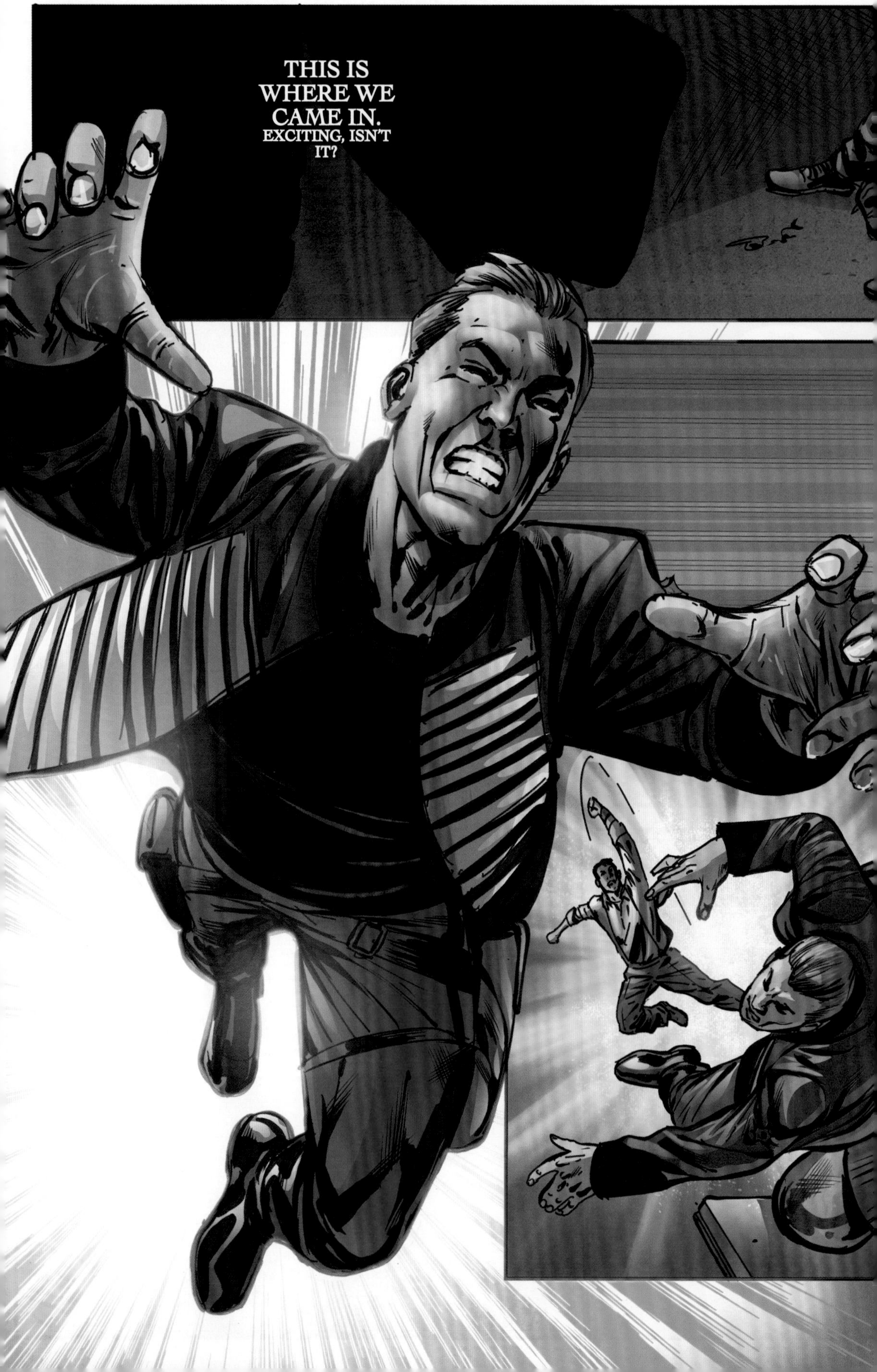
THIS IS WHERE WE CAME IN. EXCITING, ISN'T IT?

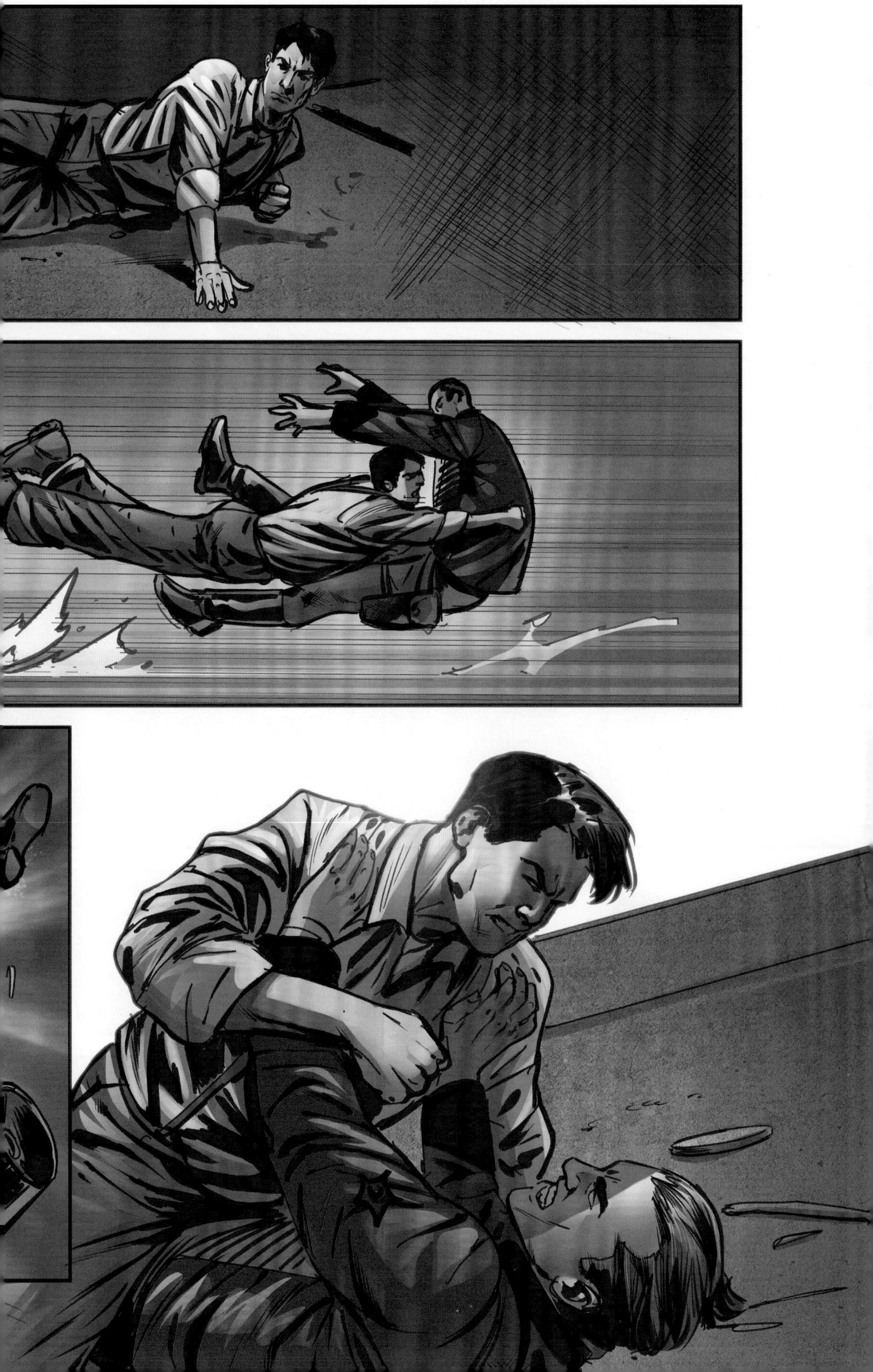

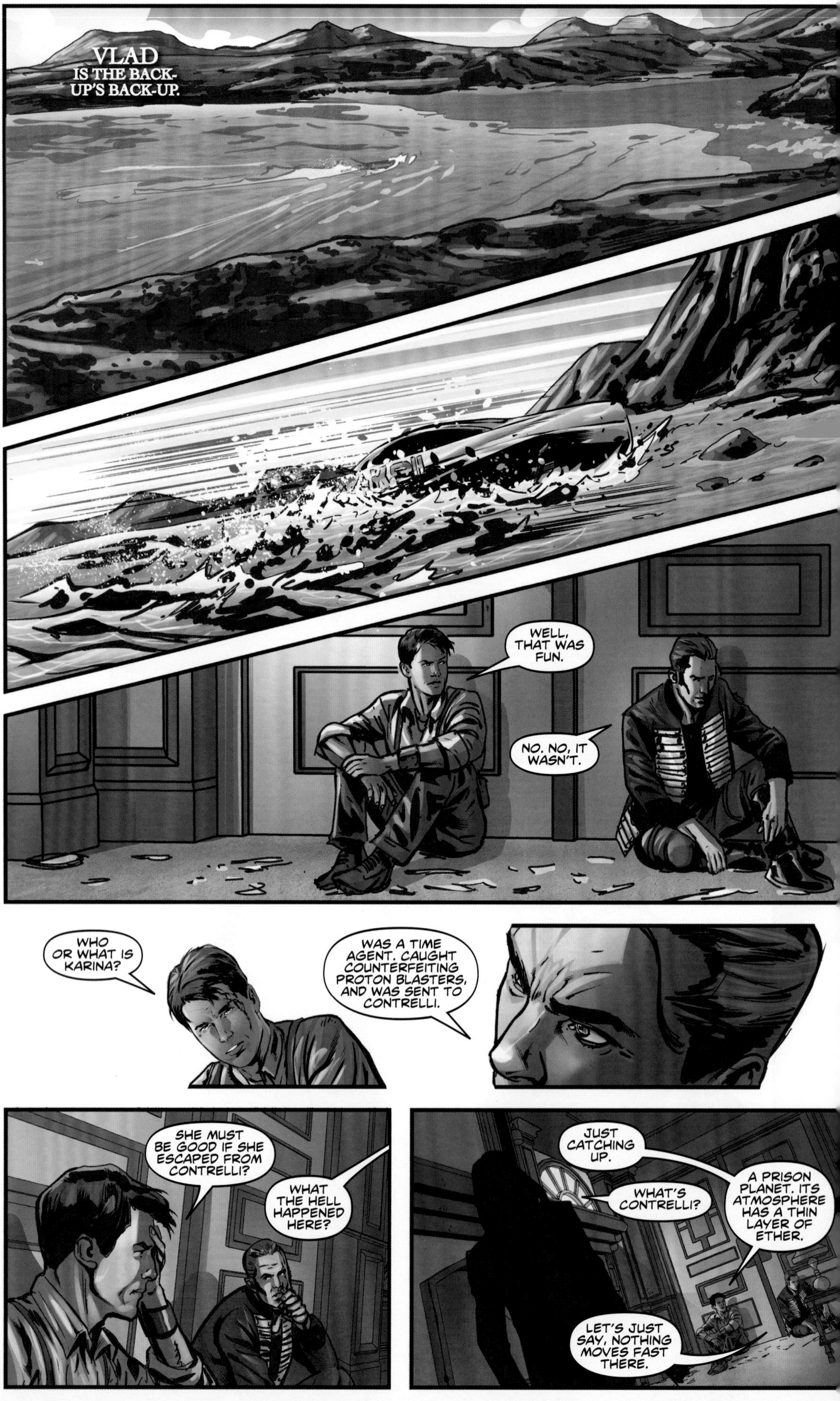
VLAD IS THE BACK-UP'S BACK-UP.
WELL, THAT WAS FUN.
NO. NO, IT WASN'T.
WHO OR WHAT IS KARINA?
WAS A TIME AGENT. CAUGHT COUNTERFEITING PROTON BLASTERS, AND WAS SENT TO CONTRELLI.
SHE MUST BE GOOD IF SHE ESCAPED FROM CONTRELLI?
WHAT THE HELL HAPPENED HERE?
JUST CATCHING UP.
WHAT'S CONTRELLI?
A PRISON PLANET. ITS ATMOSPHERE HAS A THIN LAYER OF ETHER.
LET'S JUST SAY, NOTHING MOVES FAST THERE.

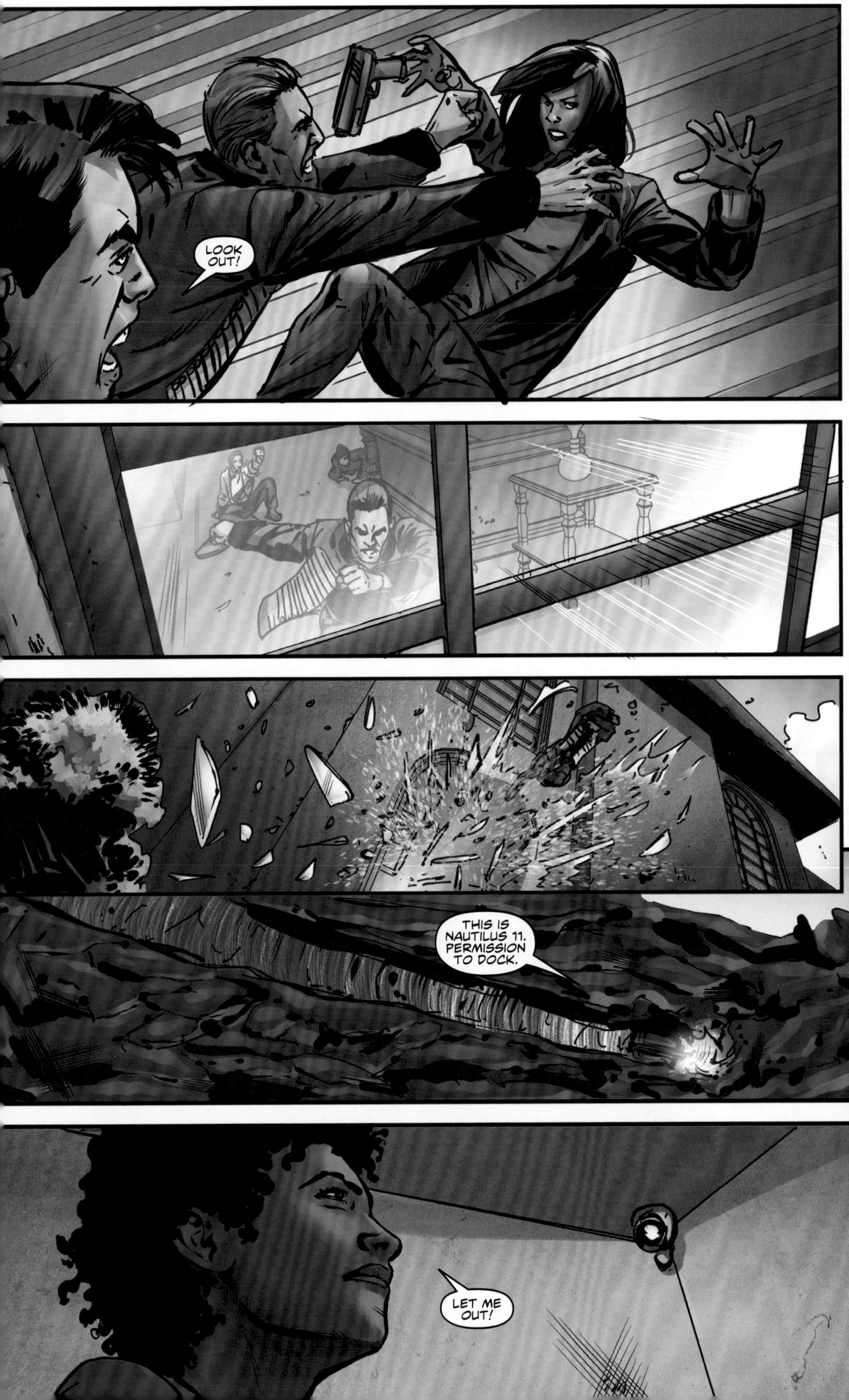
LOOK OUT!
THIS IS NAUTILUS 11. PERMISSION TO DOCK.
LET ME OUT!

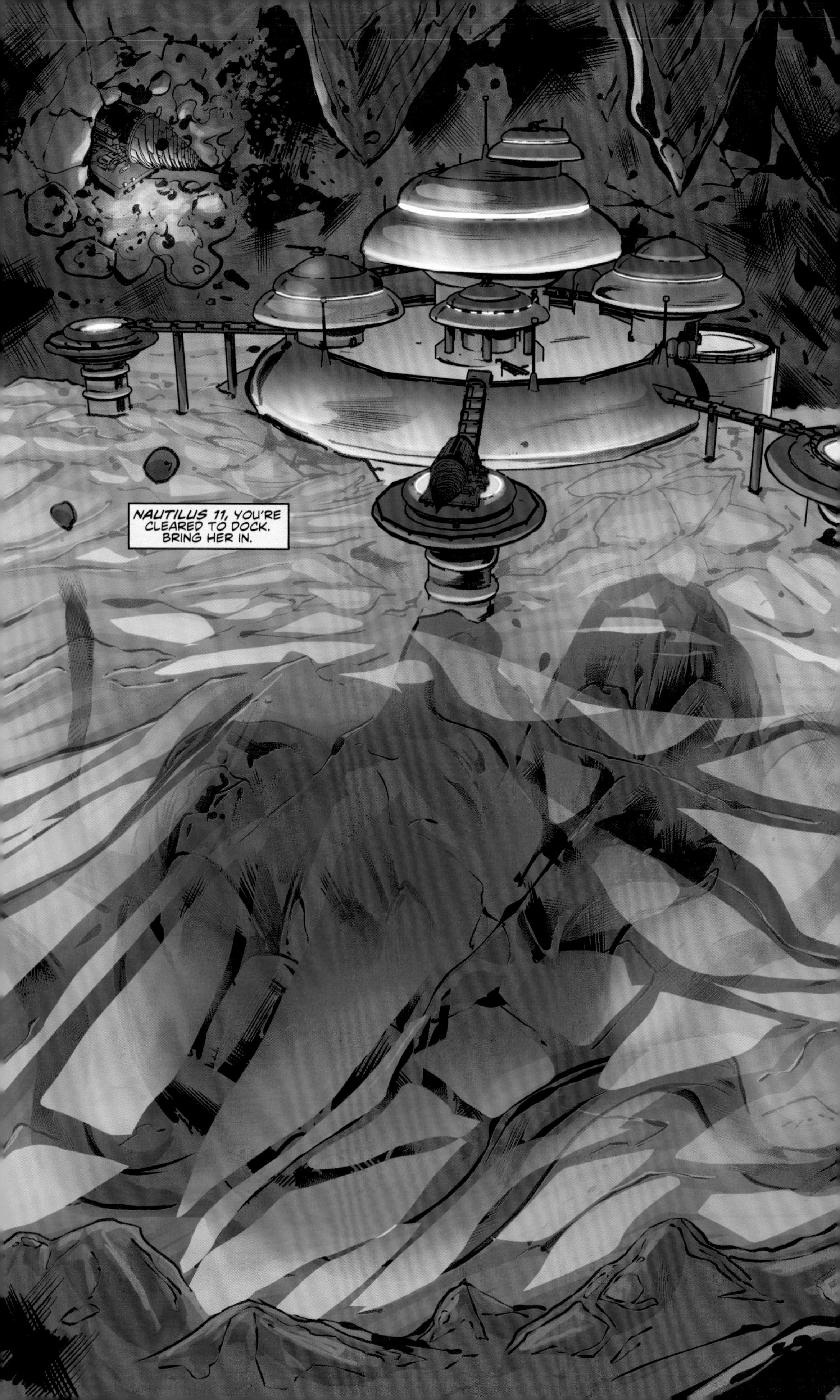
NAUTILUS 11, YOU'RE CLEARED TO DOCK. BRING HER IN.

CHAPTER 2

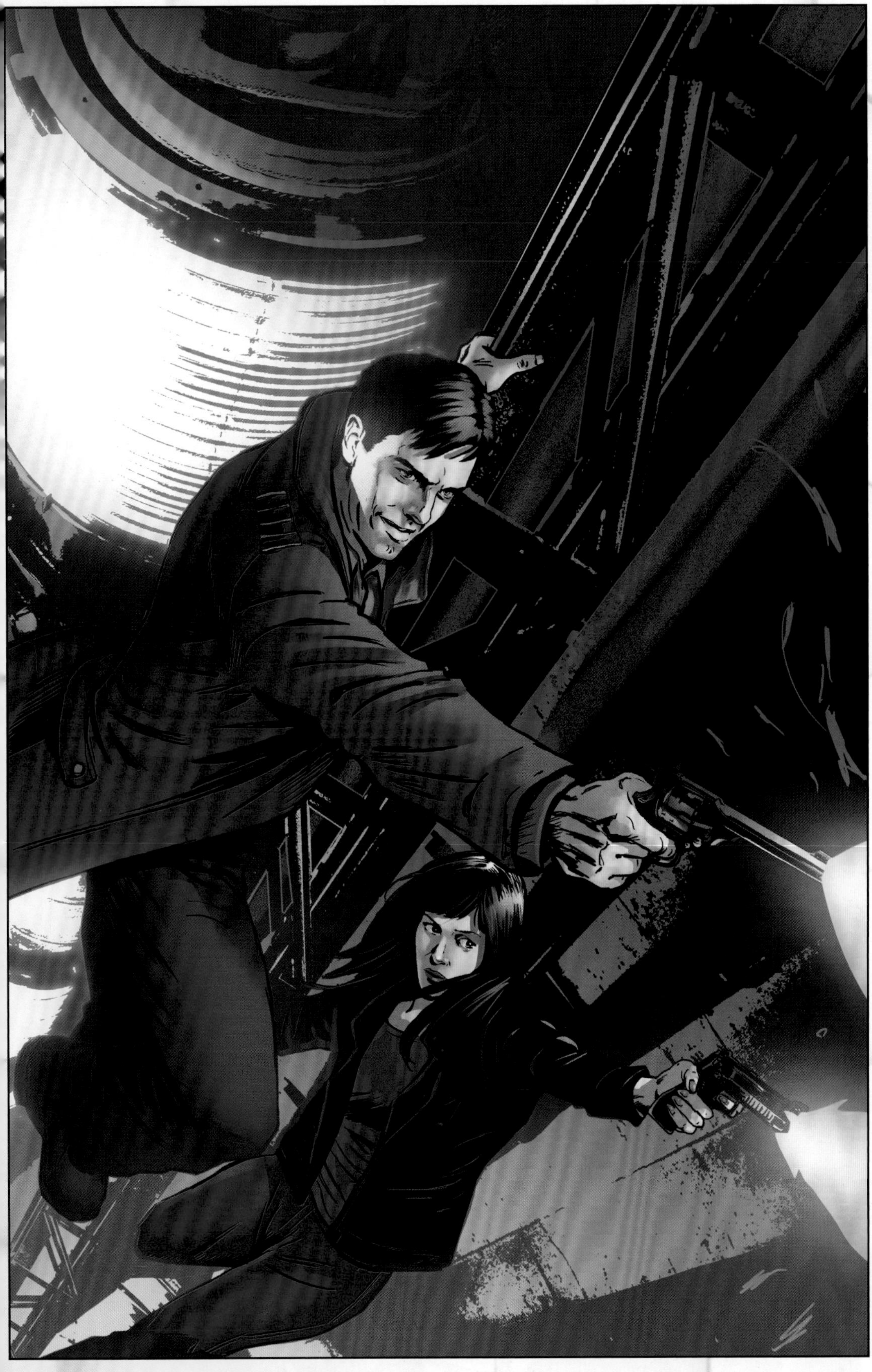

illustration by BRIAN WILLIAMSON

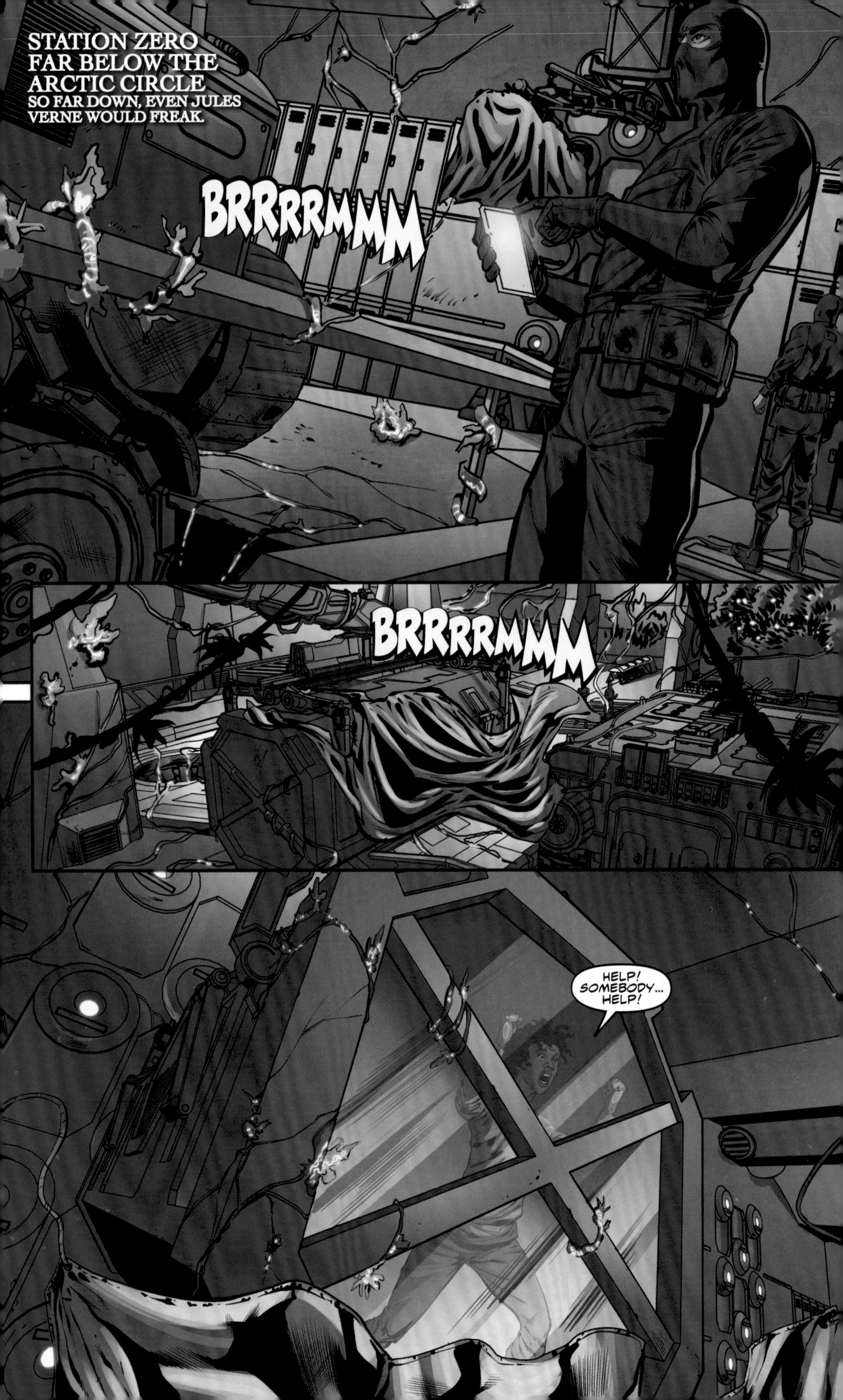
STATION ZERO
FAR BELOW THE
ARCTIC CIRCLE
SO FAR DOWN, EVEN JULES
VERNE WOULD FREAK.
BRRRRMMM
BRRRRMMM
HELP! SOMEBODY... HELP!

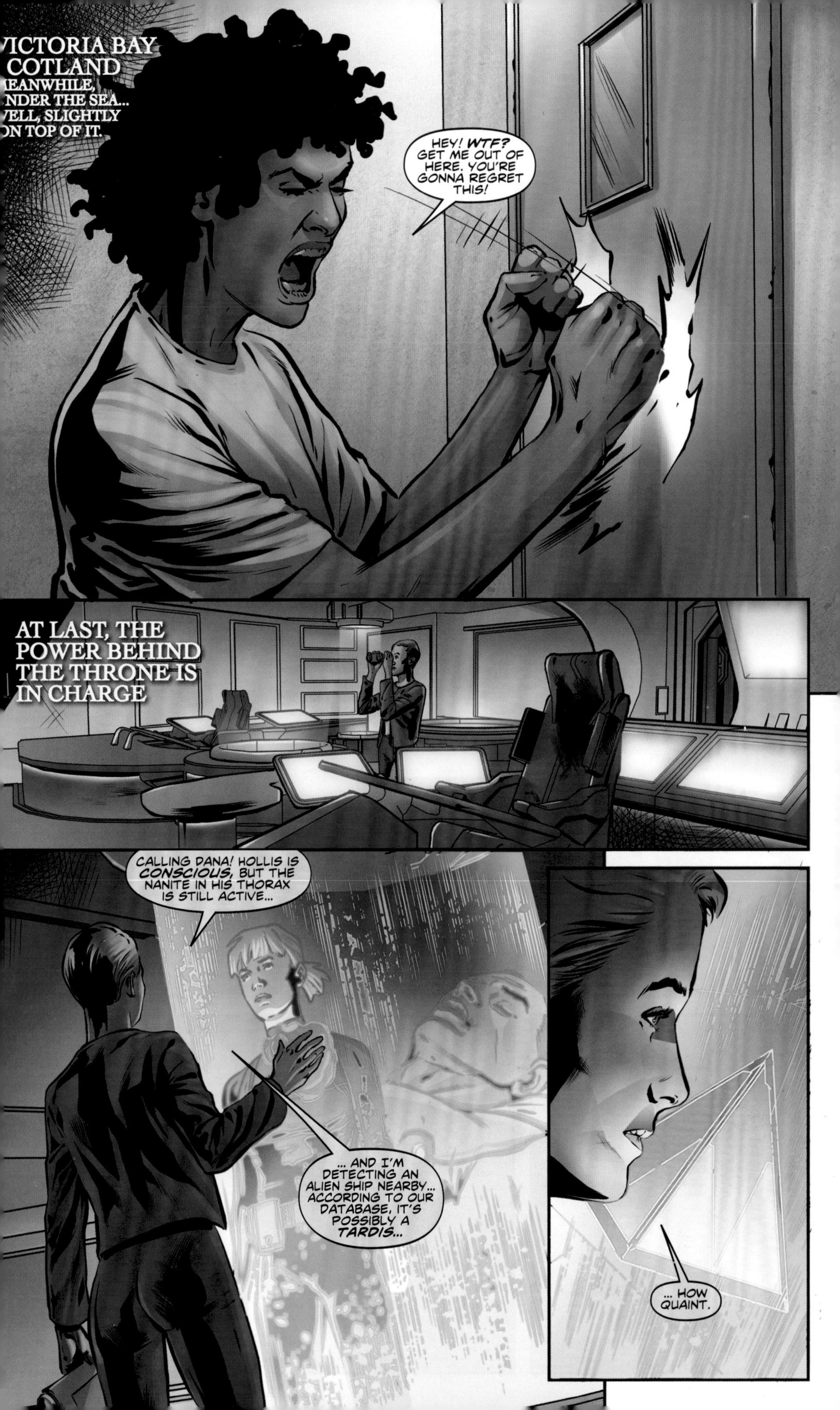
VICTORIA BAY
COTLAND
EANWHILE,
NDER THE SEA...
WELL, SLIGHTLY
ON TOP OF IT.
HEY! WTF? GET ME OUT OF HERE. YOU'RE GONNA REGRET THIS!
AT LAST, THE POWER BEHIND THE THRONE IS IN CHARGE
CALLING DANA! HOLLIS IS CONSCIOUS, BUT THE NANITE IN HIS THORAX IS STILL ACTIVE...
... AND I'M DETECTING AN ALIEN SHIP NEARBY... ACCORDING TO OUR DATABASE, IT'S POSSIBLY A TARDIS...
... HOW QUAINT.

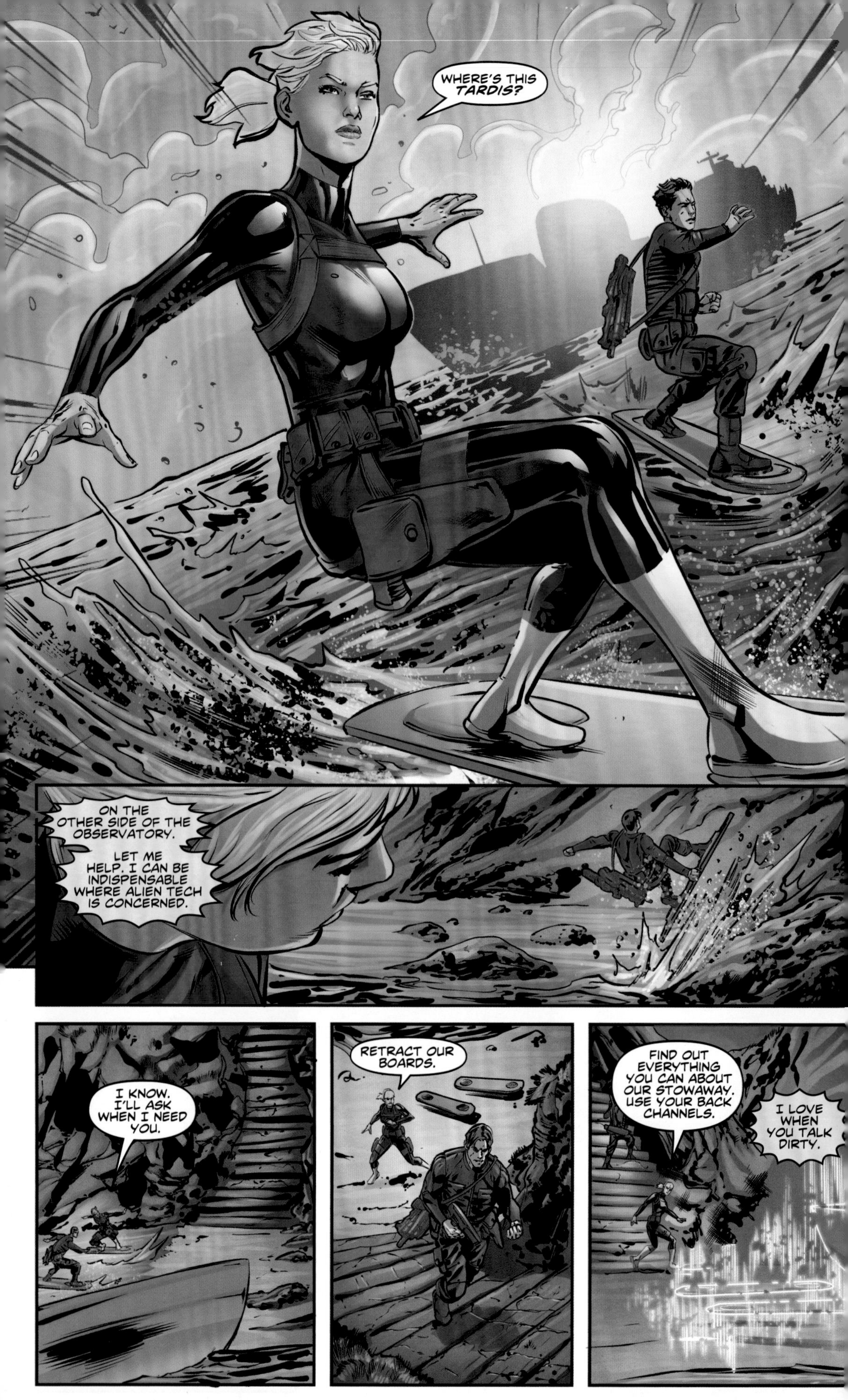
WHERE'S THIS *TARDIS?*
ON THE OTHER SIDE OF THE OBSERVATORY.
LET ME HELP. I CAN BE INDISPENSABLE WHERE ALIEN TECH IS CONCERNED.
I KNOW. I'LL ASK WHEN I NEED YOU.
RETRACT OUR BOARDS.
FIND OUT EVERYTHING YOU CAN ABOUT OUR STOWAWAY. USE YOUR BACK CHANNELS.
I LOVE WHEN YOU TALK DIRTY.

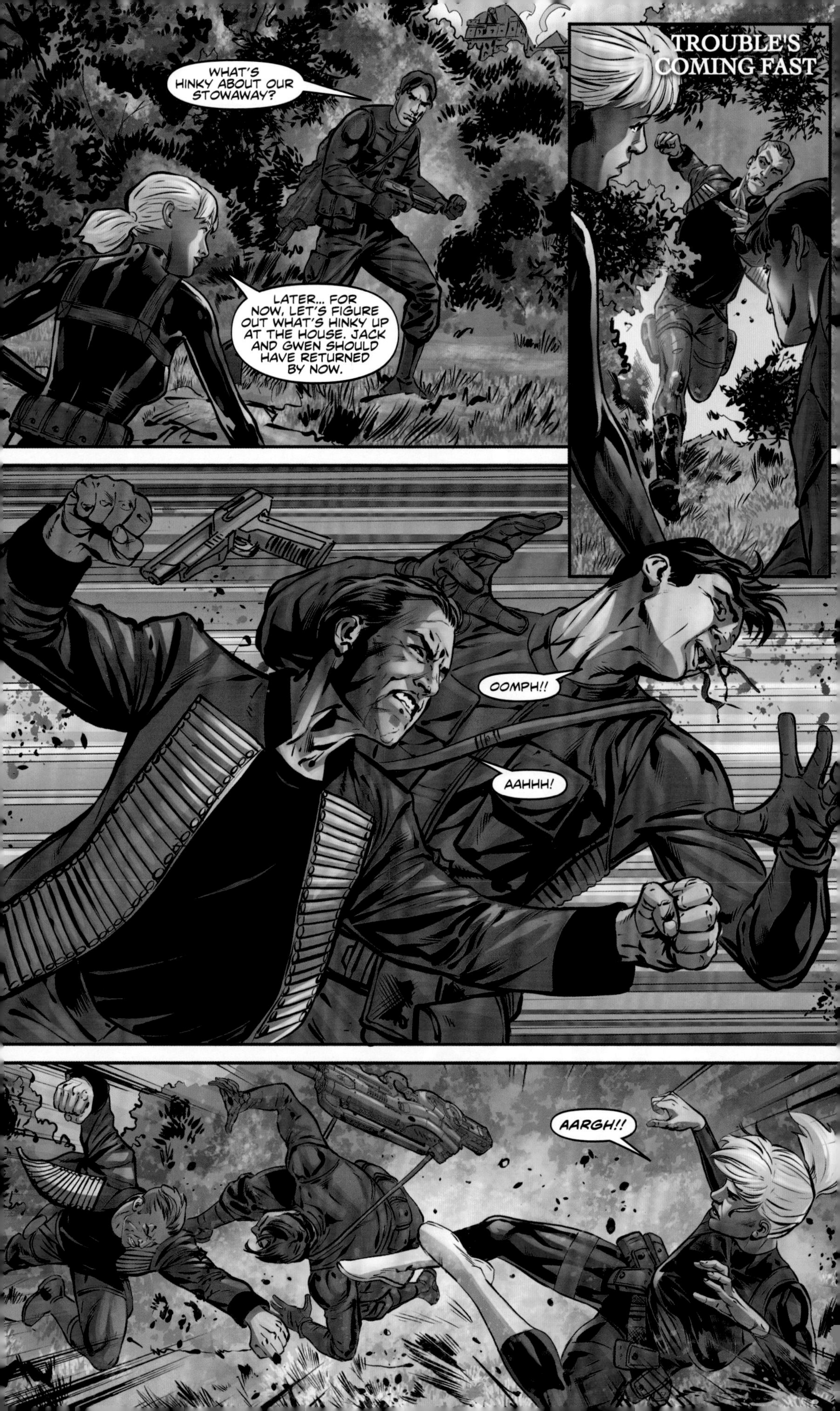
WHAT'S HINKY ABOUT OUR STOWAWAY?
LATER... FOR NOW, LET'S FIGURE OUT WHAT'S HINKY UP AT THE HOUSE. JACK AND GWEN SHOULD HAVE RETURNED BY NOW.
TROUBLE'S COMING FAST
OOMPH!!
AAHHH!
AARGH!!

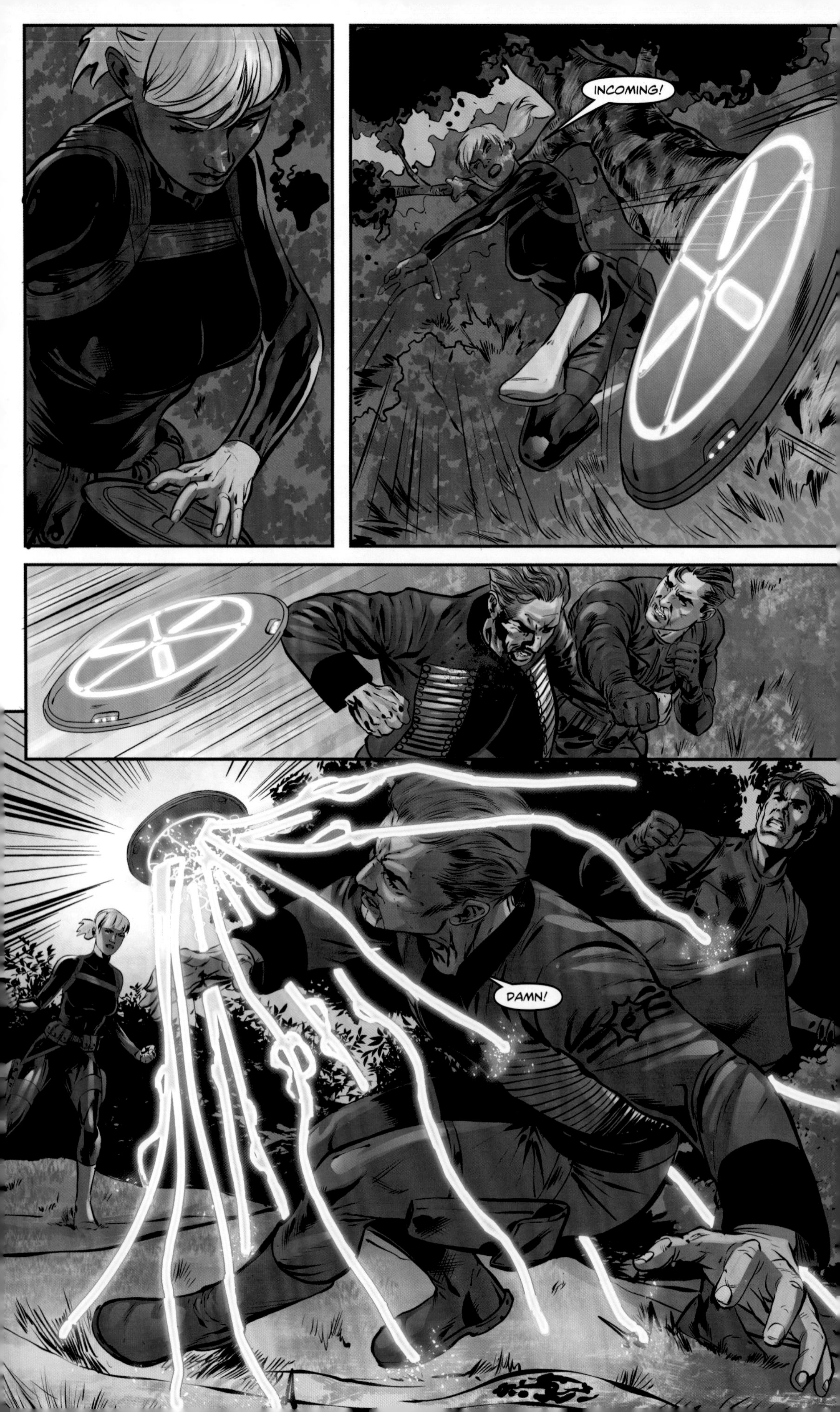
INCOMING!
DAMN!

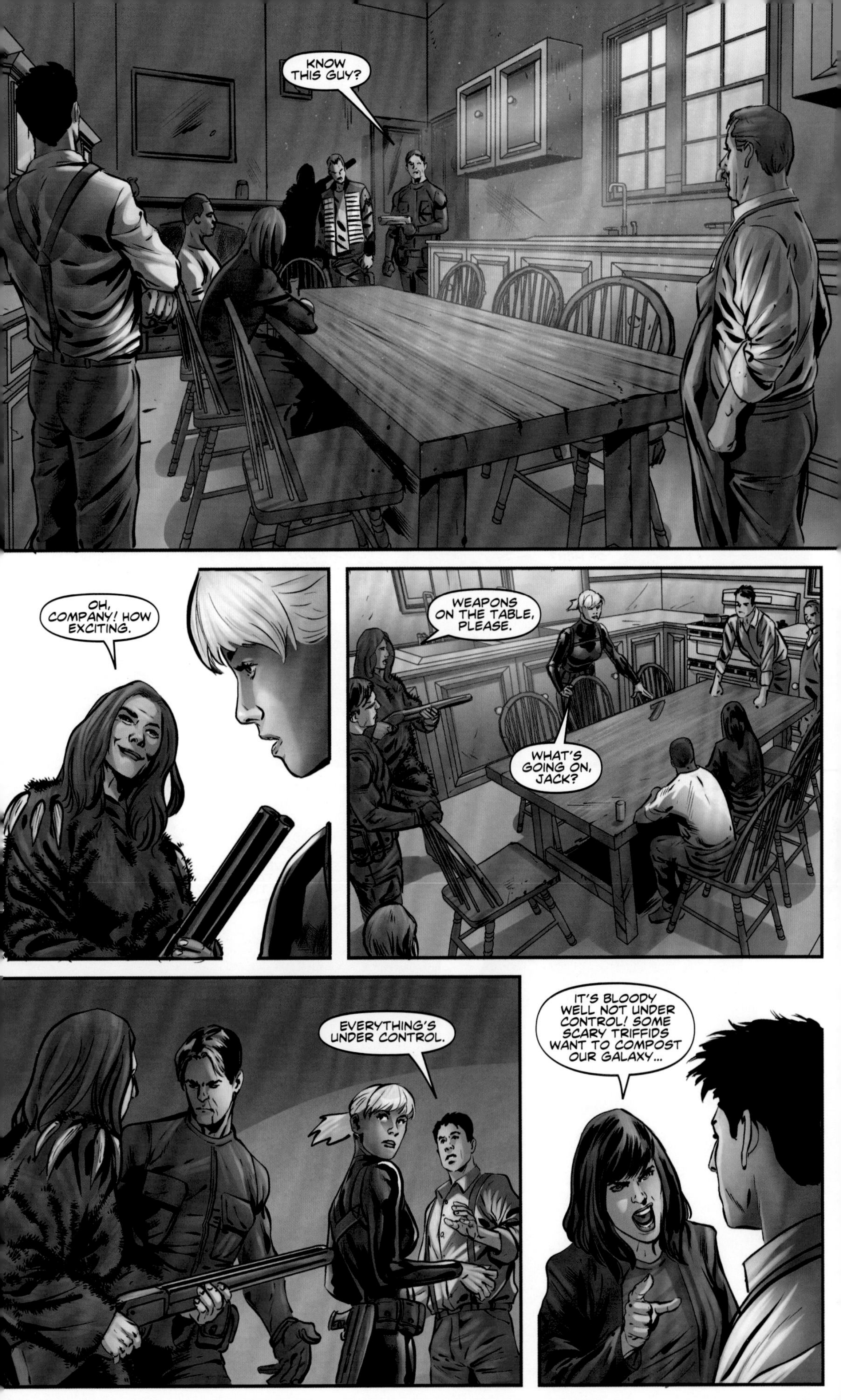
KNOW THIS GUY?
OH, COMPANY! HOW EXCITING.
WEAPONS ON THE TABLE, PLEASE.
WHAT'S GOING ON, JACK?
EVERYTHING'S UNDER CONTROL.
IT'S BLOODY WELL NOT UNDER CONTROL! SOME SCARY TRIFFIDS WANT TO COMPOST OUR GALAXY...

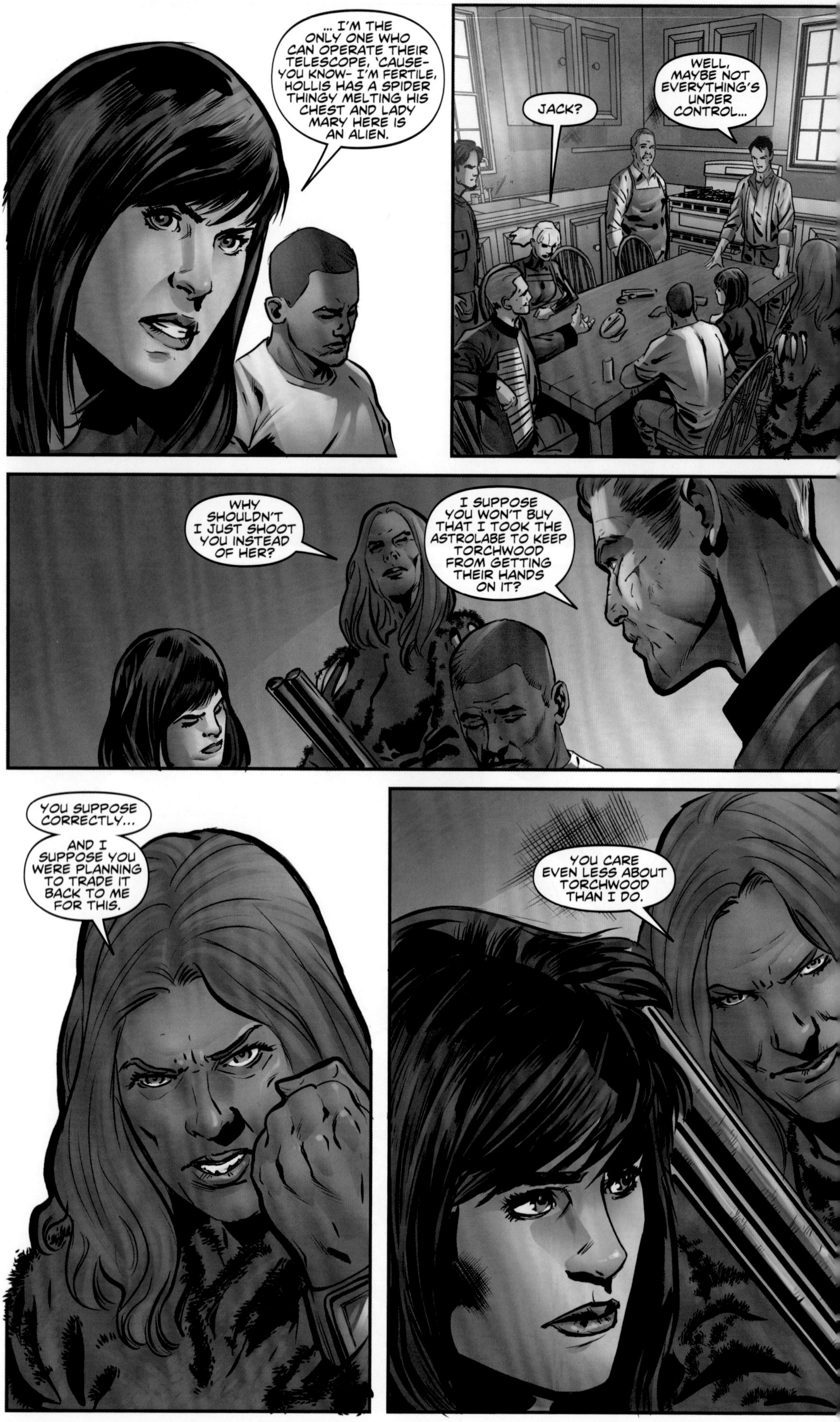
... I'M THE ONLY ONE WHO CAN OPERATE THEIR TELESCOPE, 'CAUSE- YOU KNOW- I'M FERTILE, HOLLIS HAS A SPIDER THINGY MELTING HIS CHEST AND LADY MARY HERE IS AN ALIEN.
JACK?
WELL, MAYBE NOT EVERYTHING'S UNDER CONTROL...
WHY SHOULDN'T I JUST SHOOT YOU INSTEAD OF HER?
I SUPPOSE YOU WON'T BUY THAT I TOOK THE ASTROLABE TO KEEP TORCHWOOD FROM GETTING THEIR HANDS ON IT?
YOU SUPPOSE CORRECTLY...
AND I SUPPOSE YOU WERE PLANNING TO TRADE IT BACK TO ME FOR THIS.
YOU CARE EVEN LESS ABOUT TORCHWOOD THAN I DO.

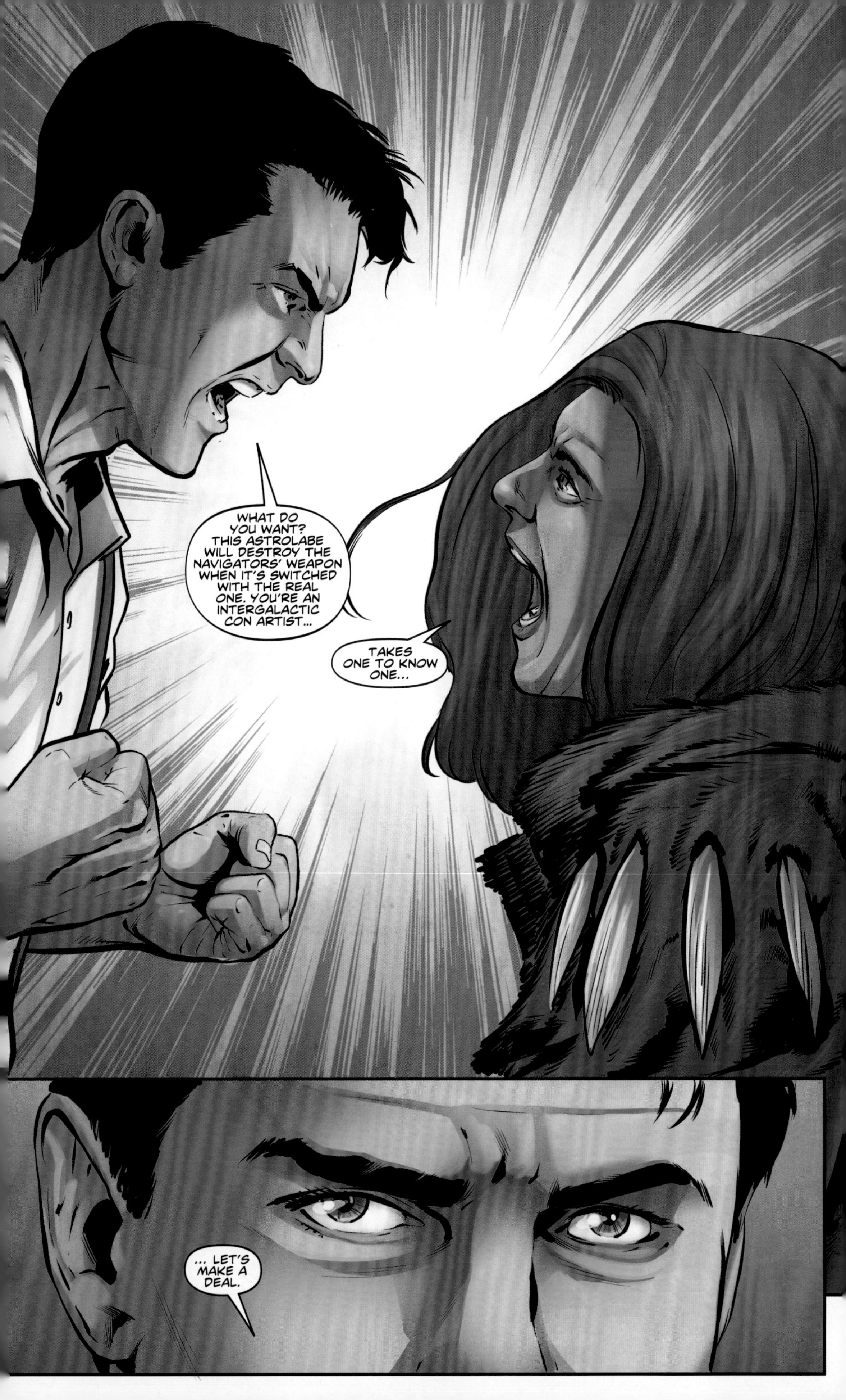
WHAT DO YOU WANT? THIS ASTROLABE WILL DESTROY THE NAVIGATORS' WEAPON WHEN IT'S SWITCHED WITH THE REAL ONE. YOU'RE AN INTERGALACTIC CON ARTIST...
TAKES ONE TO KNOW ONE...
... LET'S MAKE A DEAL.

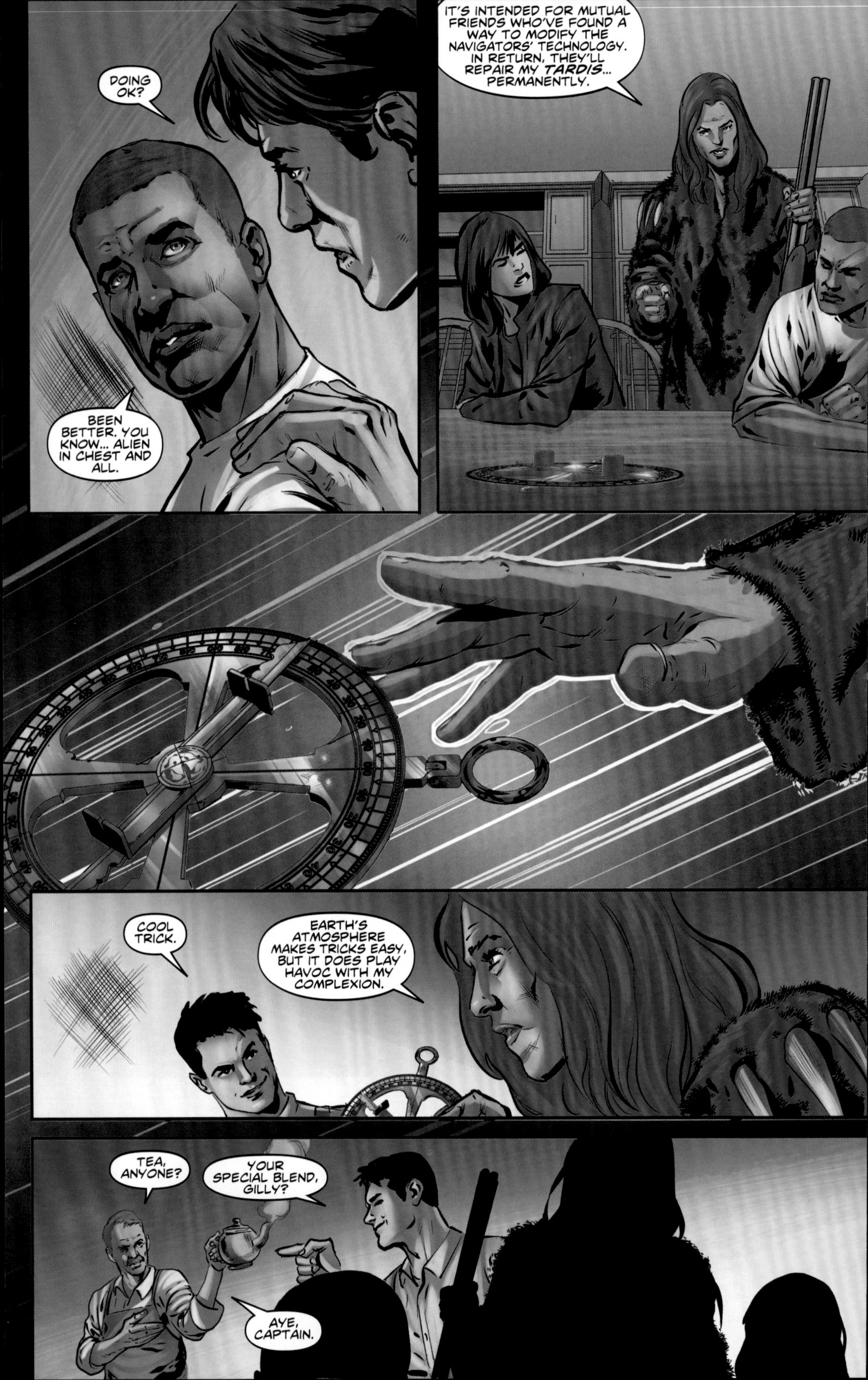

DOING OK?
BEEN BETTER. YOU KNOW... ALIEN IN CHEST AND ALL.
IT'S INTENDED FOR MUTUAL FRIENDS WHO'VE FOUND A WAY TO MODIFY THE NAVIGATORS' TECHNOLOGY. IN RETURN, THEY'LL REPAIR MY TARDIS... PERMANENTLY.
COOL TRICK.
EARTH'S ATMOSPHERE MAKES TRICKS EASY, BUT IT DOES PLAY HAVOC WITH MY COMPLEXION.
TEA, ANYONE?
YOUR SPECIAL BLEND, GILLY?
AYE, CAPTAIN.

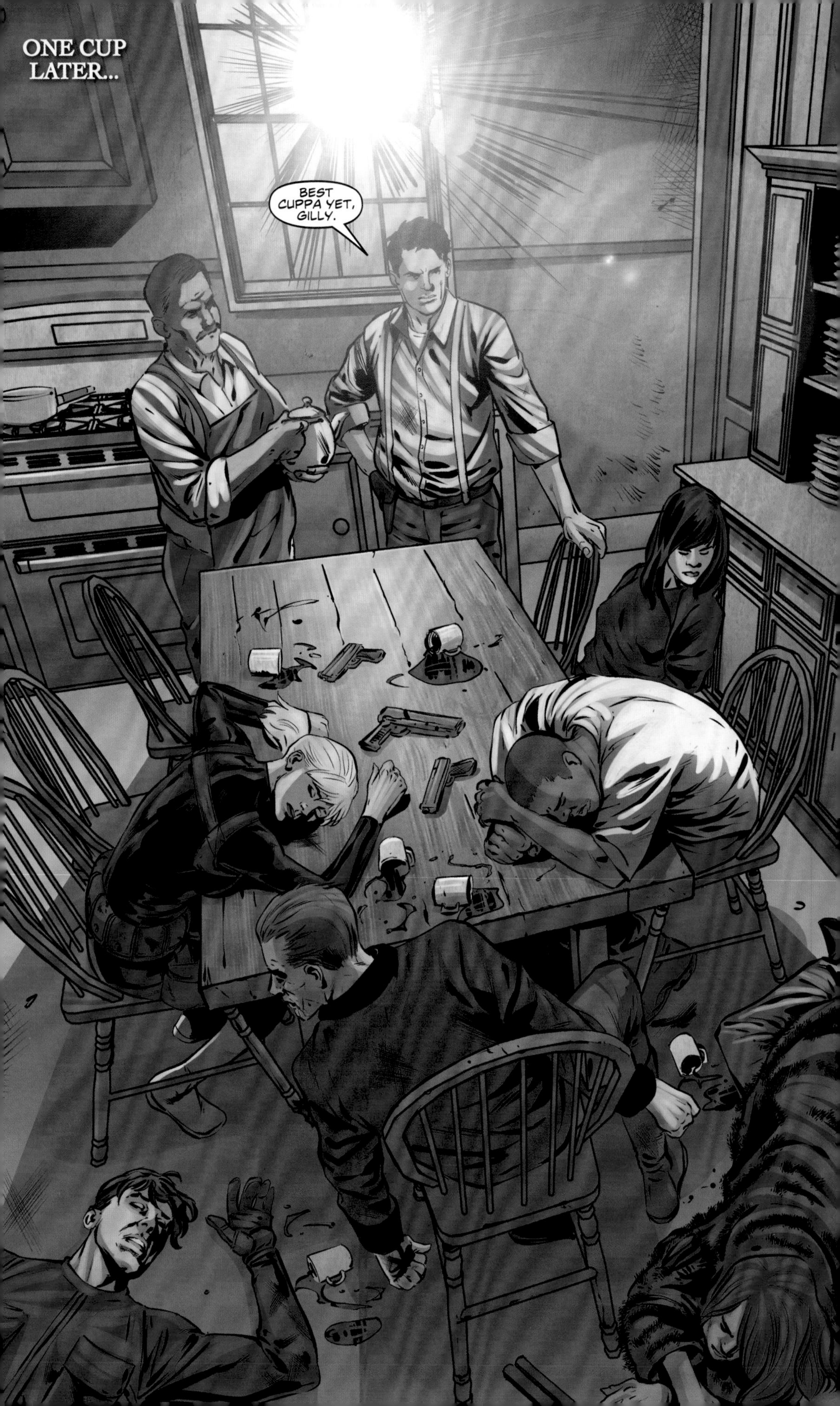
ONE CUP LATER...
BEST CUPPA YET, GILLY.

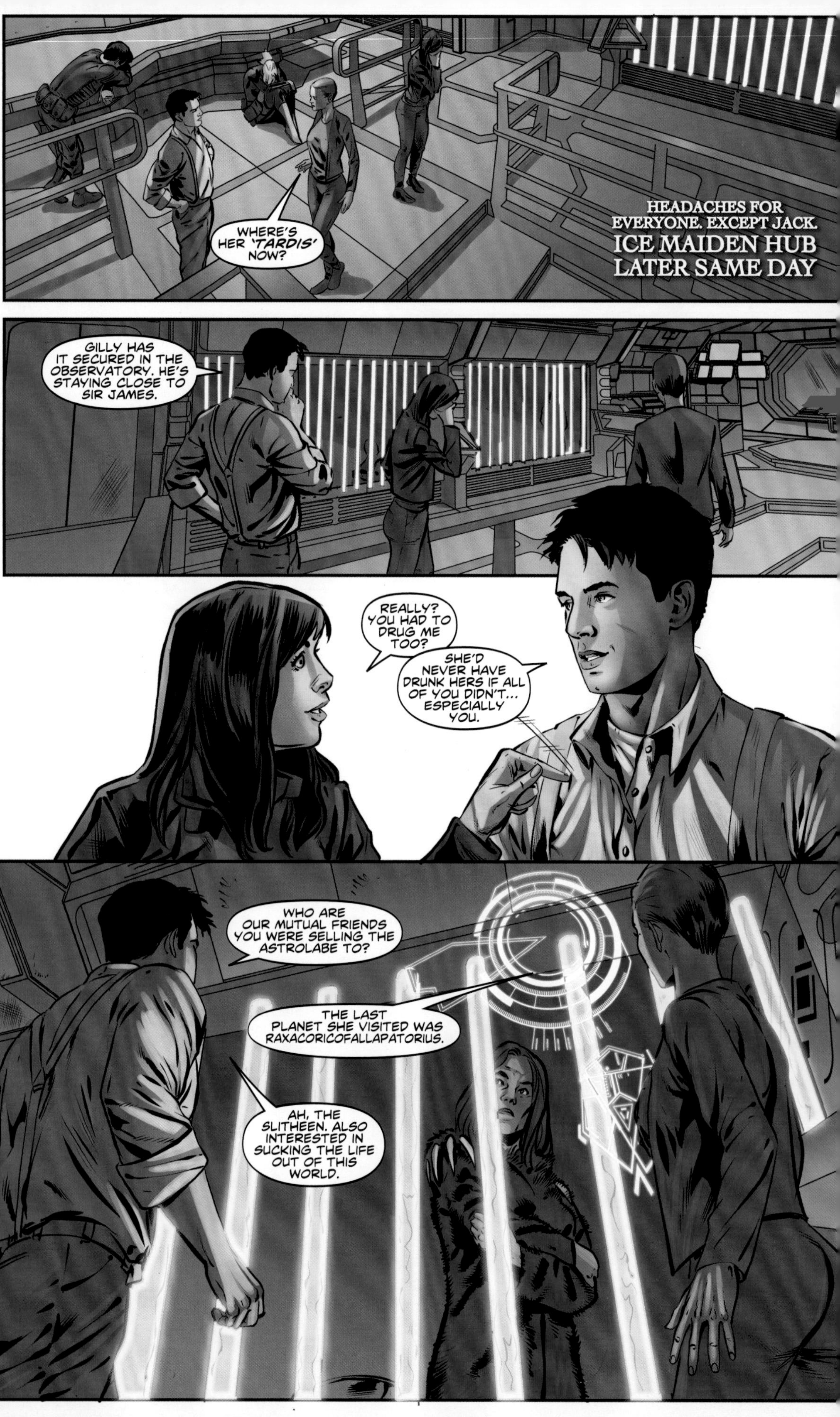
WHERE'S HER 'TARDIS' NOW?
HEADACHES FOR EVERYONE. EXCEPT JACK.
ICE MAIDEN HUB
LATER SAME DAY
GILLY HAS IT SECURED IN THE OBSERVATORY. HE'S STAYING CLOSE TO SIR JAMES.
REALLY? YOU HAD TO DRUG ME TOO?
SHE'D NEVER HAVE DRUNK HERS IF ALL OF YOU DIDN'T... ESPECIALLY YOU.
WHO ARE OUR MUTUAL FRIENDS YOU WERE SELLING THE ASTROLABE TO?
THE LAST PLANET SHE VISITED WAS RAXACORICOFALLAPATORIUS.
AH, THE SLITHEEN. ALSO INTERESTED IN SUCKING THE LIFE OUT OF THIS WORLD.

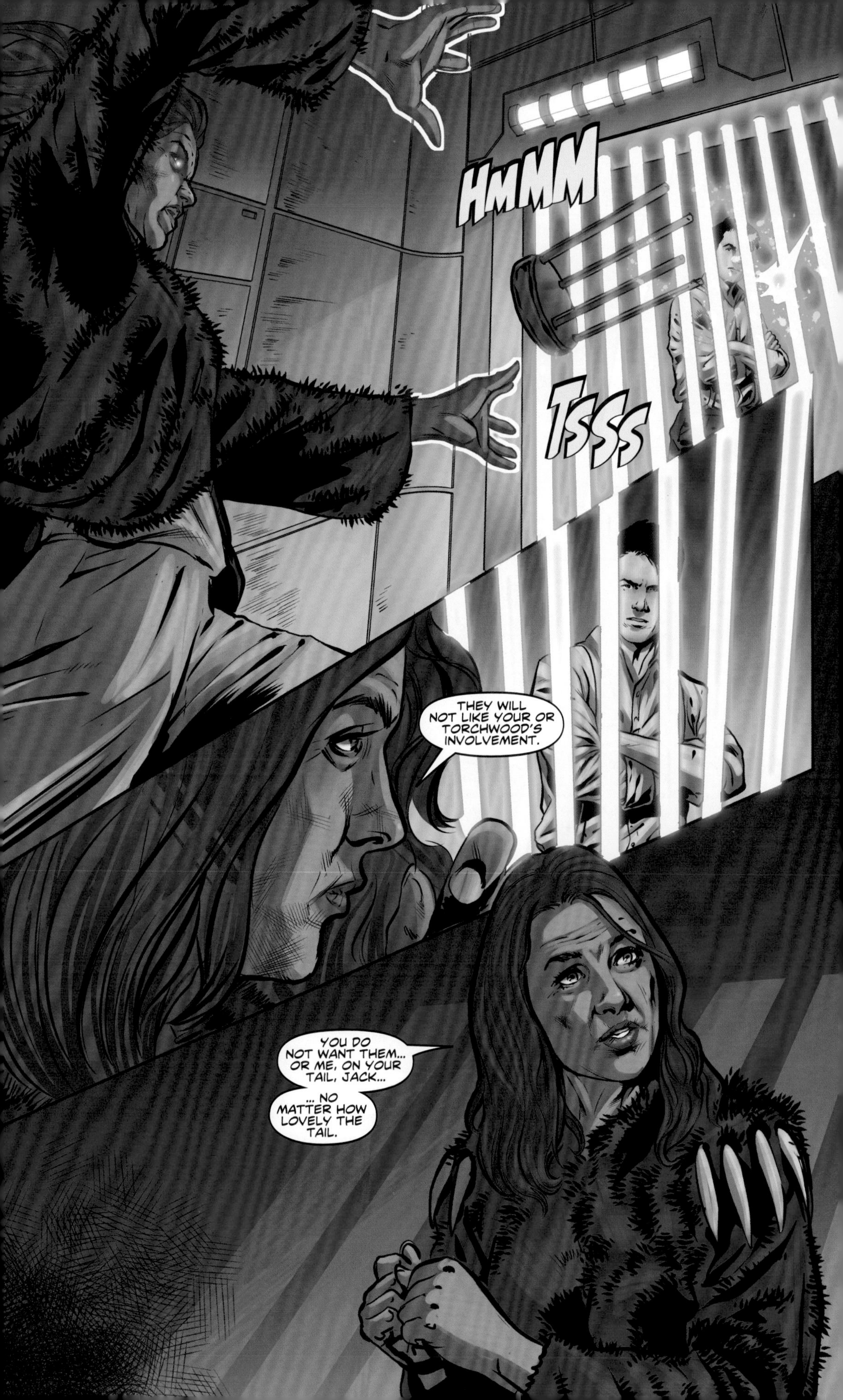
HMMM
TSSS
THEY WILL NOT LIKE YOUR OR TORCHWOOD'S INVOLVEMENT.
YOU DO NOT WANT THEM... OR ME, ON YOUR TAIL, JACK...
... NO MATTER HOW LOVELY THE TAIL.

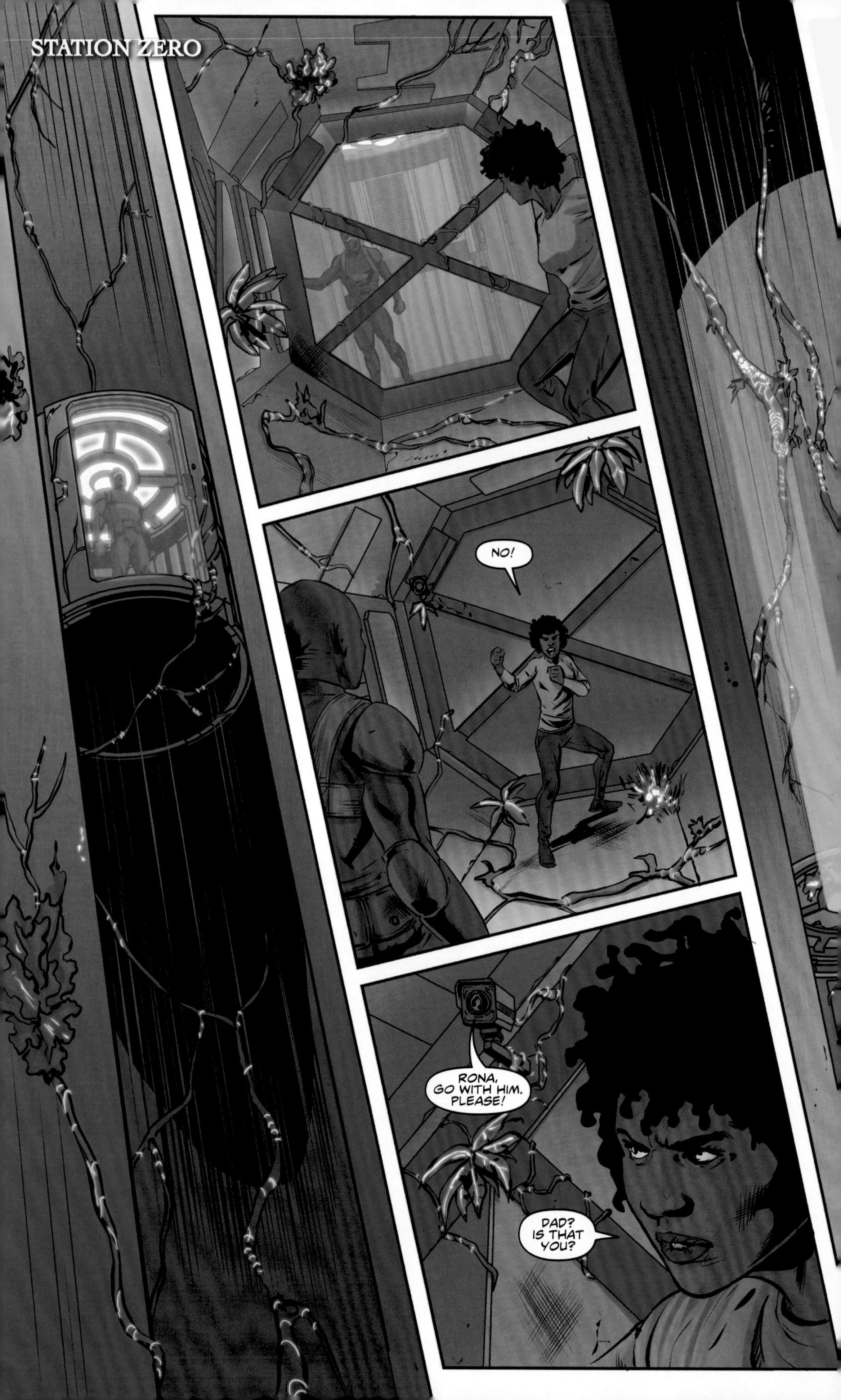
NO!
RONA, GO WITH HIM. PLEASE!
DAD? IS THAT YOU?

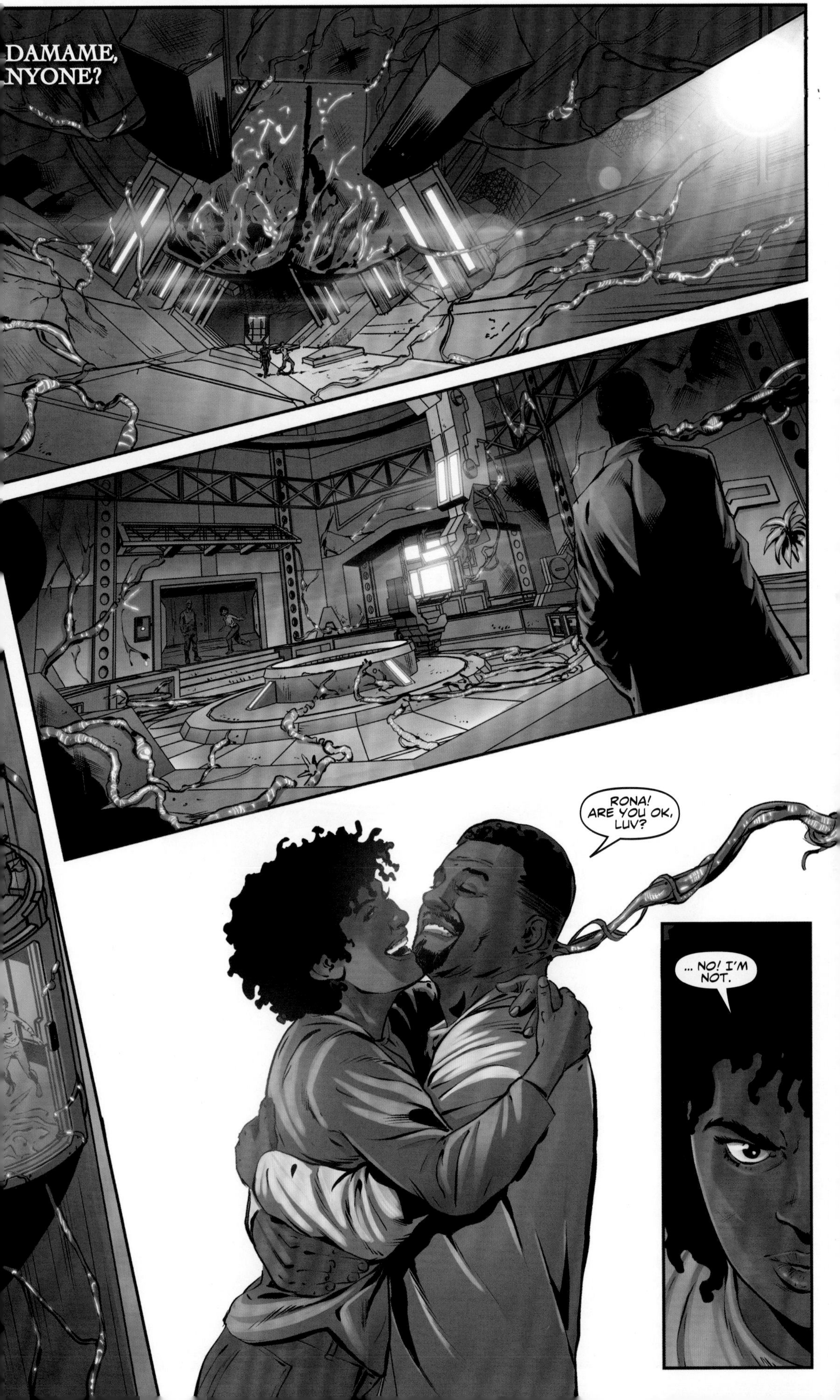
DAMAME, NYONE?
RONA! ARE YOU OK, LUV?
... NO! I'M NOT.

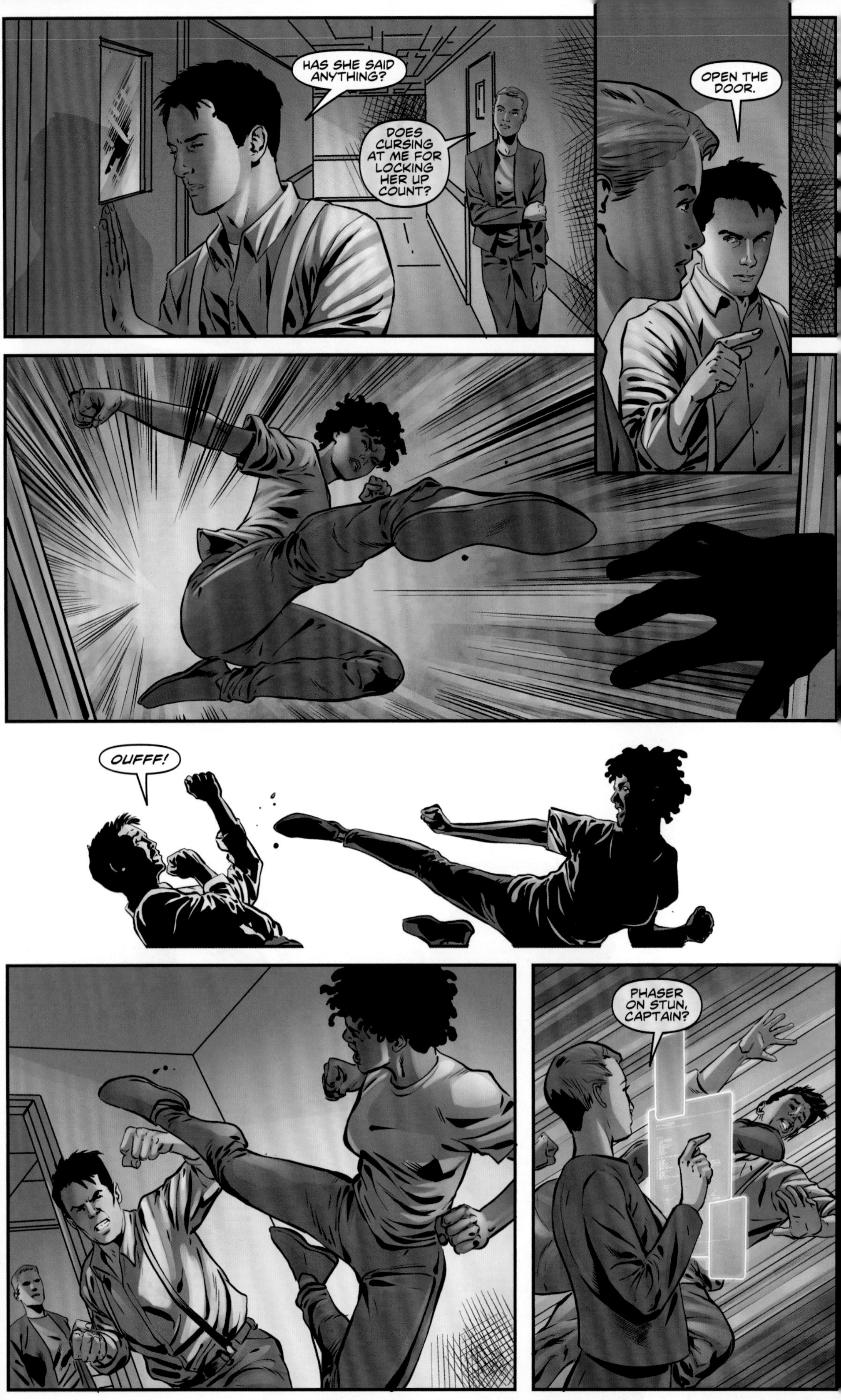
HAS SHE SAID ANYTHING?
DOES CURSING AT ME FOR LOCKING HER UP COUNT?
OPEN THE DOOR.
OUFFF!
PHASER ON STUN, CAPTAIN?

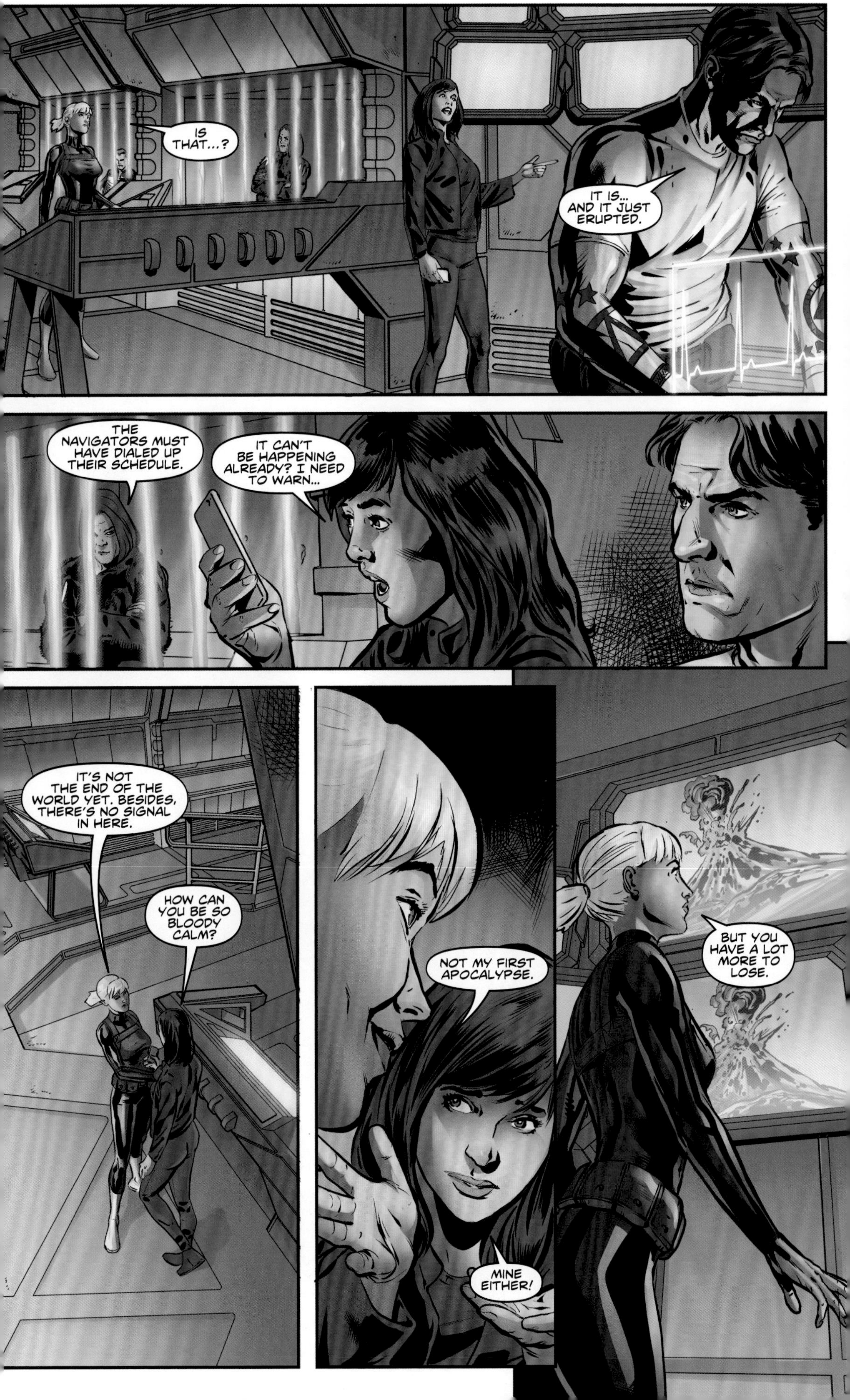

IS THAT...?
IT IS... AND IT JUST ERUPTED.
THE NAVIGATORS MUST HAVE DIALED UP THEIR SCHEDULE.
IT CAN'T BE HAPPENING ALREADY? I NEED TO WARN...
IT'S NOT THE END OF THE WORLD YET. BESIDES, THERE'S NO SIGNAL IN HERE.
HOW CAN YOU BE SO BLOODY CALM?
NOT MY FIRST APOCALYPSE.
MINE EITHER!
BUT YOU HAVE A LOT MORE TO LOSE.

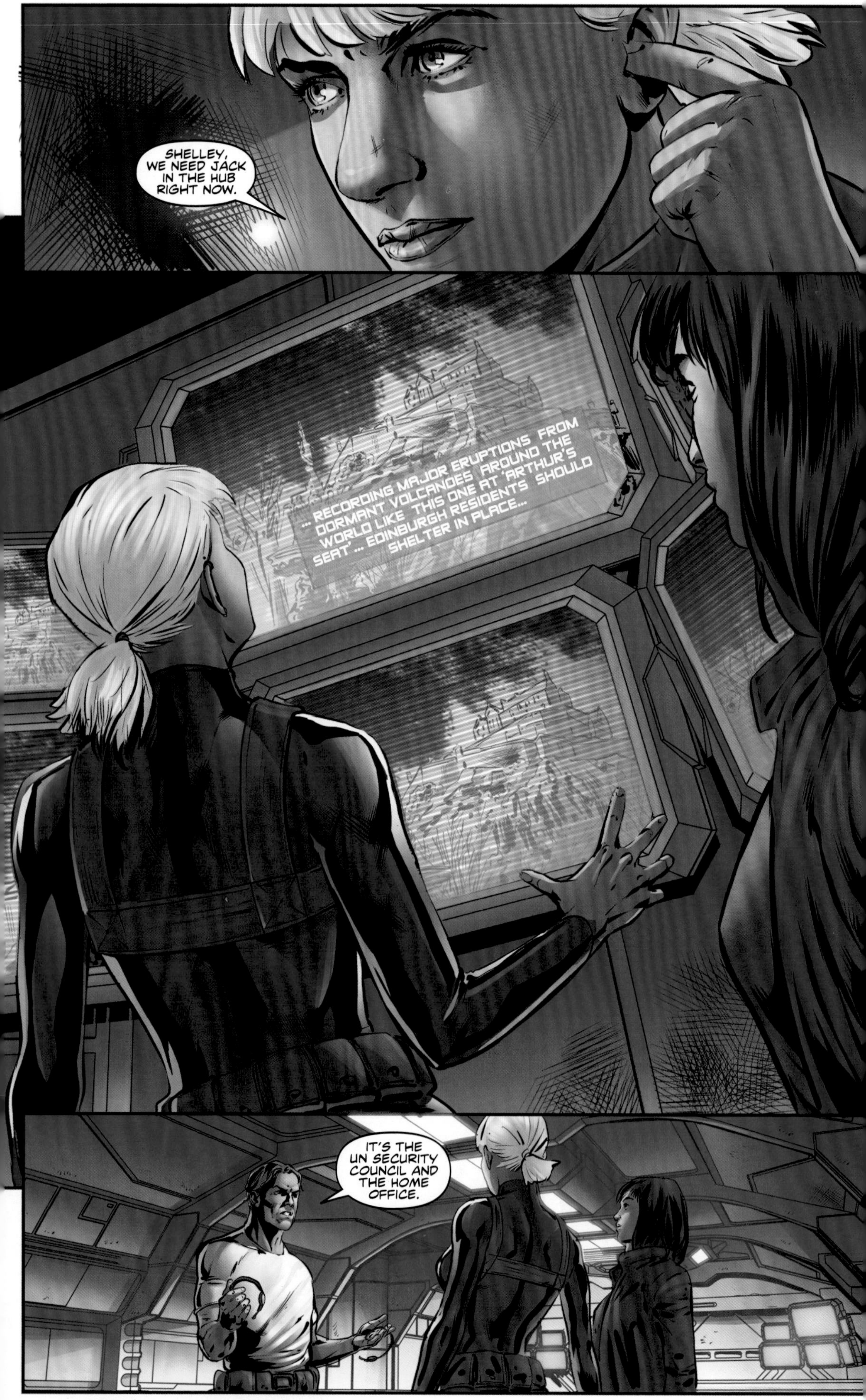
SHELLEY, WE NEED JACK IN THE HUB RIGHT NOW.
... RECORDING MAJOR ERUPTIONS FROM DORMANT VOLCANOES AROUND THE WORLD LIKE THIS ONE AT 'ARTHUR'S SEAT' ... EDINBURGH RESIDENTS SHOULD SHELTER IN PLACE...
IT'S THE UN SECURITY COUNCIL AND THE HOME OFFICE.

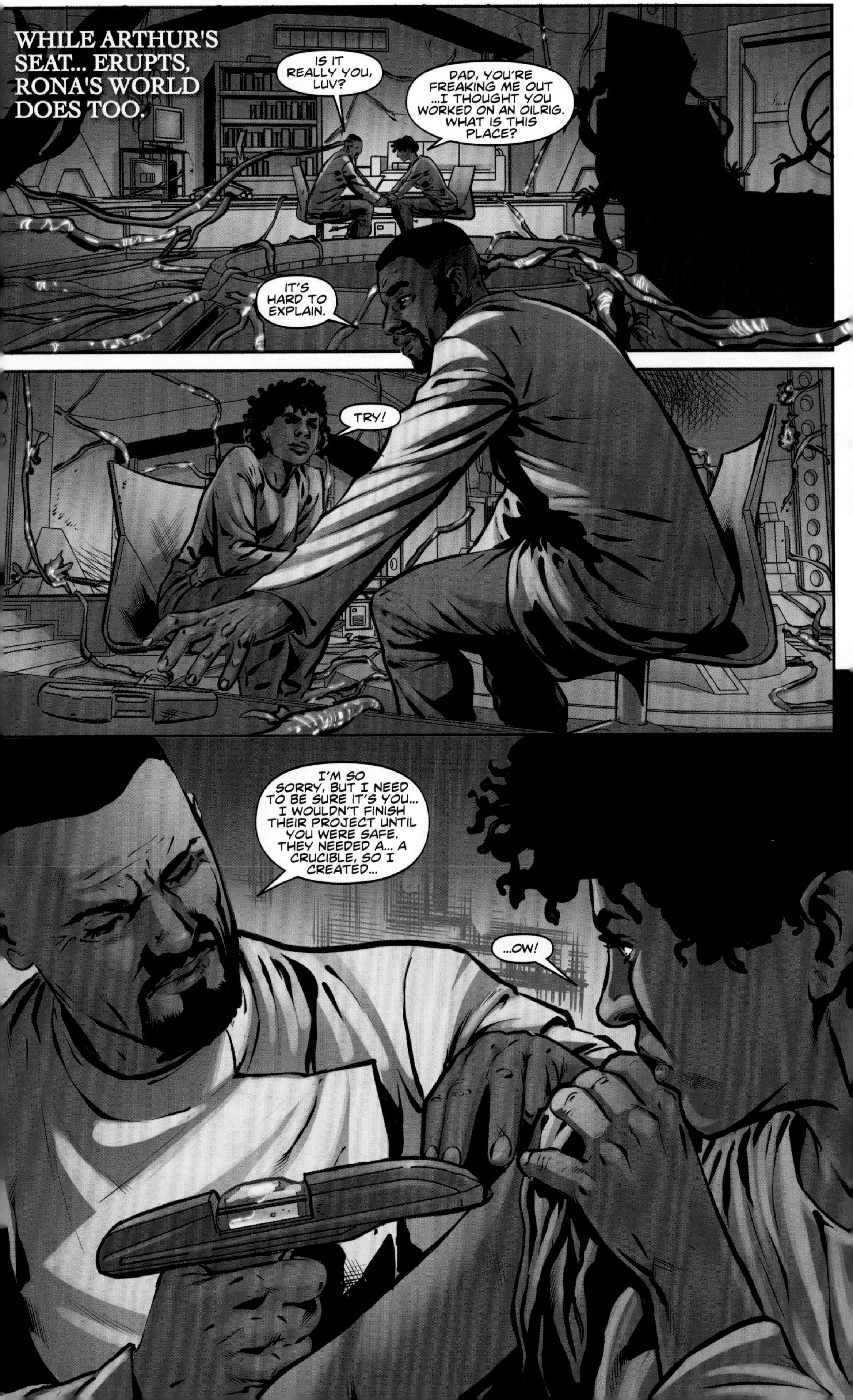
WHILE ARTHUR'S SEAT... ERUPTS, RONA'S WORLD DOES TOO.
IS IT REALLY YOU, LUV?
DAD, YOU'RE FREAKING ME OUT ...I THOUGHT YOU WORKED ON AN OILRIG. WHAT IS THIS PLACE?
IT'S HARD TO EXPLAIN.
TRY!
I'M SO SORRY, BUT I NEED TO BE SURE IT'S YOU... I WOULDN'T FINISH THEIR PROJECT UNTIL YOU WERE SAFE. THEY NEEDED A... A CRUCIBLE, SO I CREATED...
...OW!

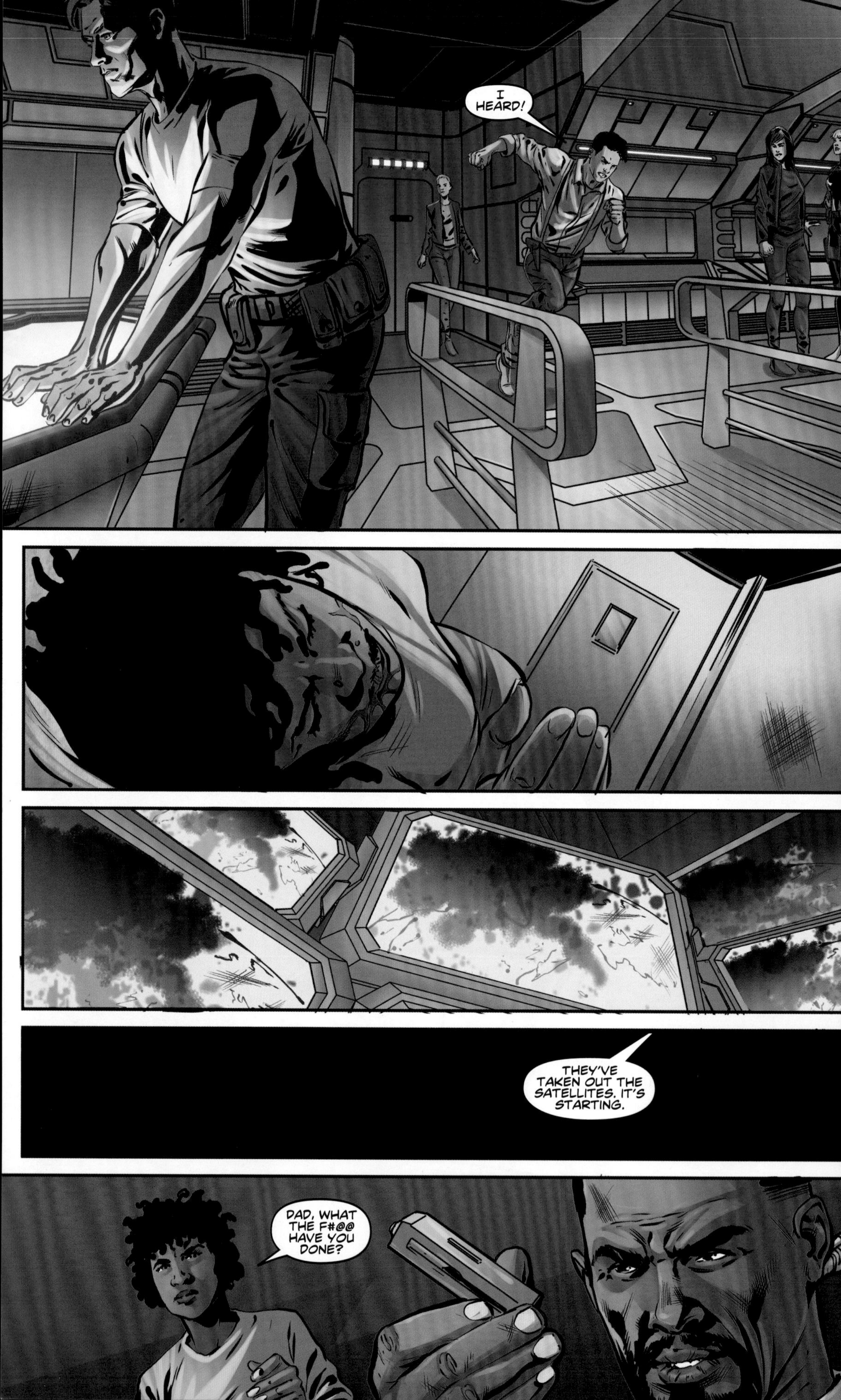
I HEARD!
THEY'VE TAKEN OUT THE SATELLITES. IT'S STARTING.
DAD, WHAT THE F#@@ HAVE YOU DONE?

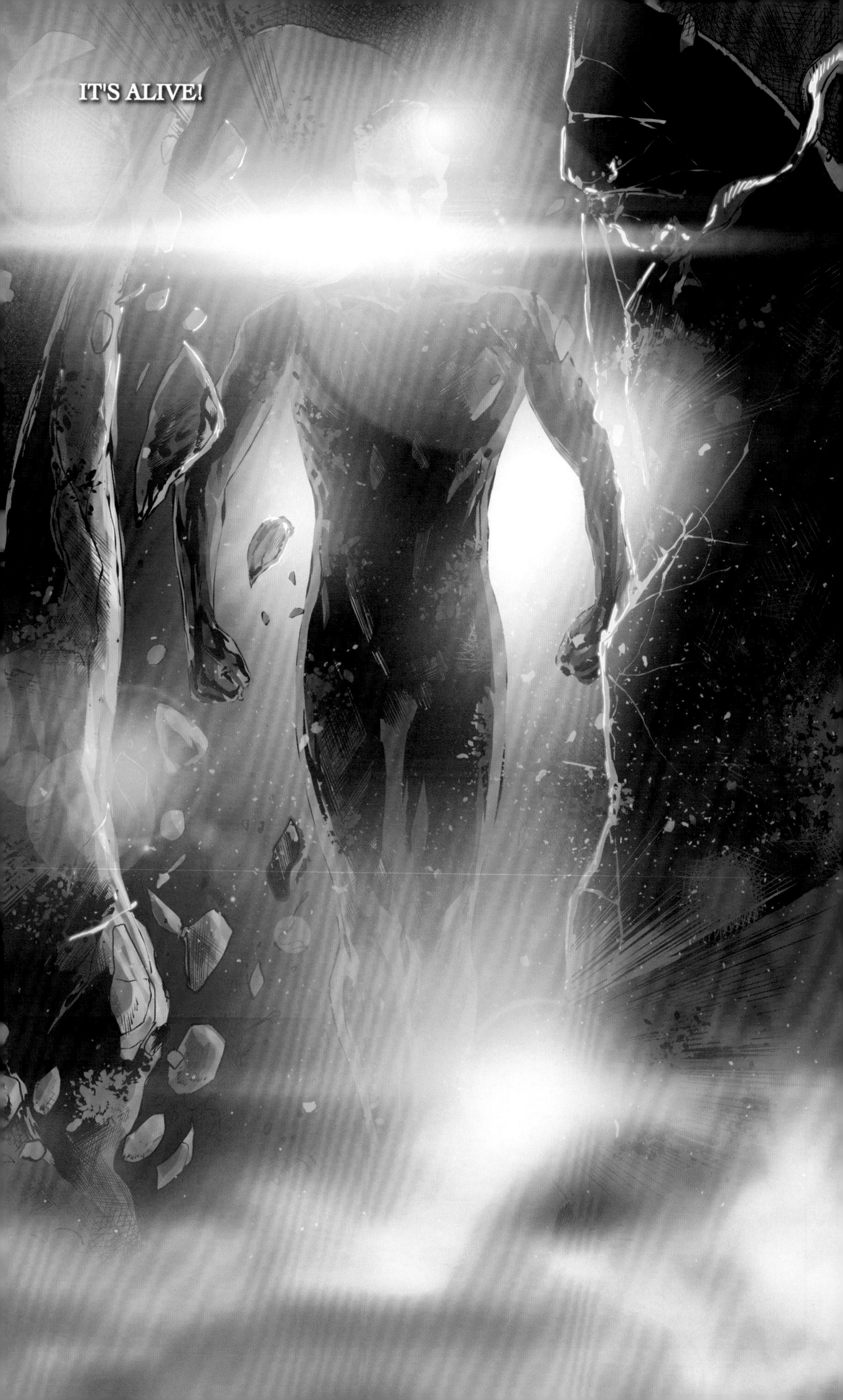
IT'S ALIVE!

CHAPTER 3

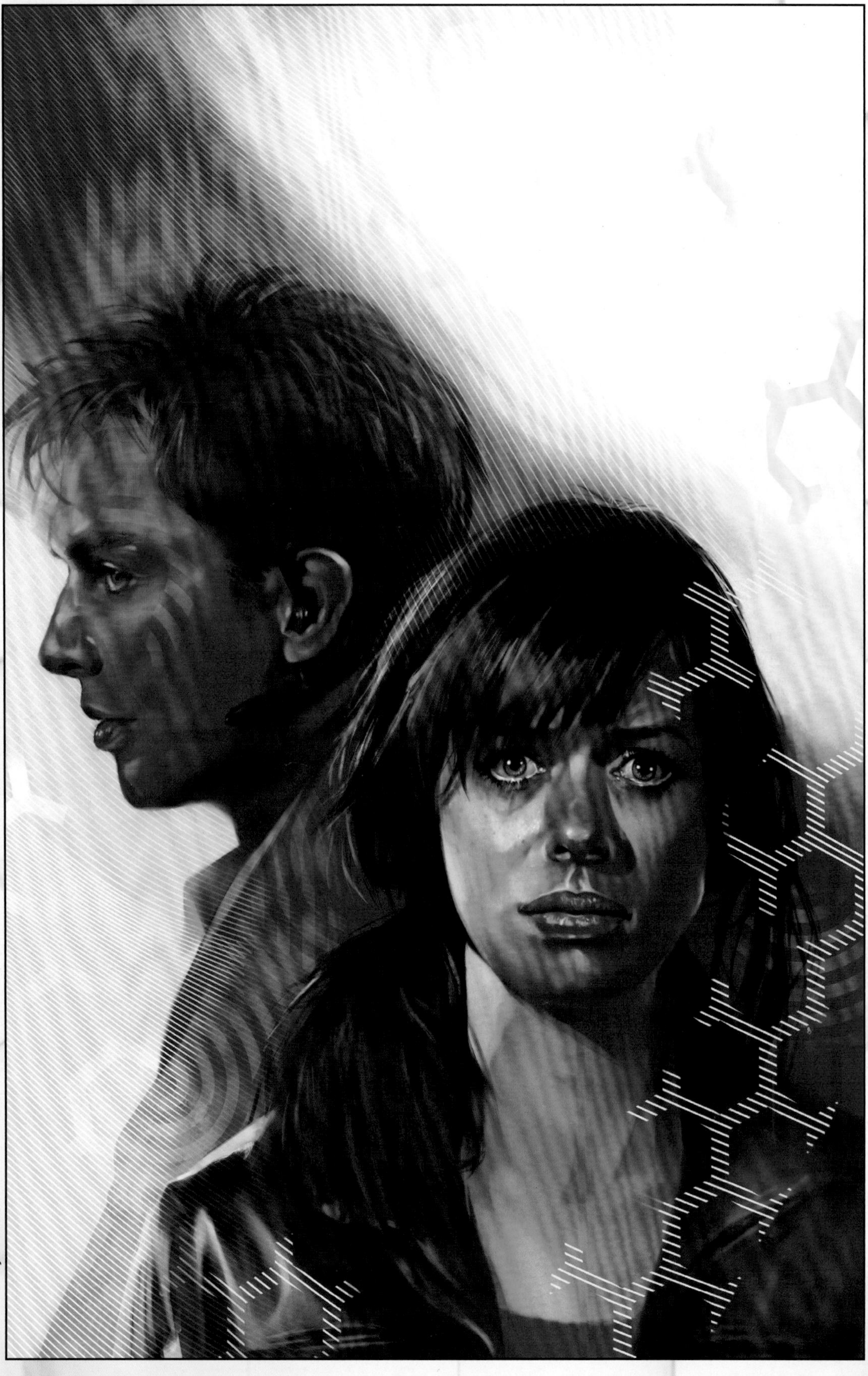

illustration by CLAUDIA CARANFA

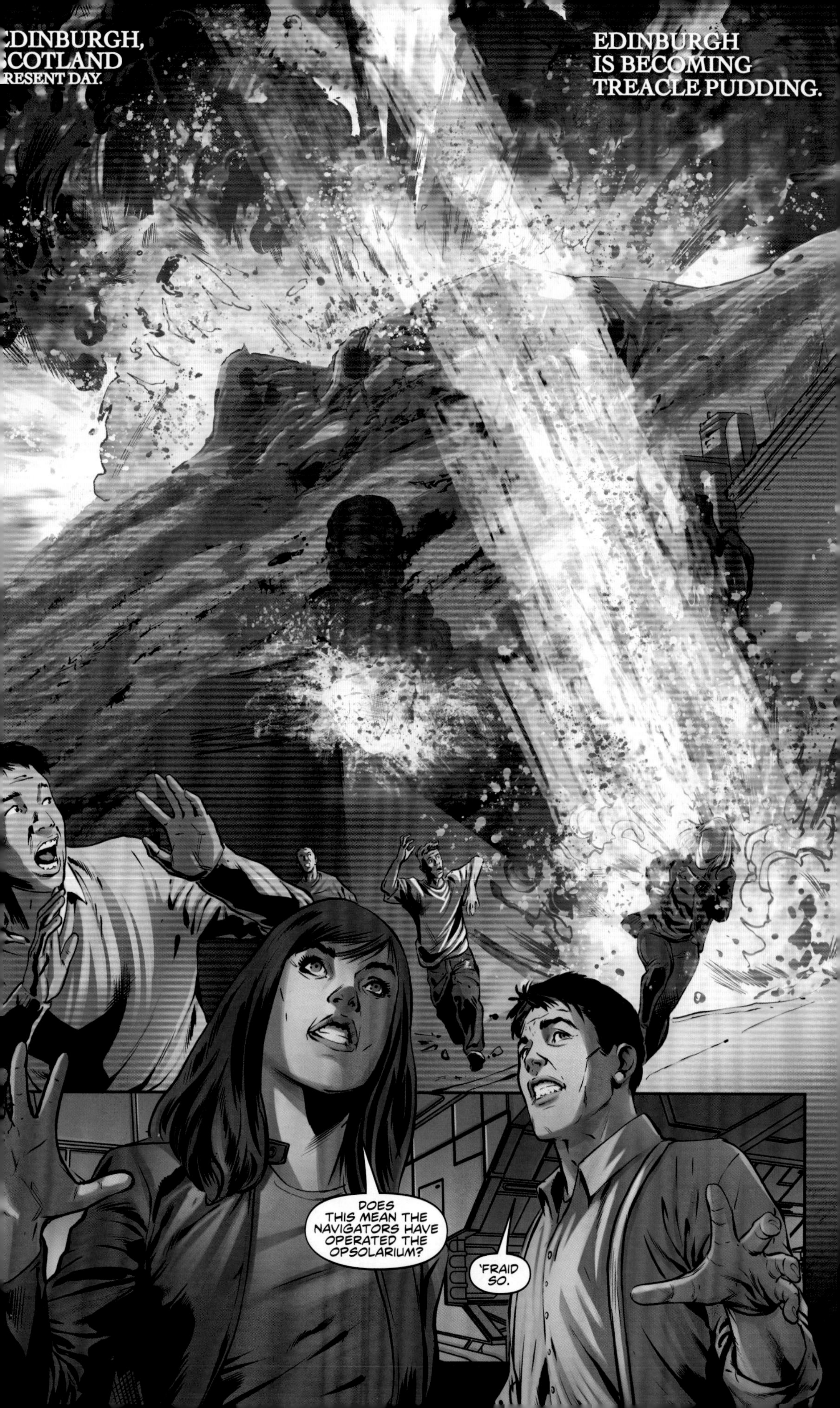

EDINBURGH,
SCOTLAND
PRESENT DAY.
EDINBURGH IS BECOMING TREACLE PUDDING.
DOES THIS MEAN THE NAVIGATORS HAVE OPERATED THE OPSOLARIUM?
'FRAID SO.

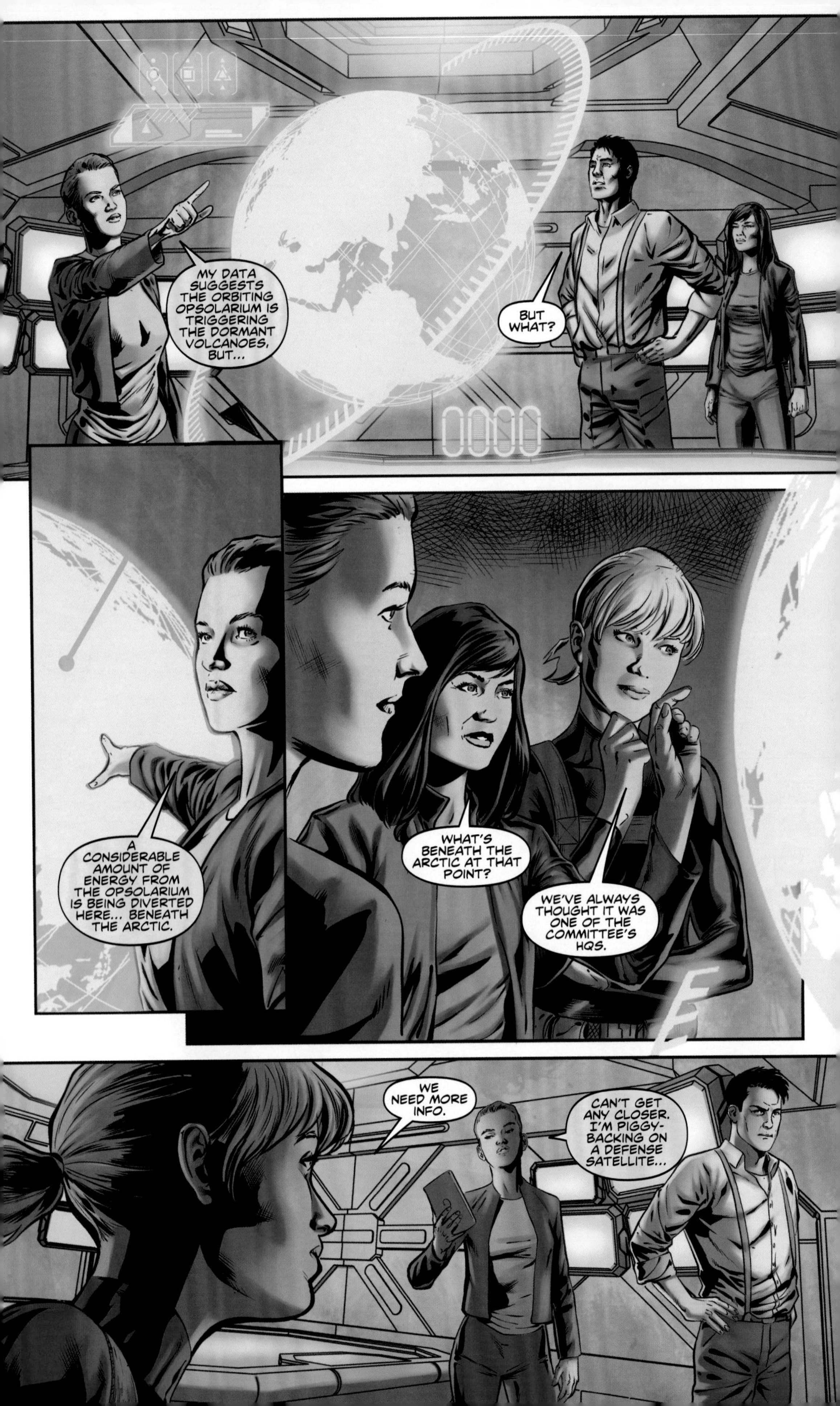
MY DATA SUGGESTS THE ORBITING OPSOLARIUM IS TRIGGERING THE DORMANT VOLCANOES, BUT...
BUT WHAT?
A CONSIDERABLE AMOUNT OF ENERGY FROM THE OPSOLARIUM IS BEING DIVERTED HERE... BENEATH THE ARCTIC.
WHAT'S BENEATH THE ARCTIC AT THAT POINT?
WE'VE ALWAYS THOUGHT IT WAS ONE OF THE COMMITTEE'S HQS.
WE NEED MORE INFO.
CAN'T GET ANY CLOSER. I'M PIGGY-BACKING ON A DEFENSE SATELLITE...

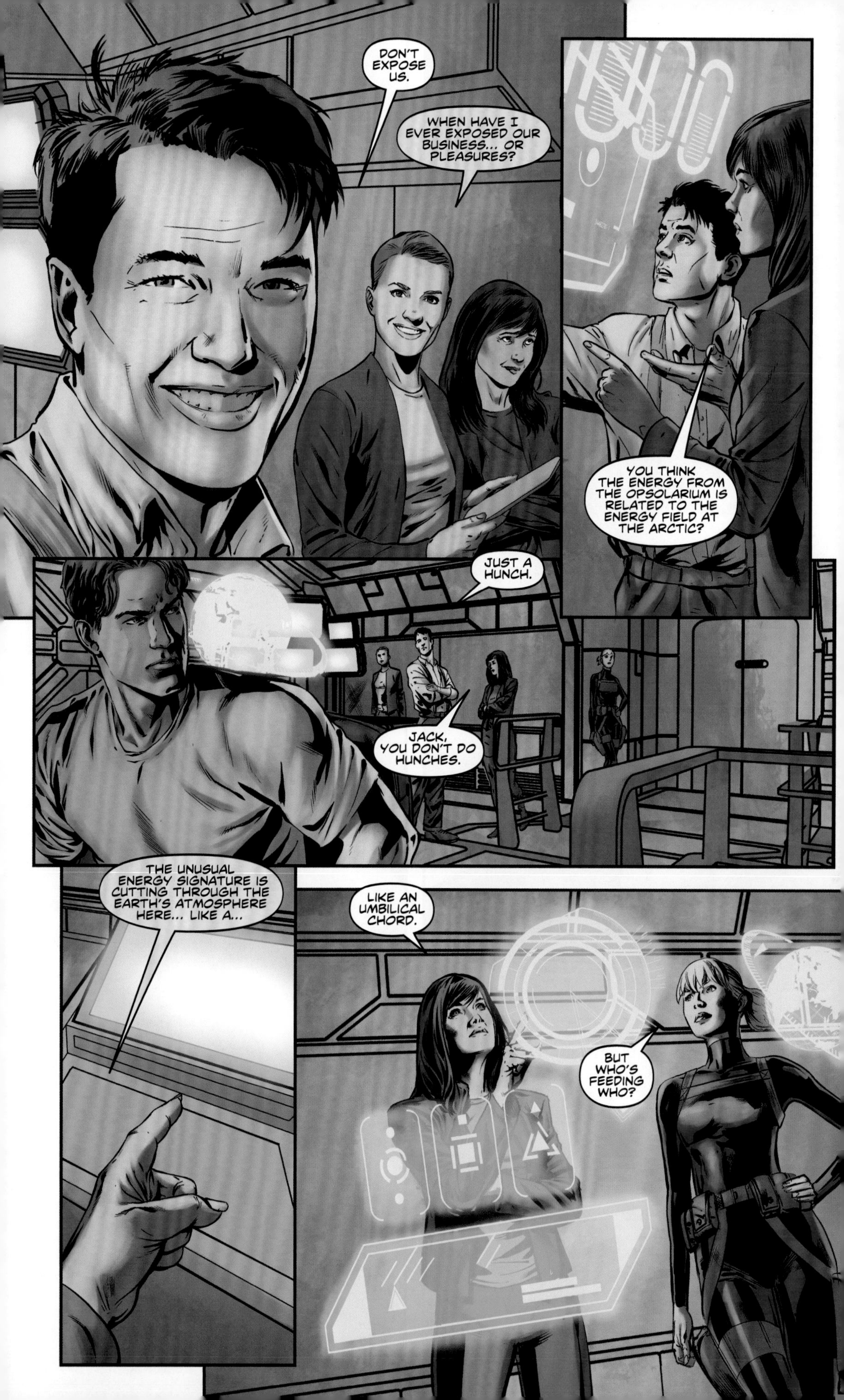
DON'T EXPOSE US.
WHEN HAVE I EVER EXPOSED OUR BUSINESS... OR PLEASURES?
YOU THINK THE ENERGY FROM THE OPSOLARIUM IS RELATED TO THE ENERGY FIELD AT THE ARCTIC?
JUST A HUNCH.
JACK, YOU DON'T DO HUNCHES.
THE UNUSUAL ENERGY SIGNATURE IS CUTTING THROUGH THE EARTH'S ATMOSPHERE HERE... LIKE A...
LIKE AN UMBILICAL CHORD.
BUT WHO'S FEEDING WHO?

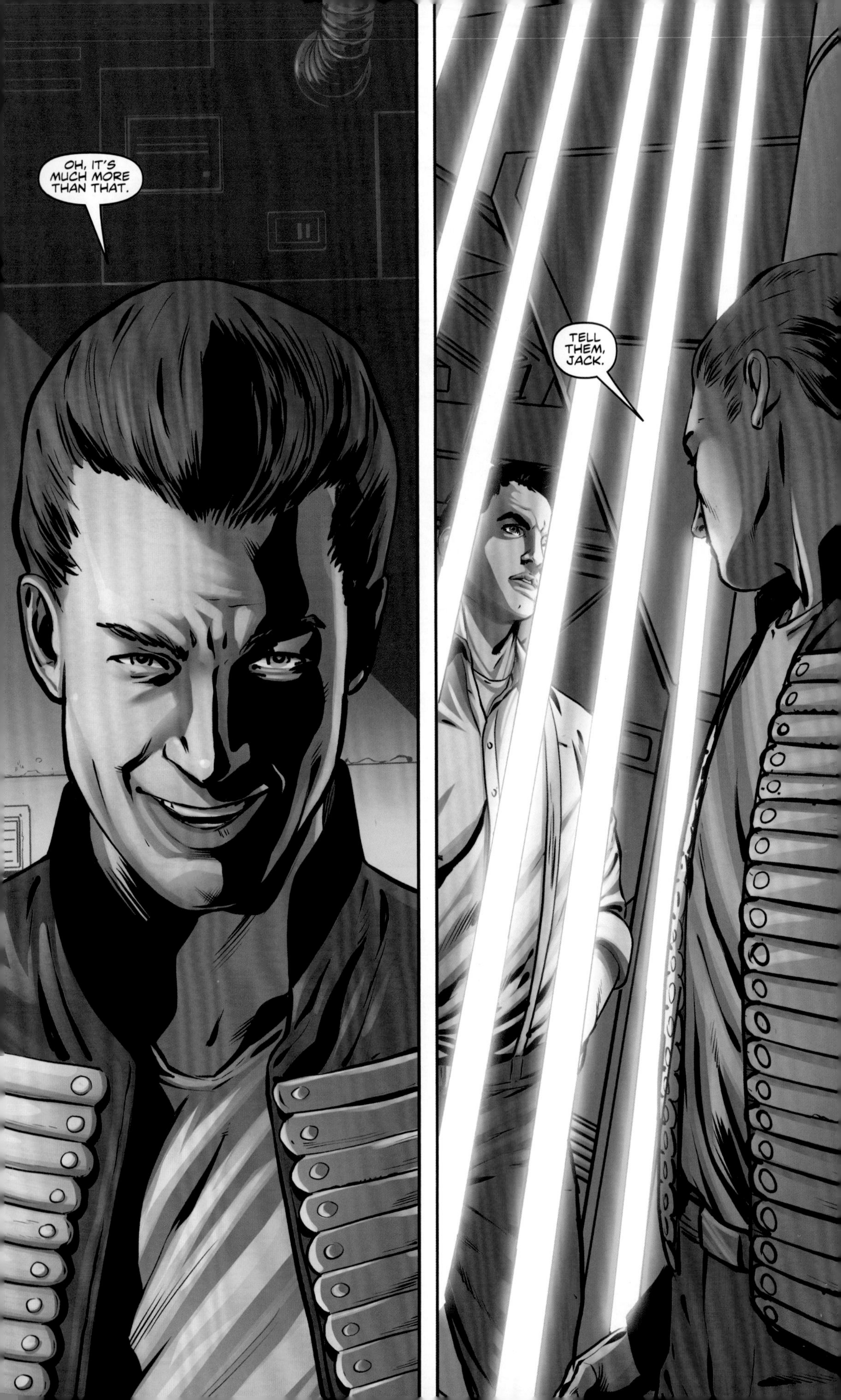
OH, IT'S MUCH MORE THAN THAT.
TELL THEM, JACK.

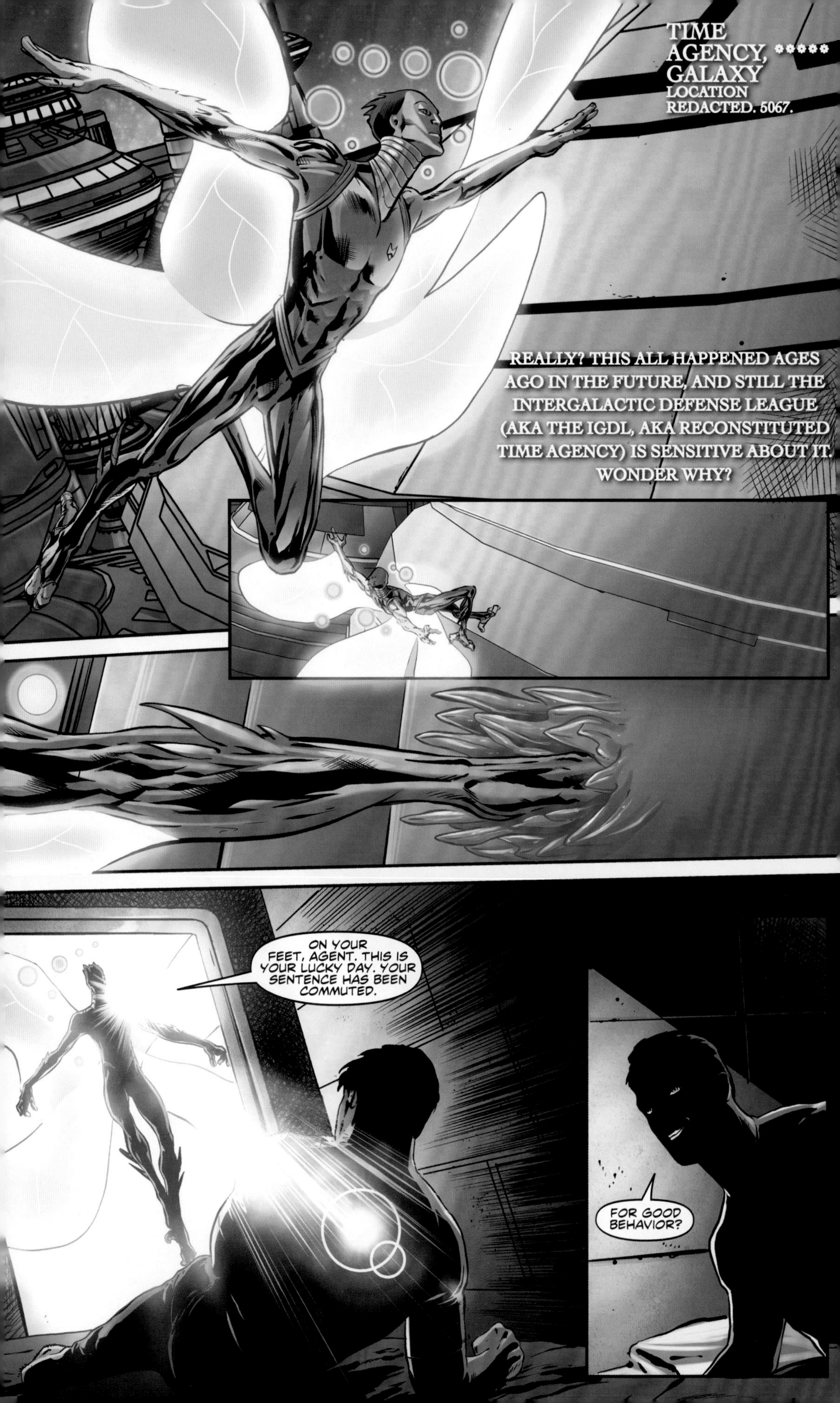
TIME AGENCY, [redacted] GALAXY LOCATION REDACTED. 5067.
REALLY? THIS ALL HAPPENED AGES AGO IN THE FUTURE, AND STILL THE INTERGALACTIC DEFENSE LEAGUE (AKA THE IGDL, AKA RECONSTITUTED TIME AGENCY) IS SENSITIVE ABOUT IT. WONDER WHY?
ON YOUR FEET, AGENT. THIS IS YOUR LUCKY DAY. YOUR SENTENCE HAS BEEN COMMUTED.
FOR GOOD BEHAVIOR?

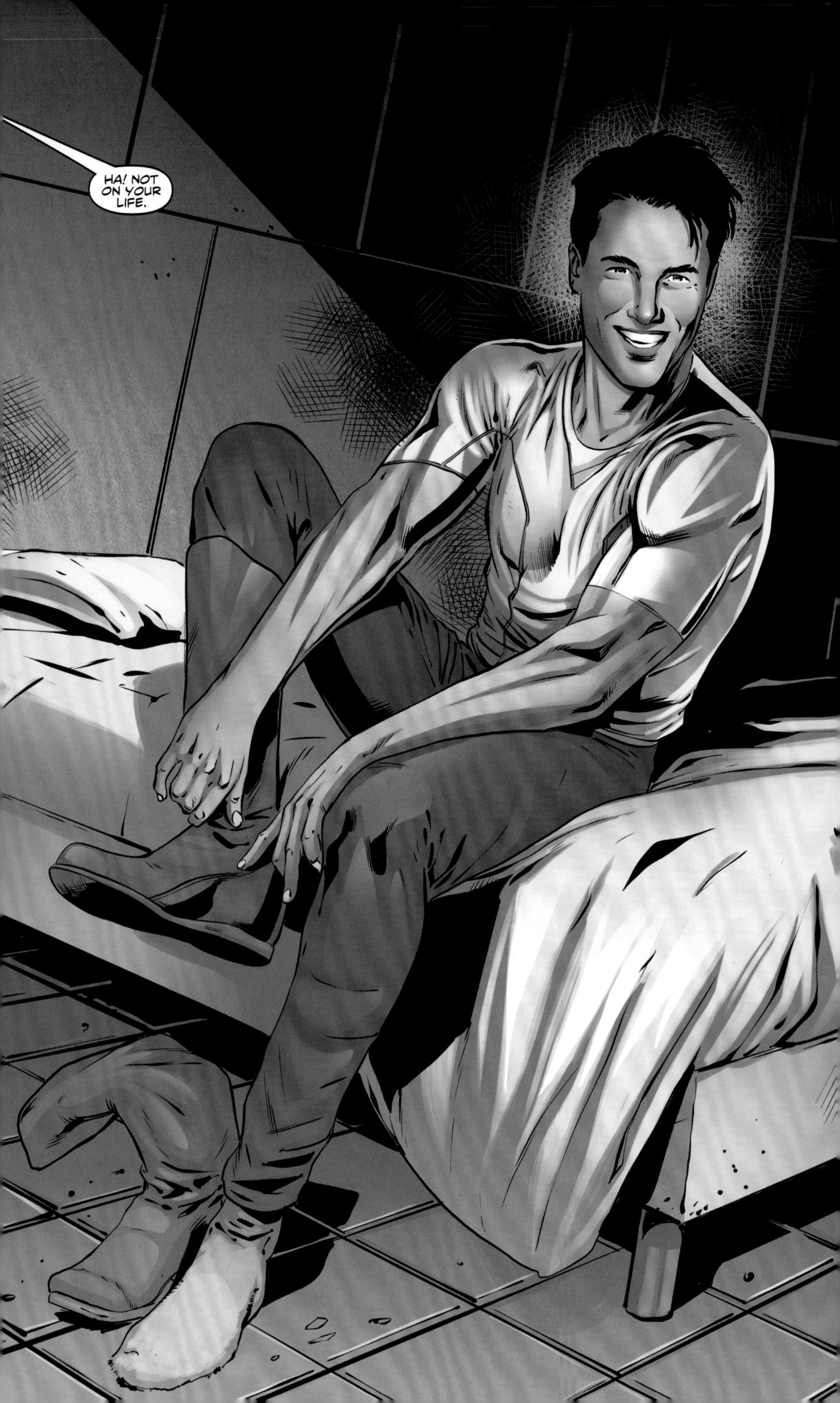
HA! NOT ON YOUR LIFE.

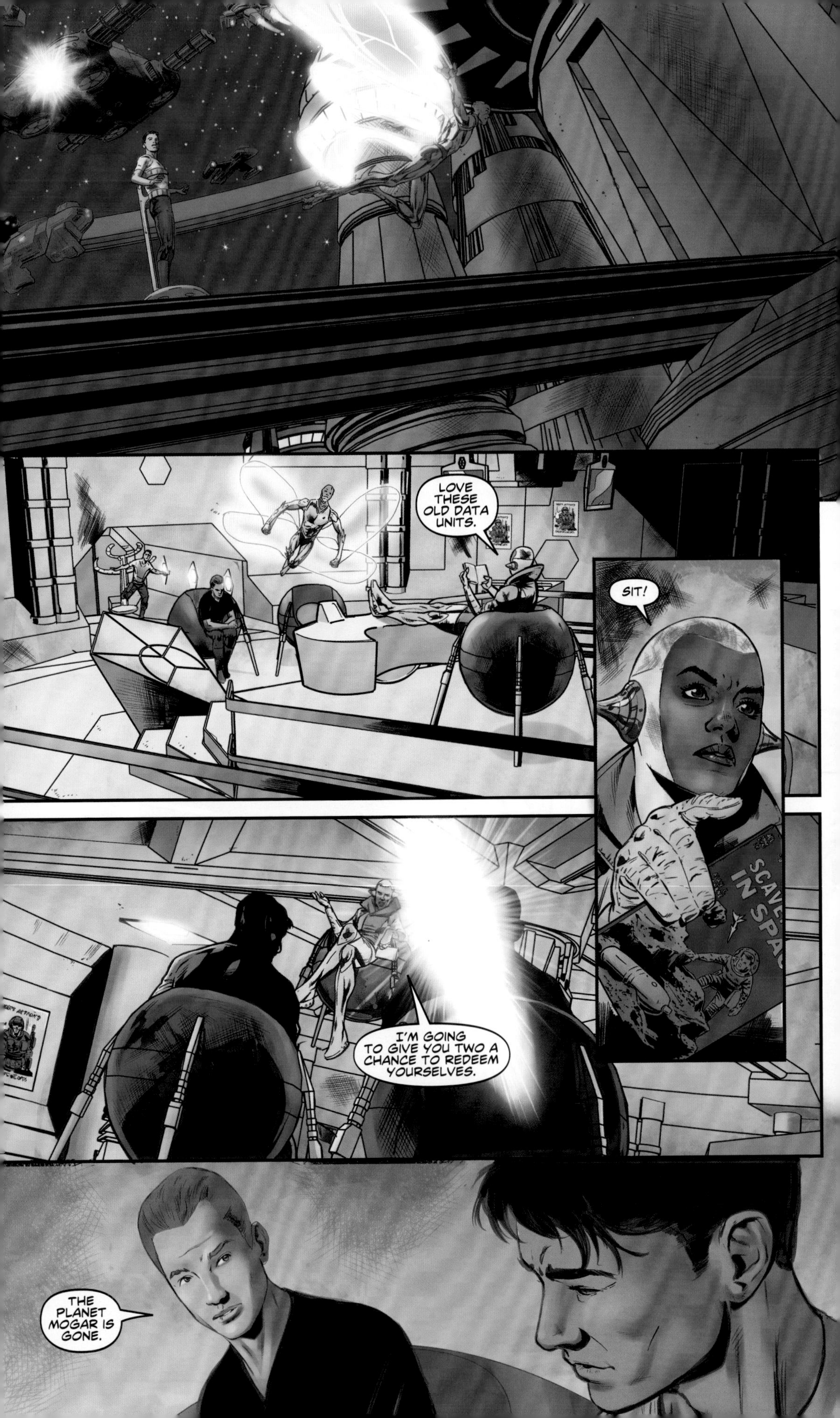
LOVE THESE OLD DATA UNITS.
SIT!
SCAVE... IN SPAC...
I'M GOING TO GIVE YOU TWO A CHANCE TO REDEEM YOURSELVES.
THE PLANET MOGAR IS GONE.

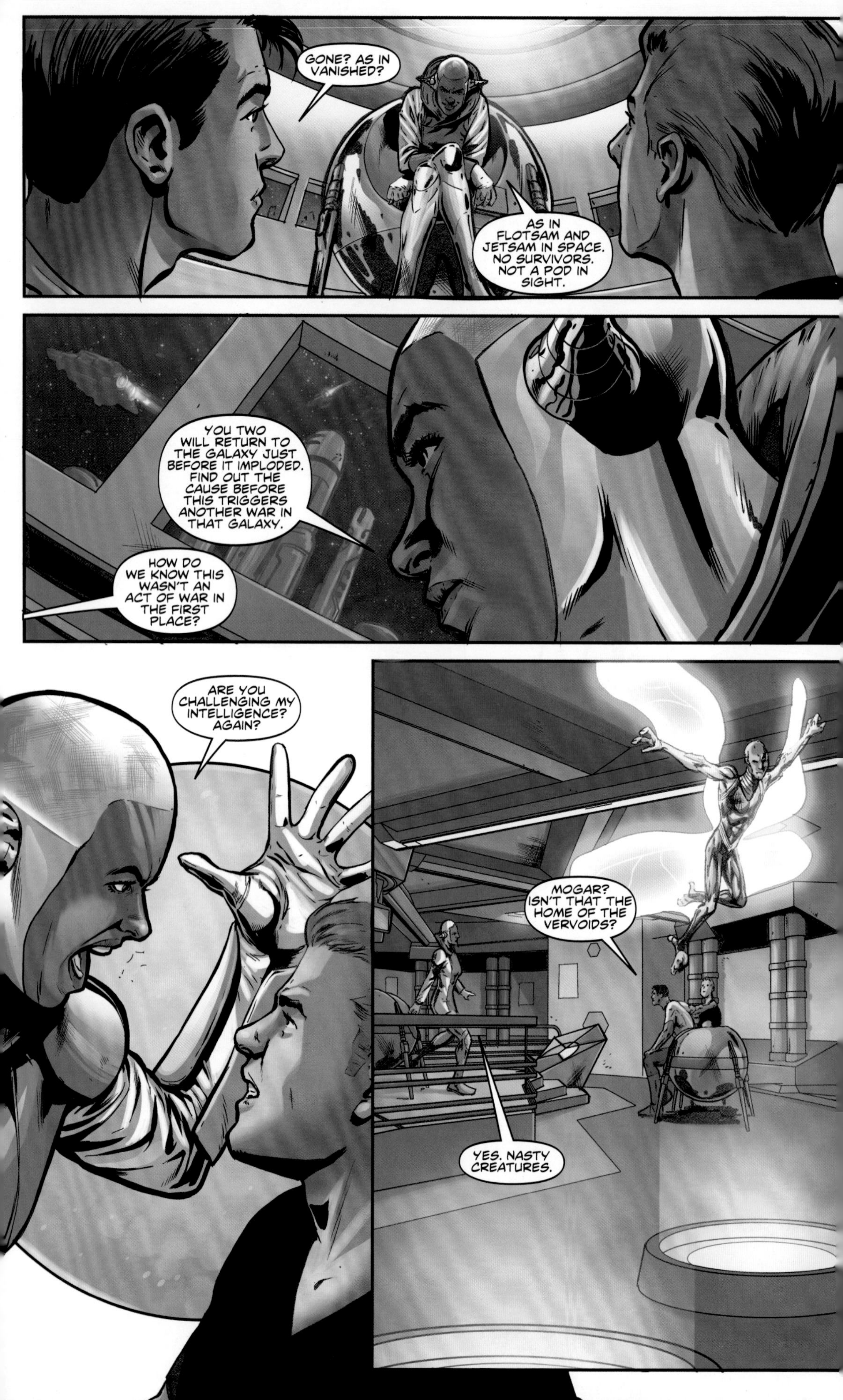
GONE? AS IN VANISHED?
AS IN FLOTSAM AND JETSAM IN SPACE. NO SURVIVORS. NOT A POD IN SIGHT.
YOU TWO WILL RETURN TO THE GALAXY JUST BEFORE IT IMPLODED. FIND OUT THE CAUSE BEFORE THIS TRIGGERS ANOTHER WAR IN THAT GALAXY.
HOW DO WE KNOW THIS WASN'T AN ACT OF WAR IN THE FIRST PLACE?
ARE YOU CHALLENGING MY INTELLIGENCE? AGAIN?
MOGAR? ISN'T THAT THE HOME OF THE VERVOIDS?
YES. NASTY CREATURES.

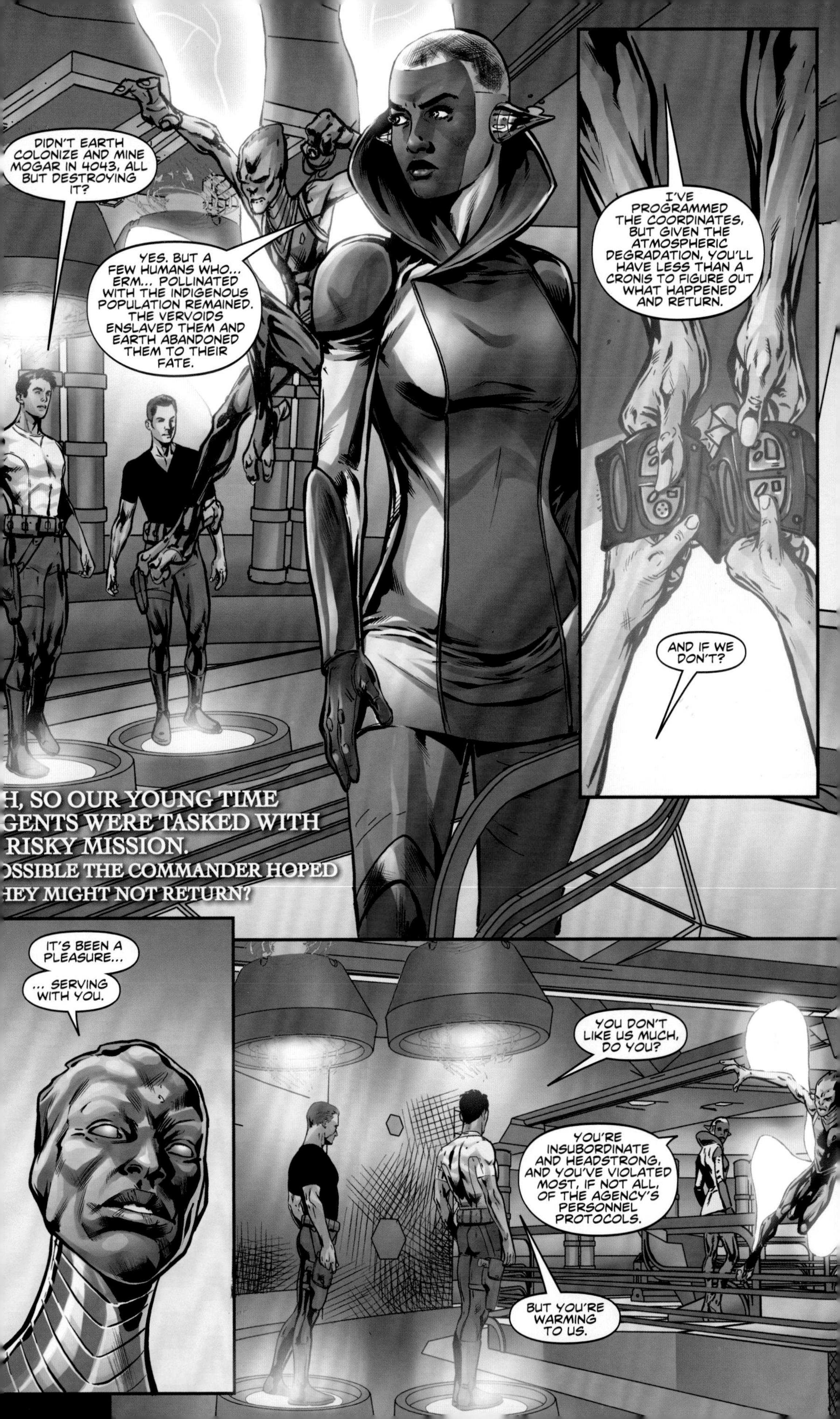
DIDN'T EARTH COLONIZE AND MINE MOGAR IN 4043, ALL BUT DESTROYING IT?
YES. BUT A FEW HUMANS WHO... ERM... POLLINATED WITH THE INDIGENOUS POPULATION REMAINED. THE VERVOIDS ENSLAVED THEM AND EARTH ABANDONED THEM TO THEIR FATE.
I'VE PROGRAMMED THE COORDINATES, BUT GIVEN THE ATMOSPHERIC DEGRADATION, YOU'LL HAVE LESS THAN A CRONIS TO FIGURE OUT WHAT HAPPENED AND RETURN.
AND IF WE DON'T?
H, SO OUR YOUNG TIME
GENTS WERE TASKED WITH
RISKY MISSION.
OSSIBLE THE COMMANDER HOPED
HEY MIGHT NOT RETURN?
IT'S BEEN A PLEASURE...
... SERVING WITH YOU.
YOU DON'T LIKE US MUCH, DO YOU?
YOU'RE INSUBORDINATE AND HEADSTRONG, AND YOU'VE VIOLATED MOST, IF NOT ALL, OF THE AGENCY'S PERSONNEL PROTOCOLS.
BUT YOU'RE WARMING TO US.

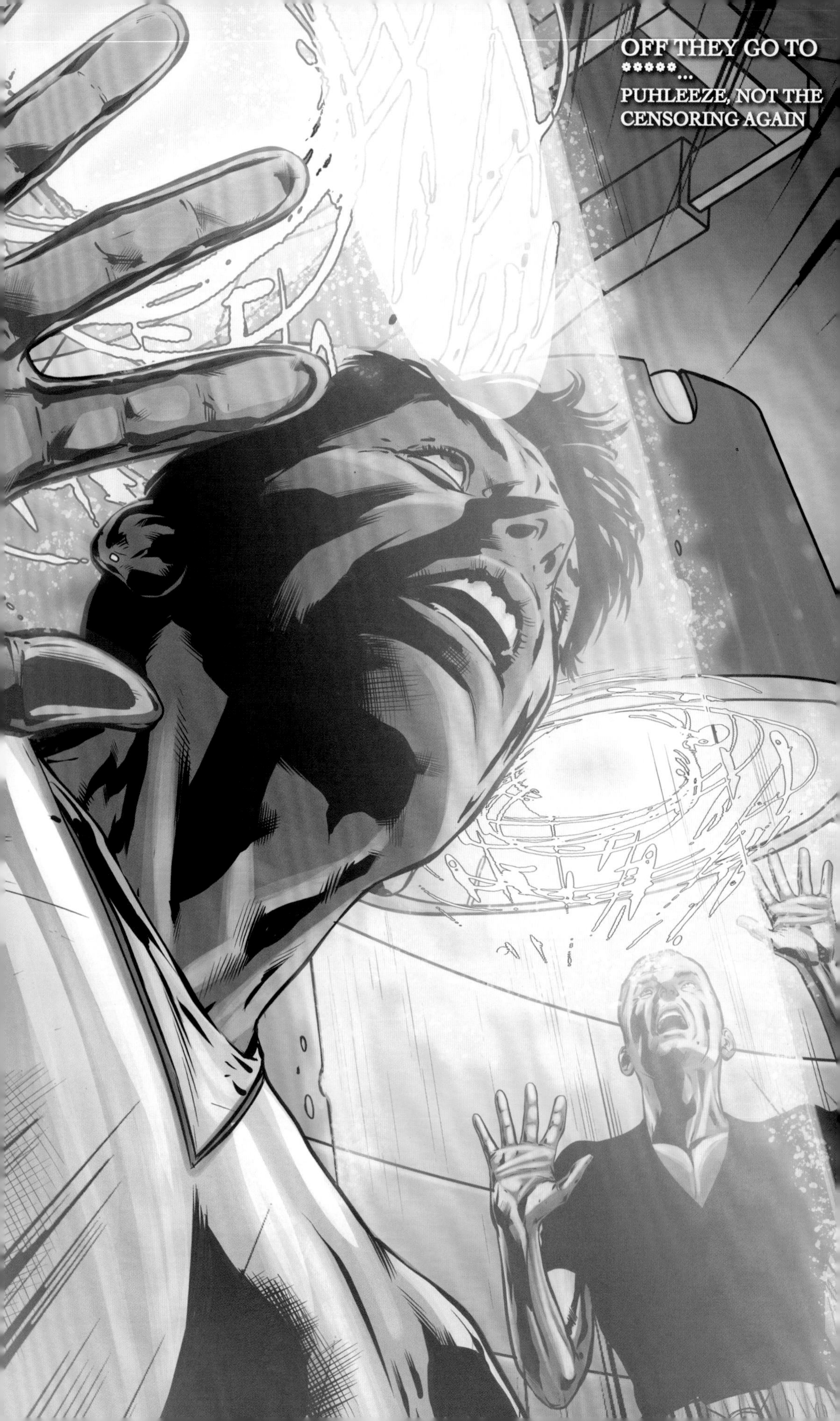
OFF THEY GO TO
*****...
PUHLEEZE, NOT THE
CENSORING AGAIN

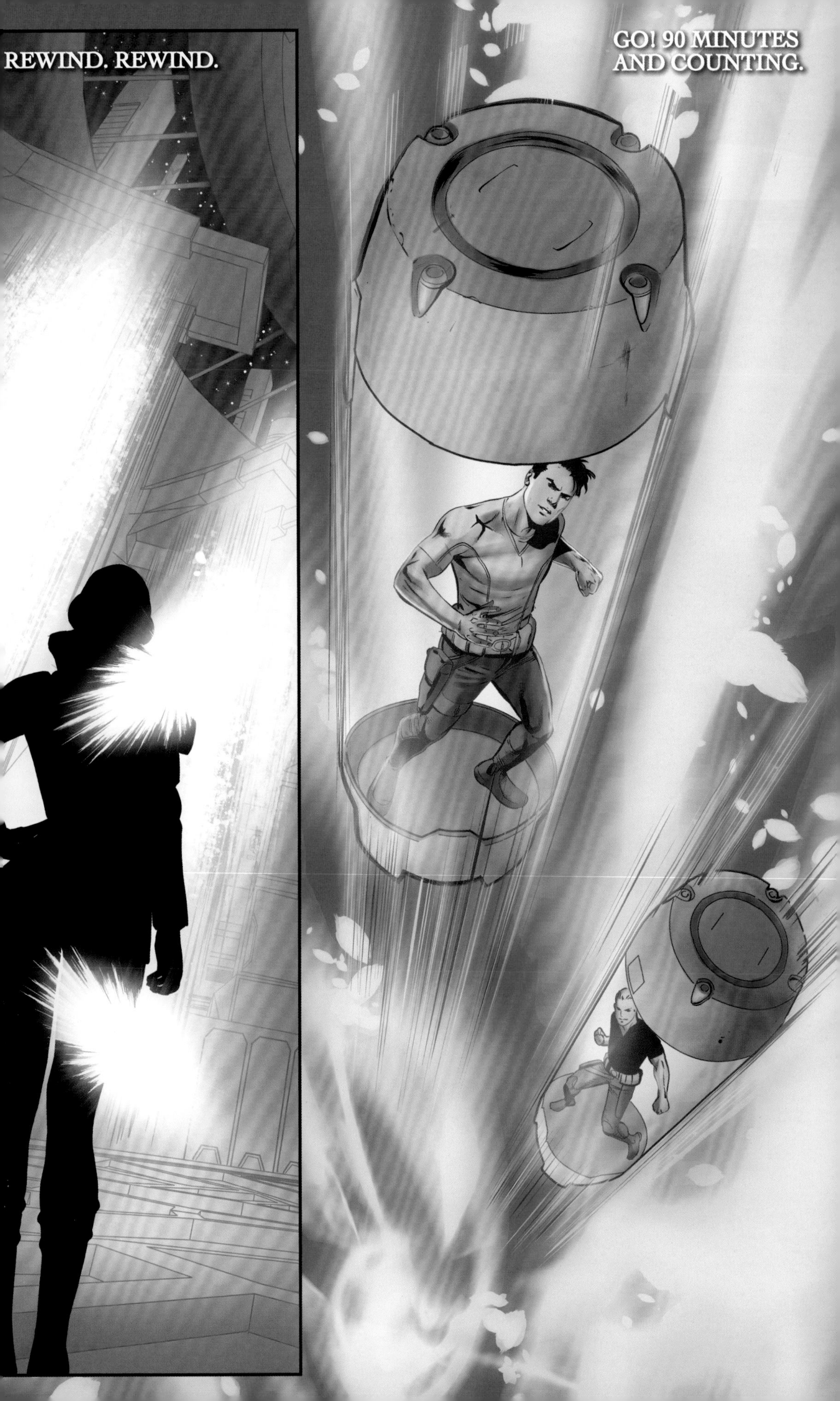

REWIND. REWIND.
GO! 90 MINUTES AND COUNTING.

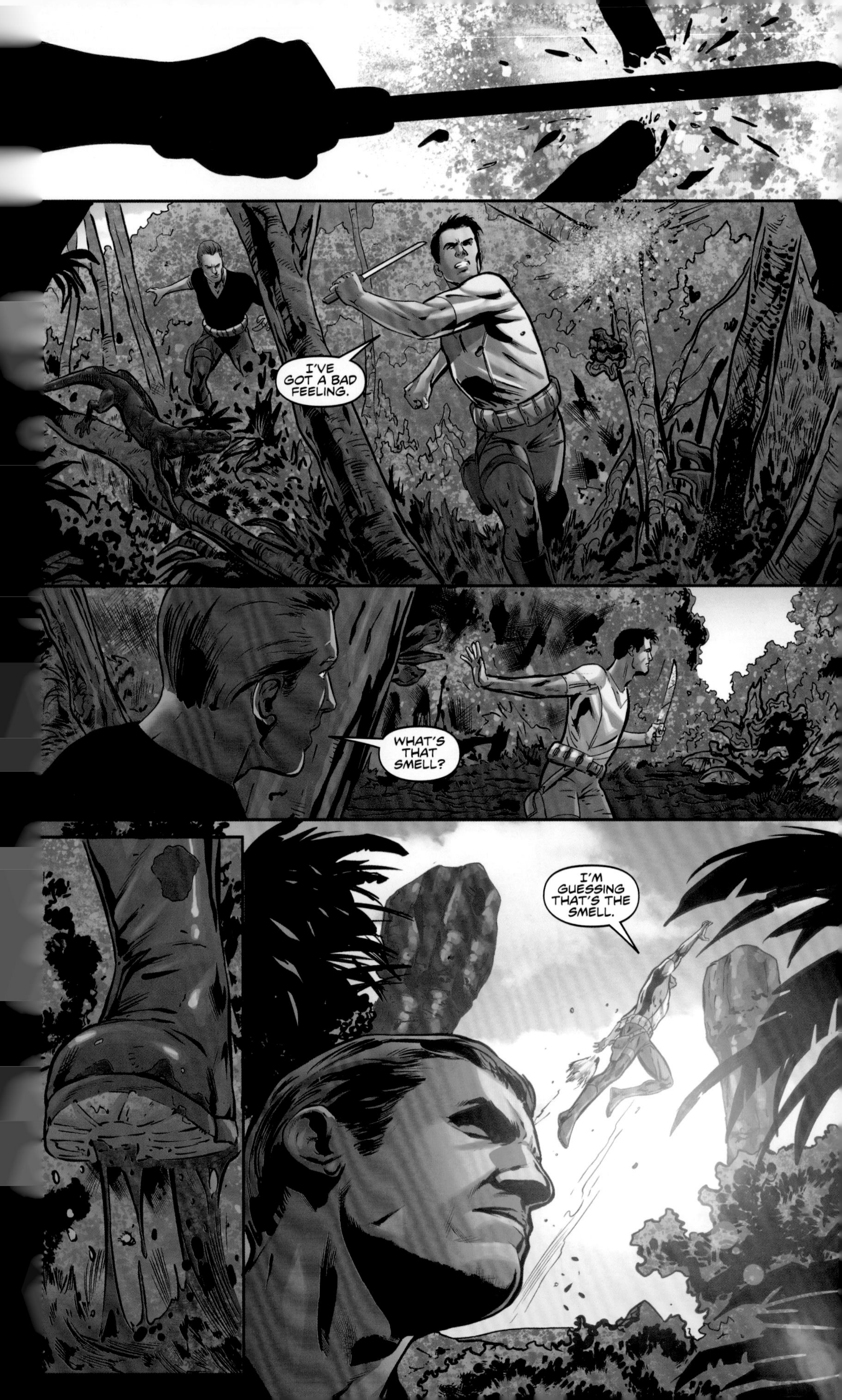
I'VE GOT A BAD FEELING.
WHAT'S THAT SMELL?
I'M GUESSING THAT'S THE SMELL.

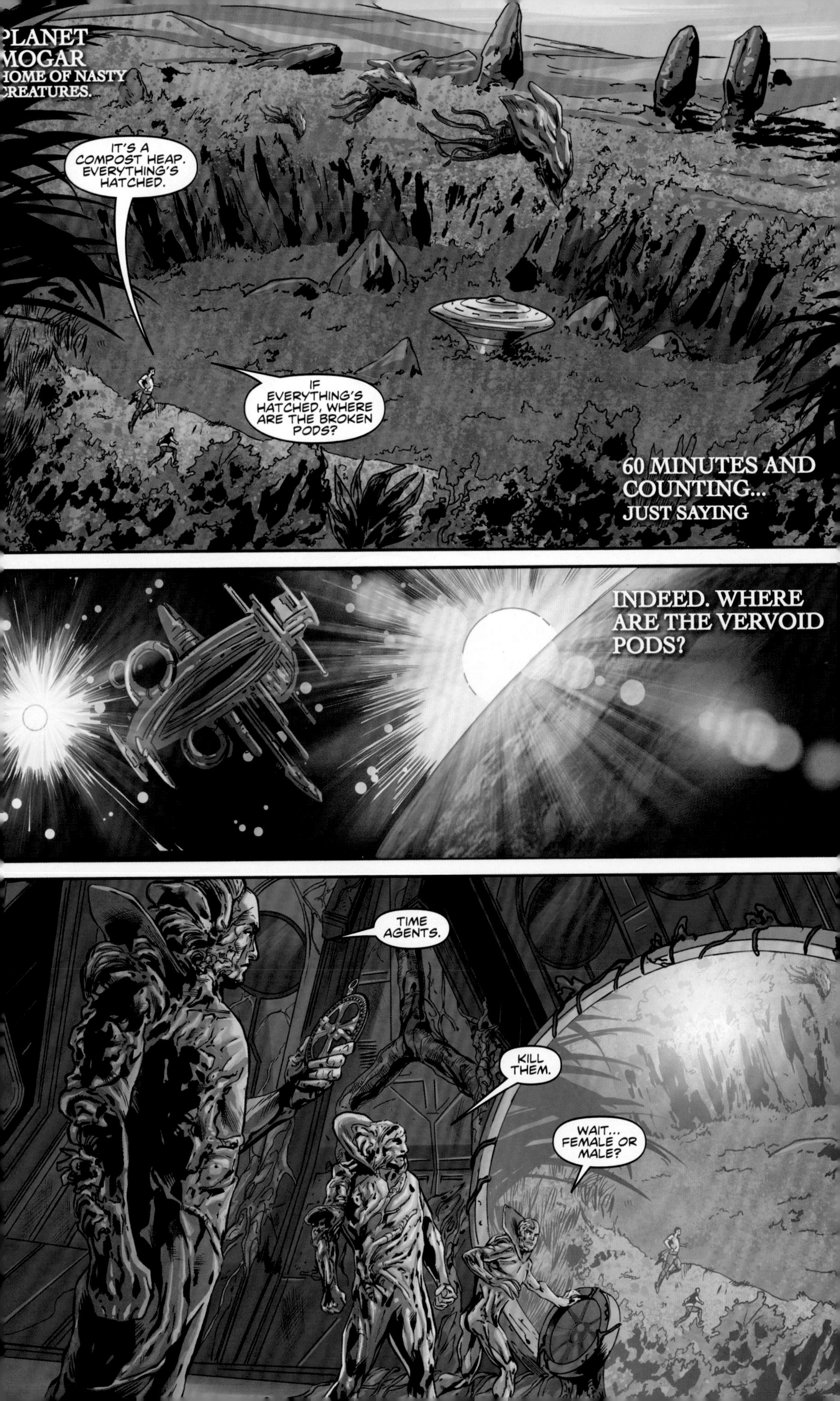
PLANET MOGAR
HOME OF NASTY CREATURES.
IT'S A COMPOST HEAP. EVERYTHING'S HATCHED.
IF EVERYTHING'S HATCHED, WHERE ARE THE BROKEN PODS?
60 MINUTES AND COUNTING... JUST SAYING
INDEED. WHERE ARE THE VERVOID PODS?
TIME AGENTS.
KILL THEM.
WAIT... FEMALE OR MALE?

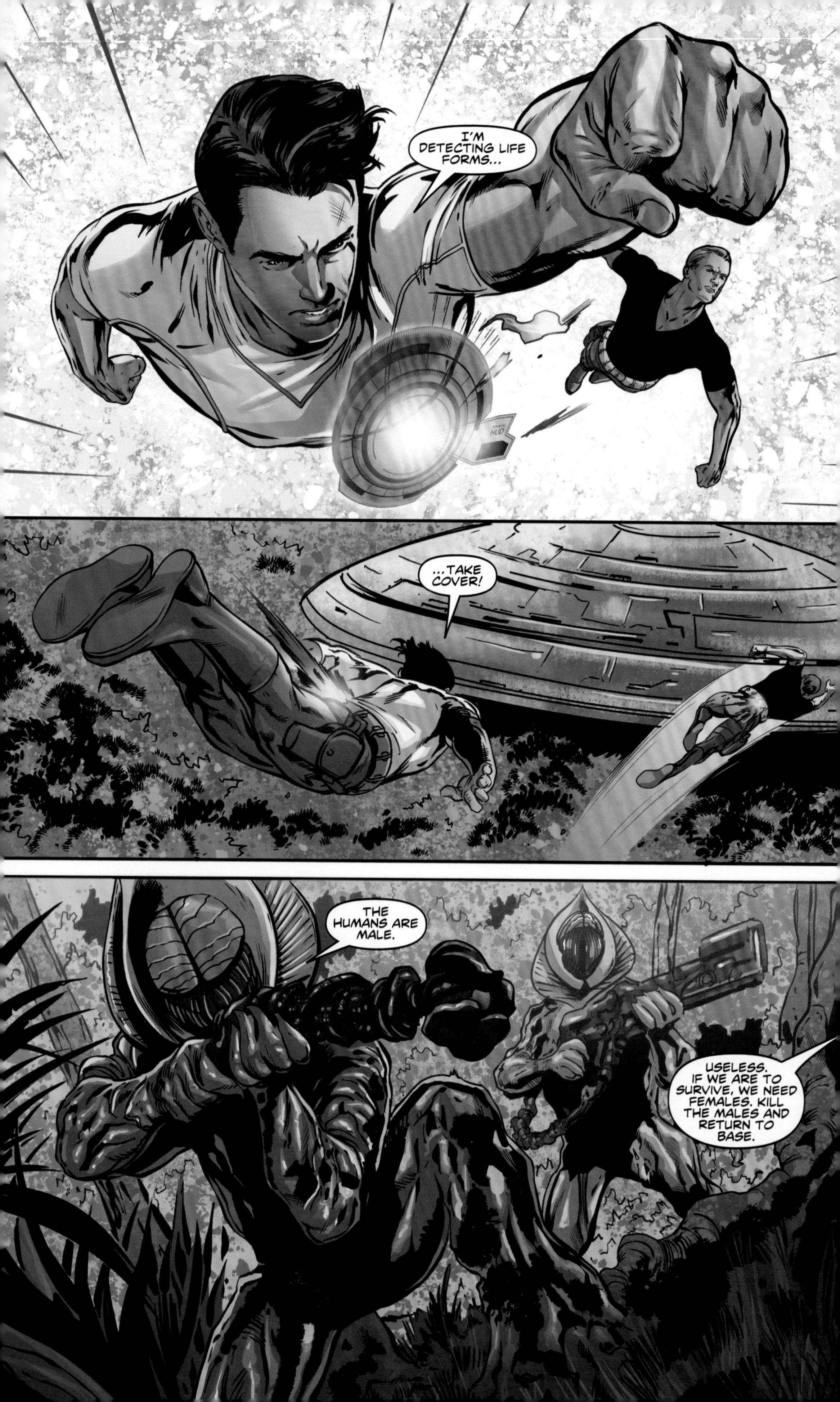
I'M DETECTING LIFE FORMS...
HUD
...TAKE COVER!
THE HUMANS ARE MALE.
USELESS. IF WE ARE TO SURVIVE, WE NEED FEMALES. KILL THE MALES AND RETURN TO BASE.

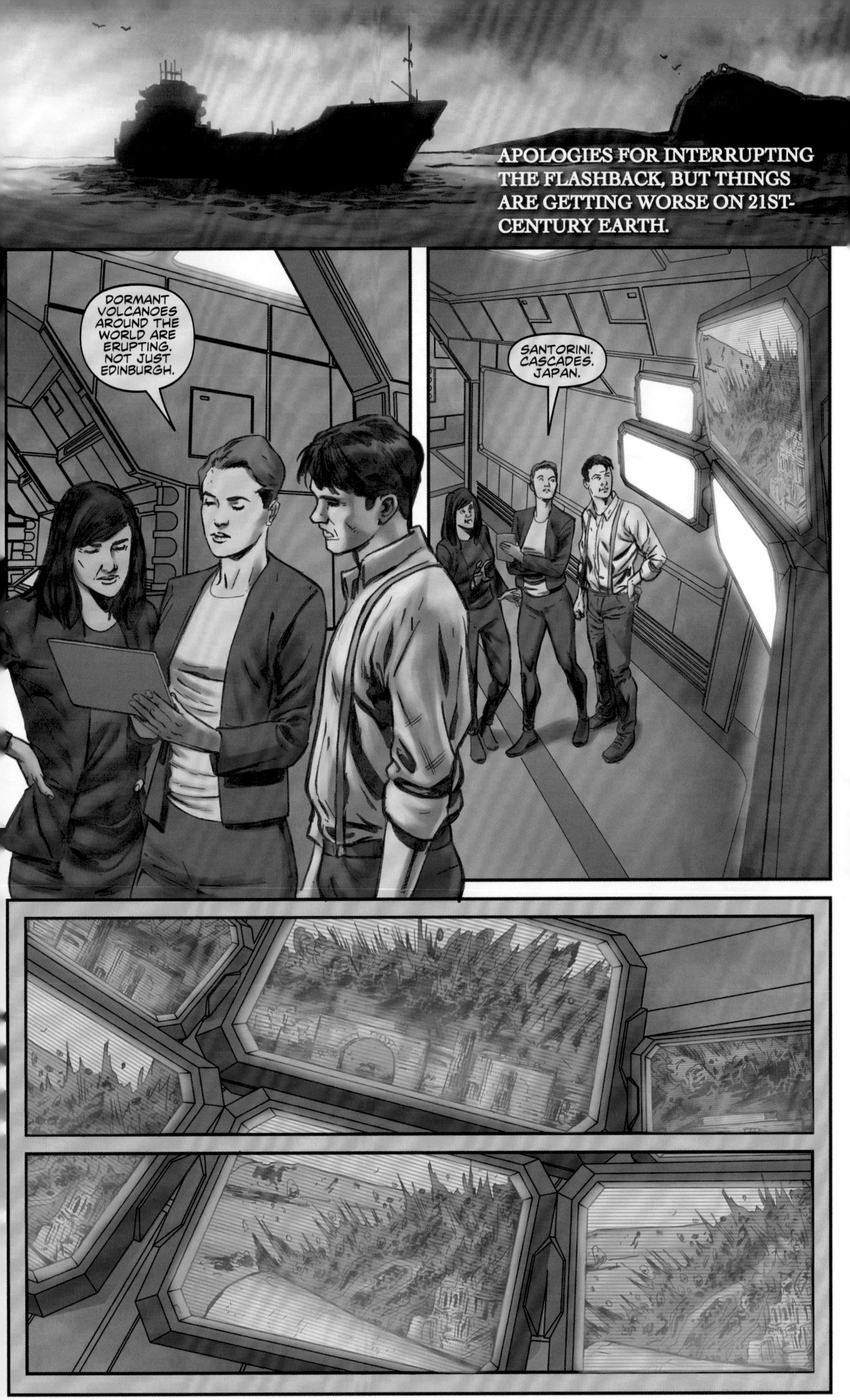
APOLOGIES FOR INTERRUPTING THE FLASHBACK, BUT THINGS ARE GETTING WORSE ON 21ST-CENTURY EARTH.
DORMANT VOLCANOES AROUND THE WORLD ARE ERUPTING. NOT JUST EDINBURGH.
SANTORINI. CASCADES. JAPAN.

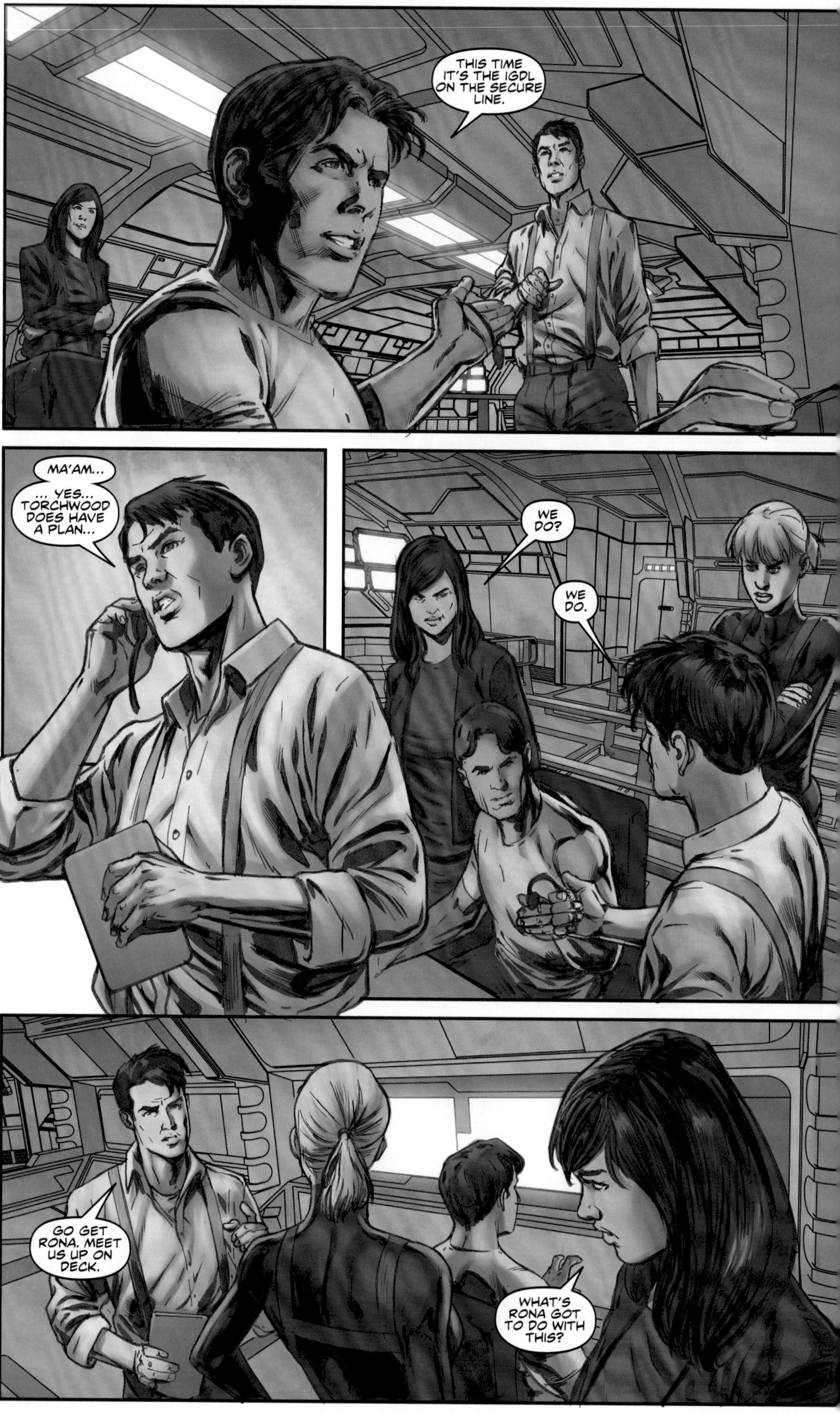
THIS TIME IT'S THE IGDL ON THE SECURE LINE.
MA'AM...
... YES... TORCHWOOD DOES HAVE A PLAN...
WE DO?
WE DO.
GO GET RONA. MEET US UP ON DECK.
WHAT'S RONA GOT TO DO WITH THIS?

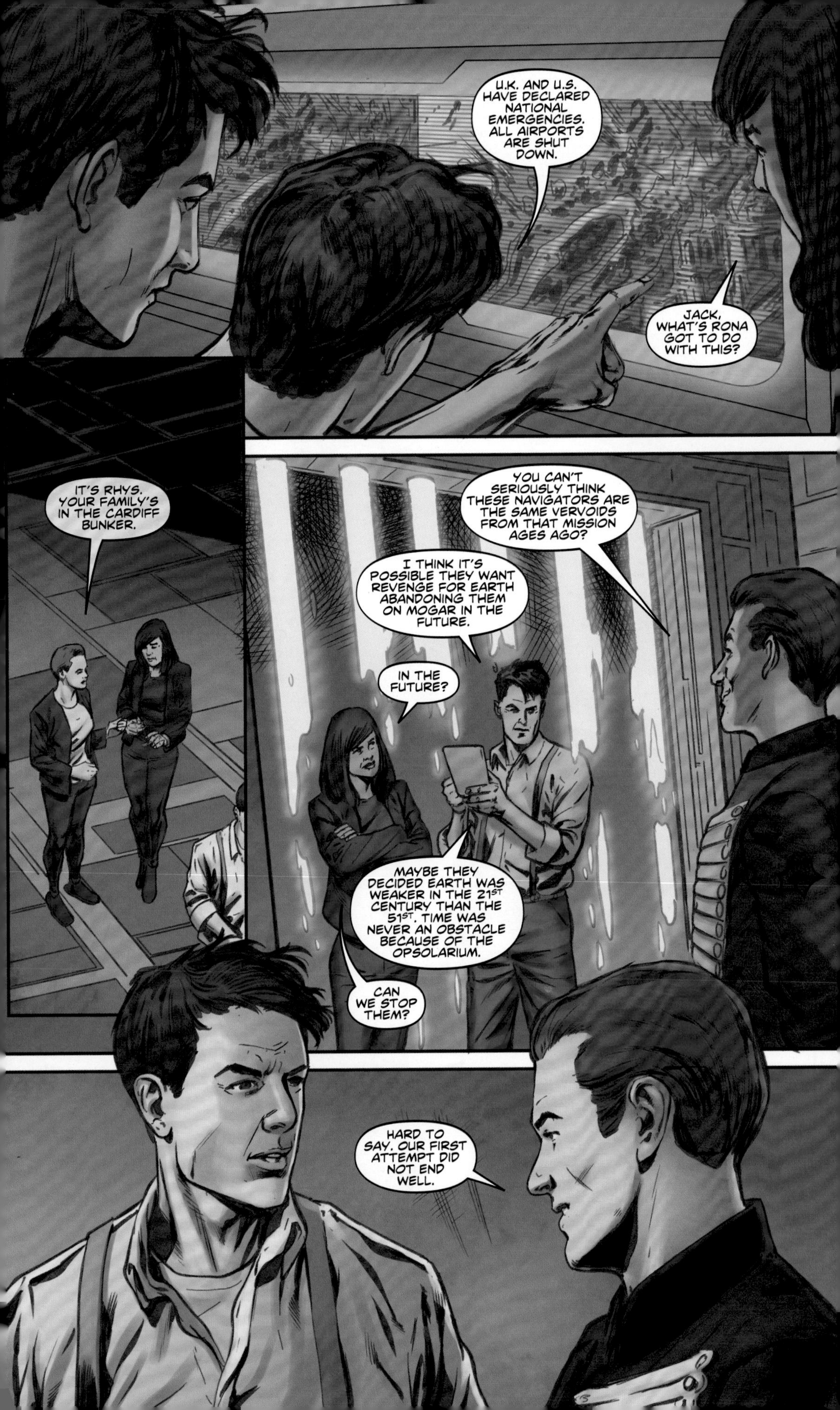
U.K. AND U.S. HAVE DECLARED NATIONAL EMERGENCIES. ALL AIRPORTS ARE SHUT DOWN.
JACK, WHAT'S RONA GOT TO DO WITH THIS?
IT'S RHYS. YOUR FAMILY'S IN THE CARDIFF BUNKER.
YOU CAN'T SERIOUSLY THINK THESE NAVIGATORS ARE THE SAME VERVOIDS FROM THAT MISSION AGES AGO?
I THINK IT'S POSSIBLE THEY WANT REVENGE FOR EARTH ABANDONING THEM ON MOGAR IN THE FUTURE.
IN THE FUTURE?
MAYBE THEY DECIDED EARTH WAS WEAKER IN THE 21ST CENTURY THAN THE 51ST. TIME WAS NEVER AN OBSTACLE BECAUSE OF THE OPSOLARIUM.
CAN WE STOP THEM?
HARD TO SAY. OUR FIRST ATTEMPT DID NOT END WELL.

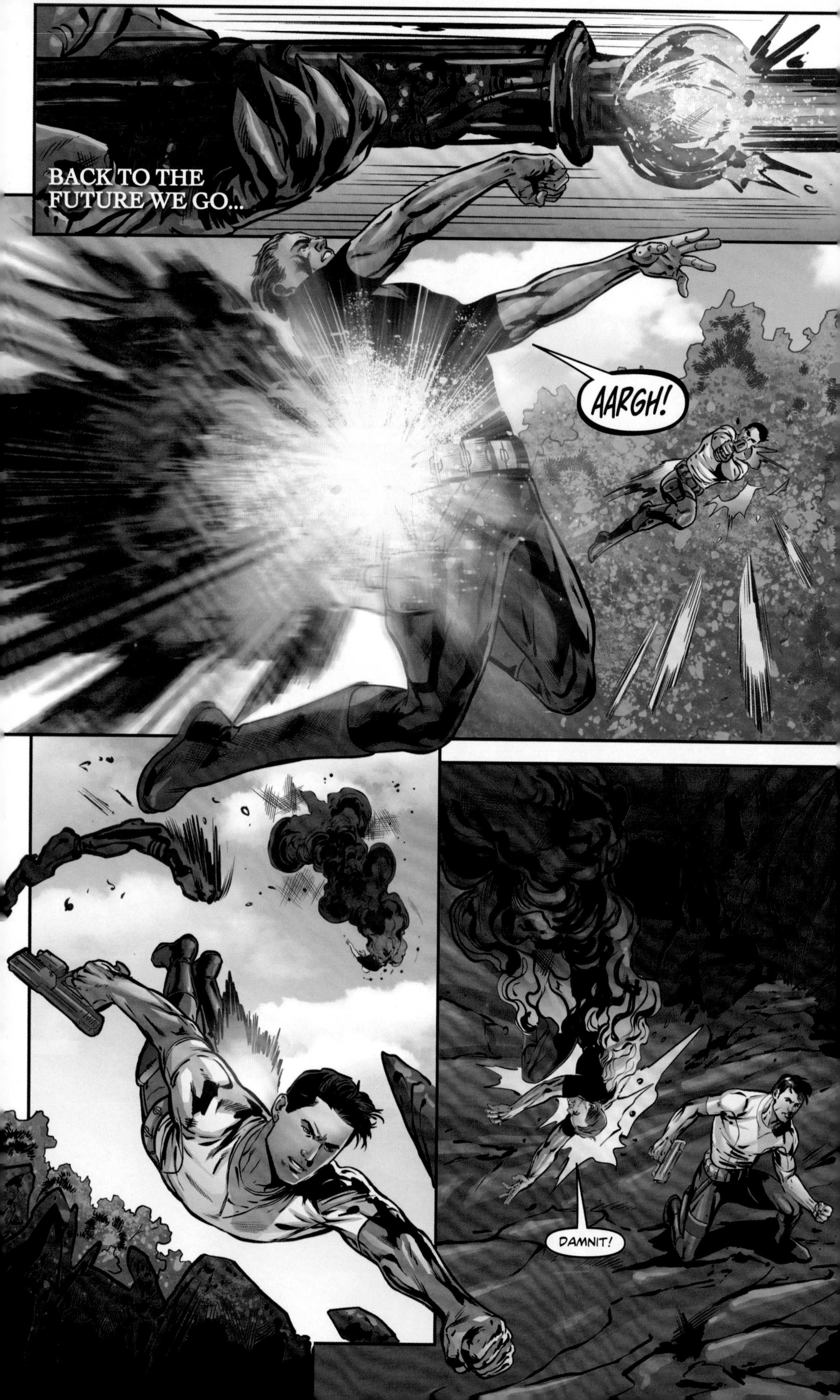
BACK TO THE FUTURE WE GO...
AARGH!
DAMNIT!

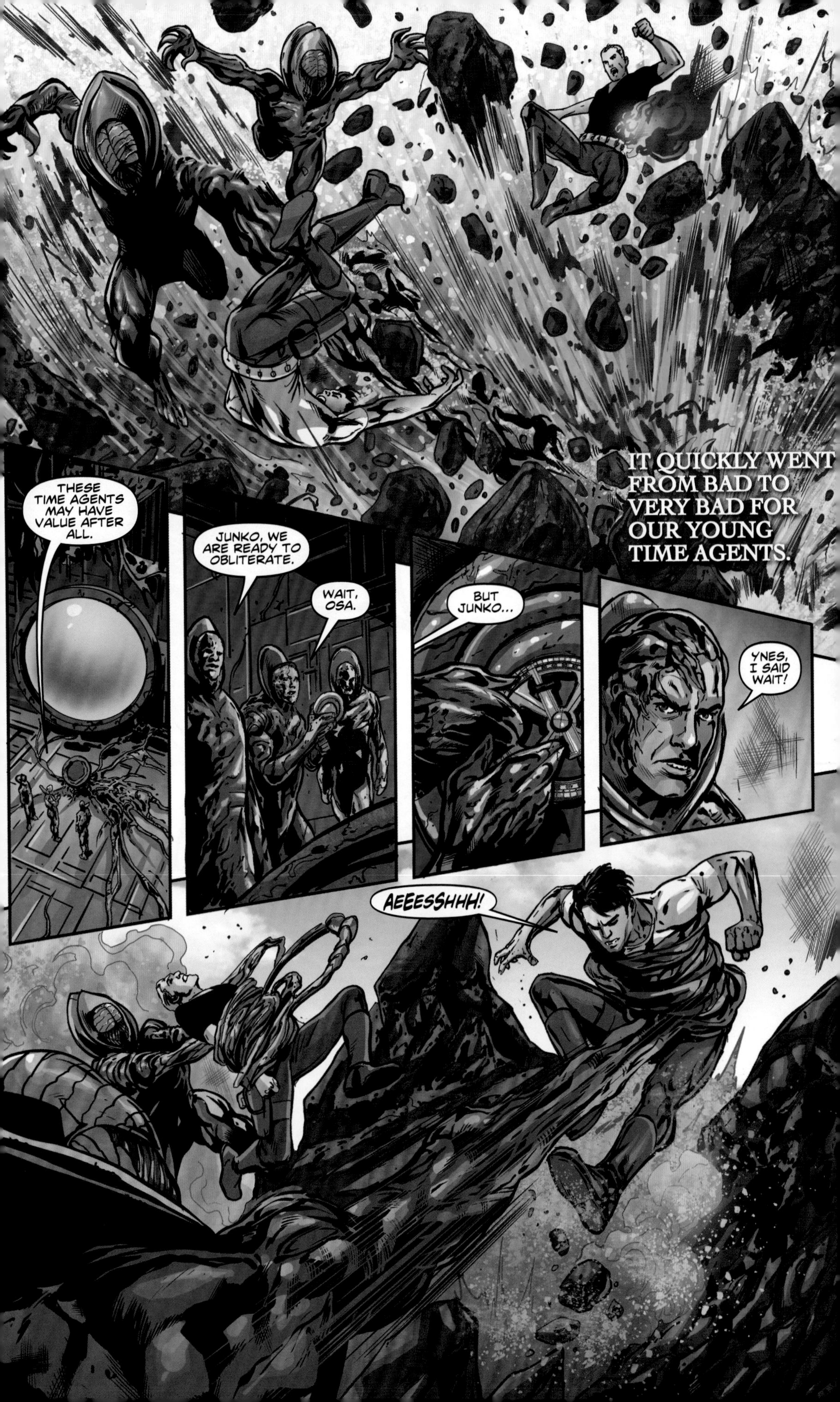
IT QUICKLY WENT FROM BAD TO VERY BAD FOR OUR YOUNG TIME AGENTS.
THESE TIME AGENTS MAY HAVE VALUE AFTER ALL.
JUNKO, WE ARE READY TO OBLITERATE.
WAIT, OSA.
BUT JUNKO...
YNES, I SAID WAIT!
AEEESSHHH!

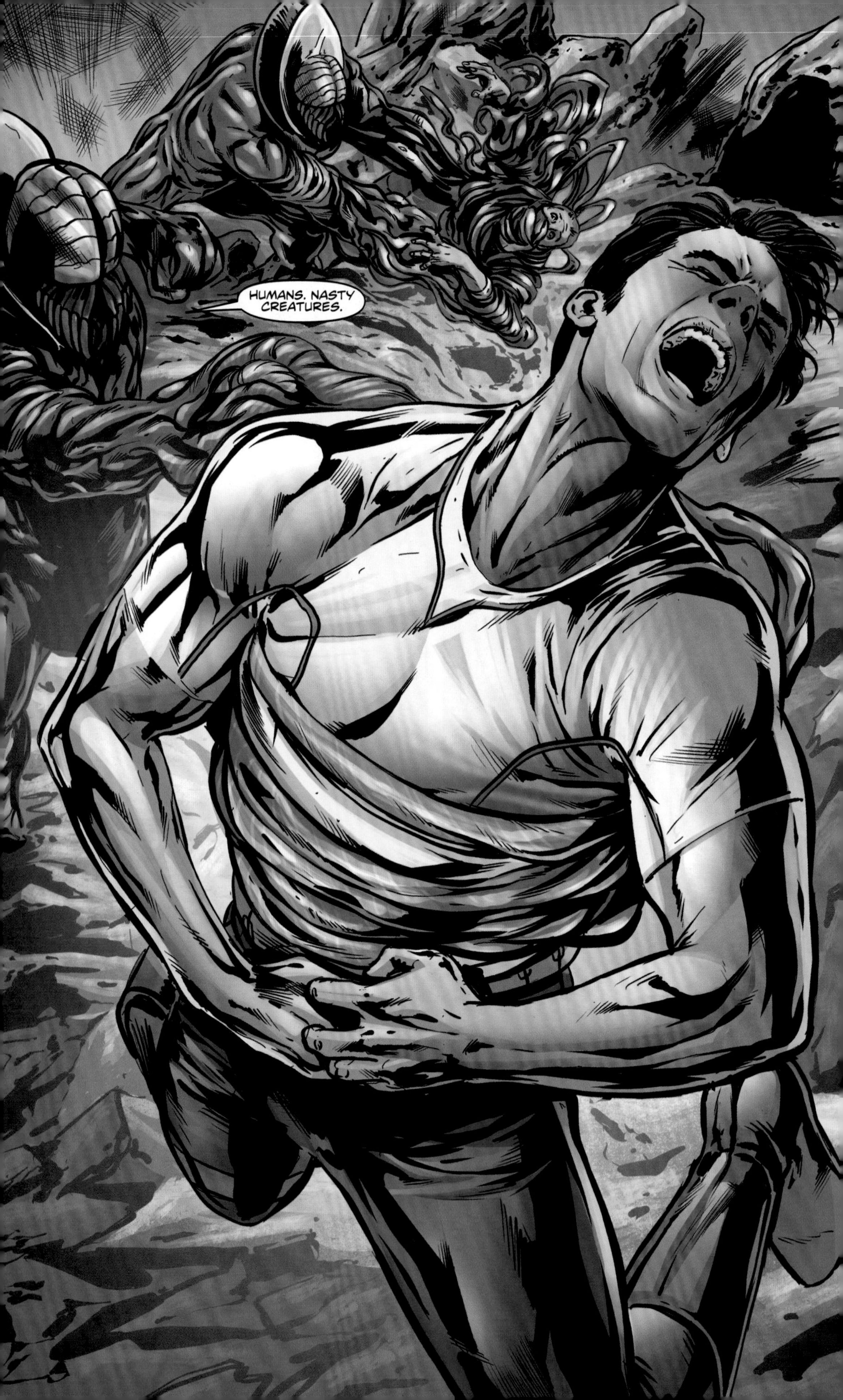
HUMANS. NASTY CREATURES.

CHAPTER 4

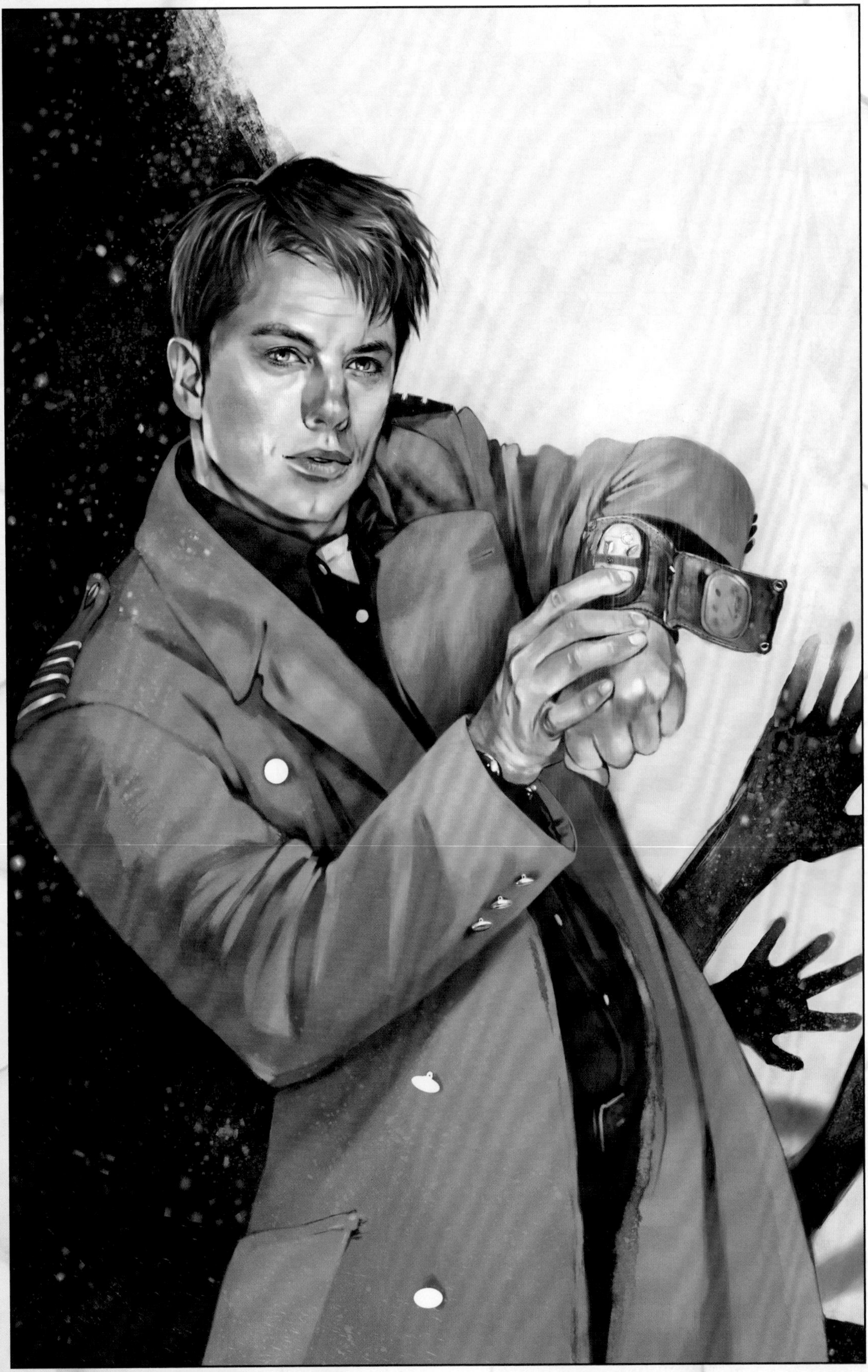

illustration by CLAUDIA CARANFA

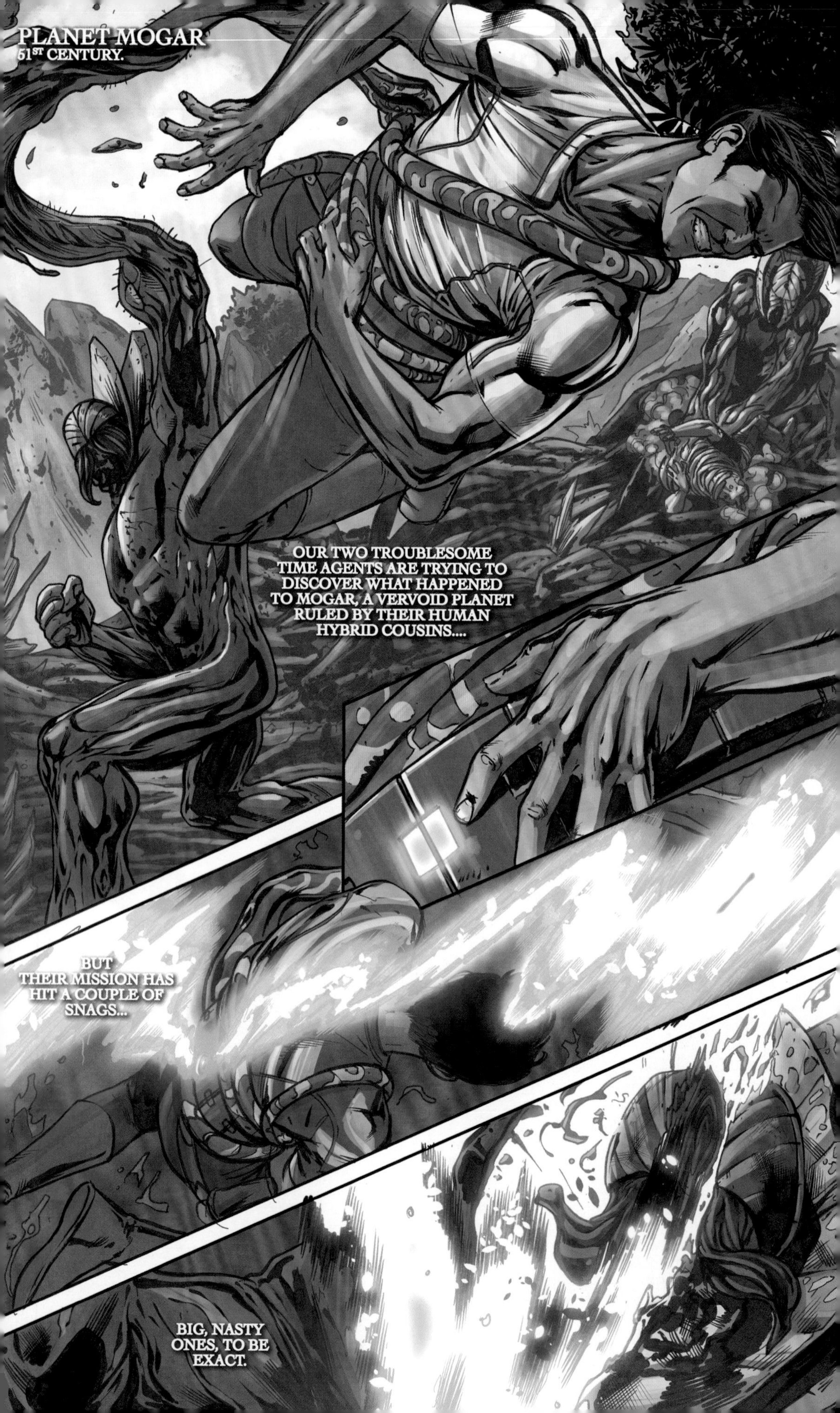
PLANET MOGAR
51ST CENTURY.
OUR TWO TROUBLESOME TIME AGENTS ARE TRYING TO DISCOVER WHAT HAPPENED TO MOGAR, A VERVOID PLANET RULED BY THEIR HUMAN HYBRID COUSINS....
BUT THEIR MISSION HAS HIT A COUPLE OF SNAGS...
BIG, NASTY ONES, TO BE EXACT.

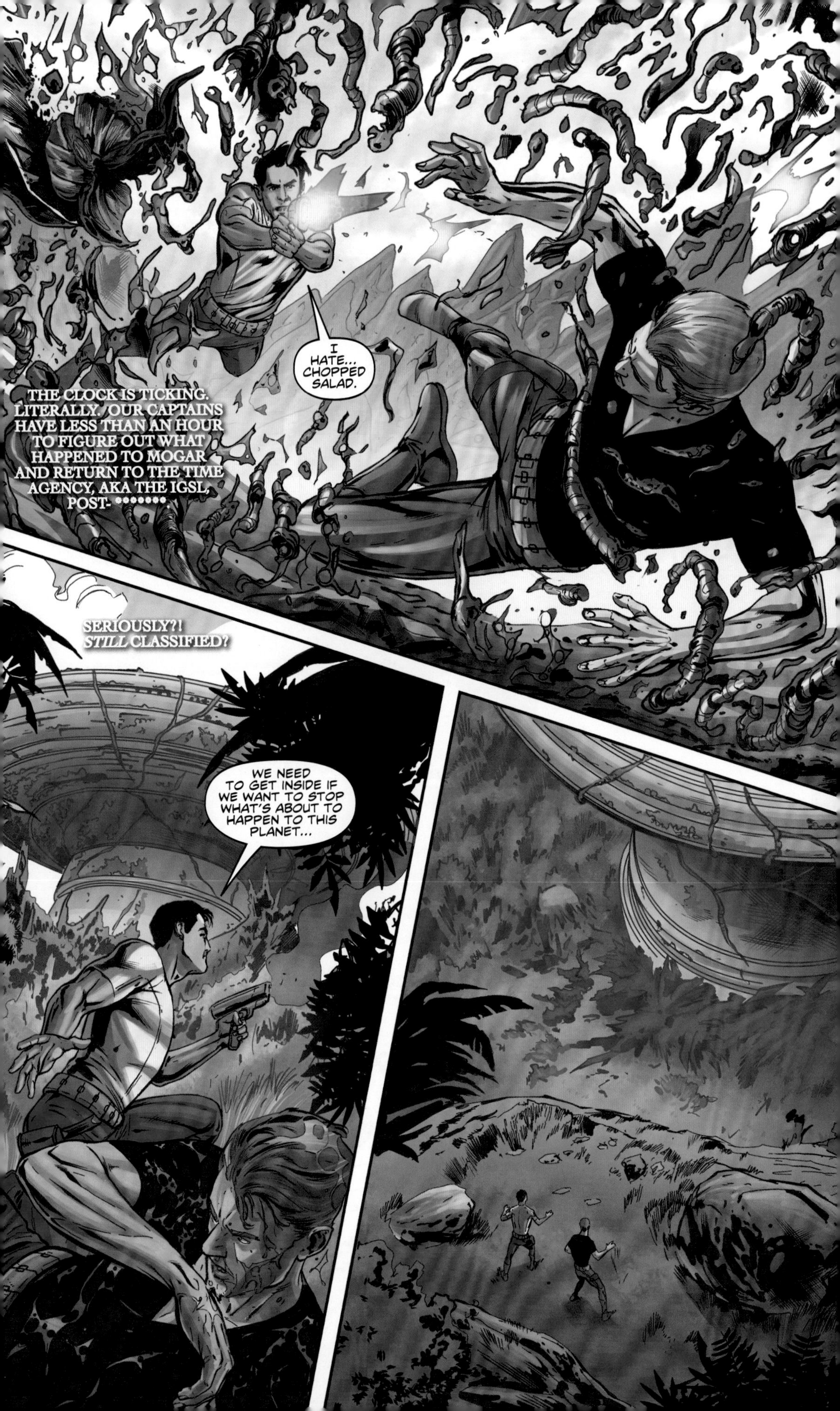
I HATE... CHOPPED SALAD.
THE CLOCK IS TICKING. LITERALLY. OUR CAPTAINS HAVE LESS THAN AN HOUR TO FIGURE OUT WHAT HAPPENED TO MOGAR AND RETURN TO THE TIME AGENCY, AKA THE IGSL, POST-*******.
SERIOUSLY?! *STILL* CLASSIFIED?
WE NEED TO GET INSIDE IF WE WANT TO STOP WHAT'S ABOUT TO HAPPEN TO THIS PLANET...

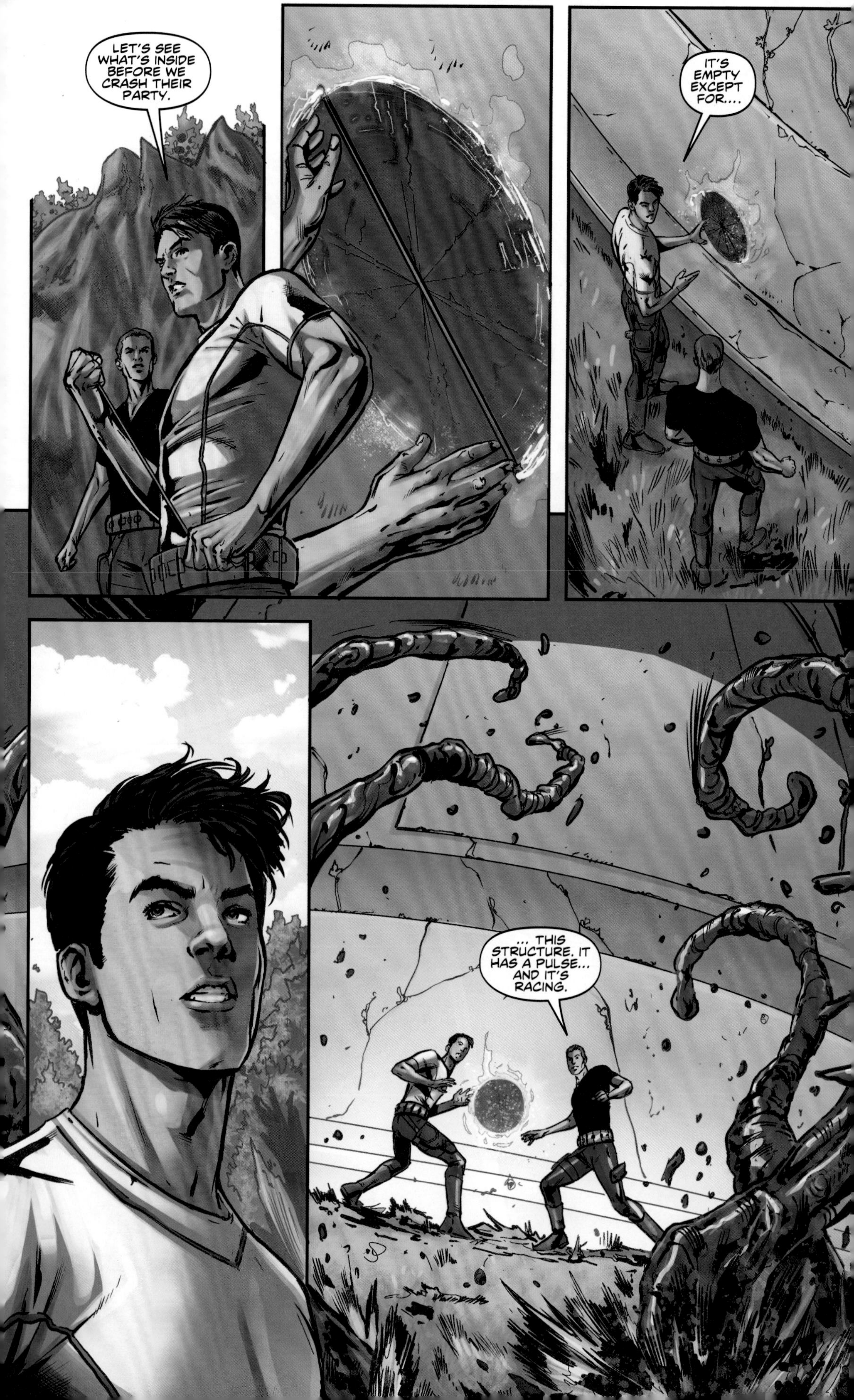
LET'S SEE WHAT'S INSIDE BEFORE WE CRASH THEIR PARTY.
IT'S EMPTY EXCEPT FOR....
... THIS STRUCTURE. IT HAS A PULSE... AND IT'S RACING.

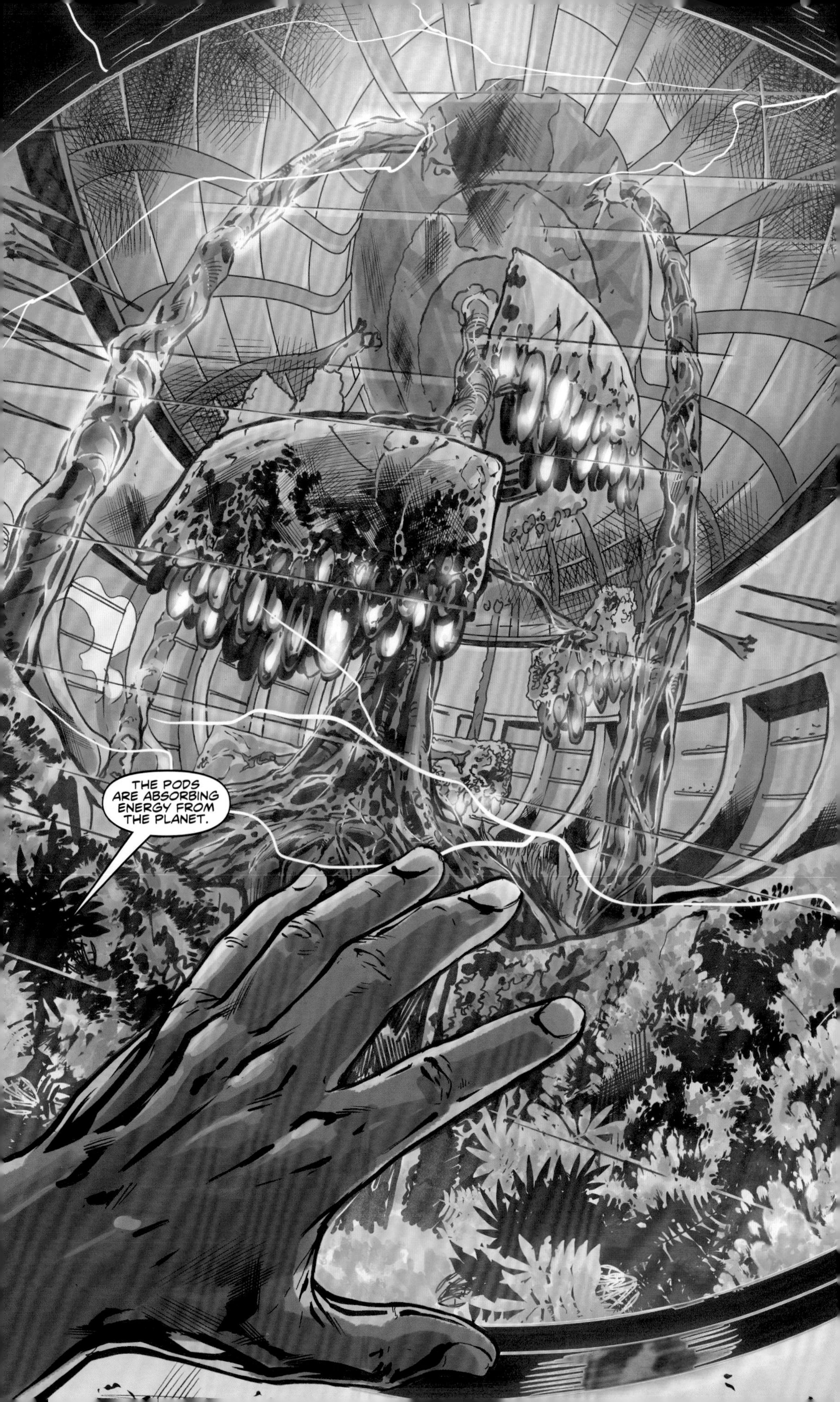
THE PODS ARE ABSORBING ENERGY FROM THE PLANET.

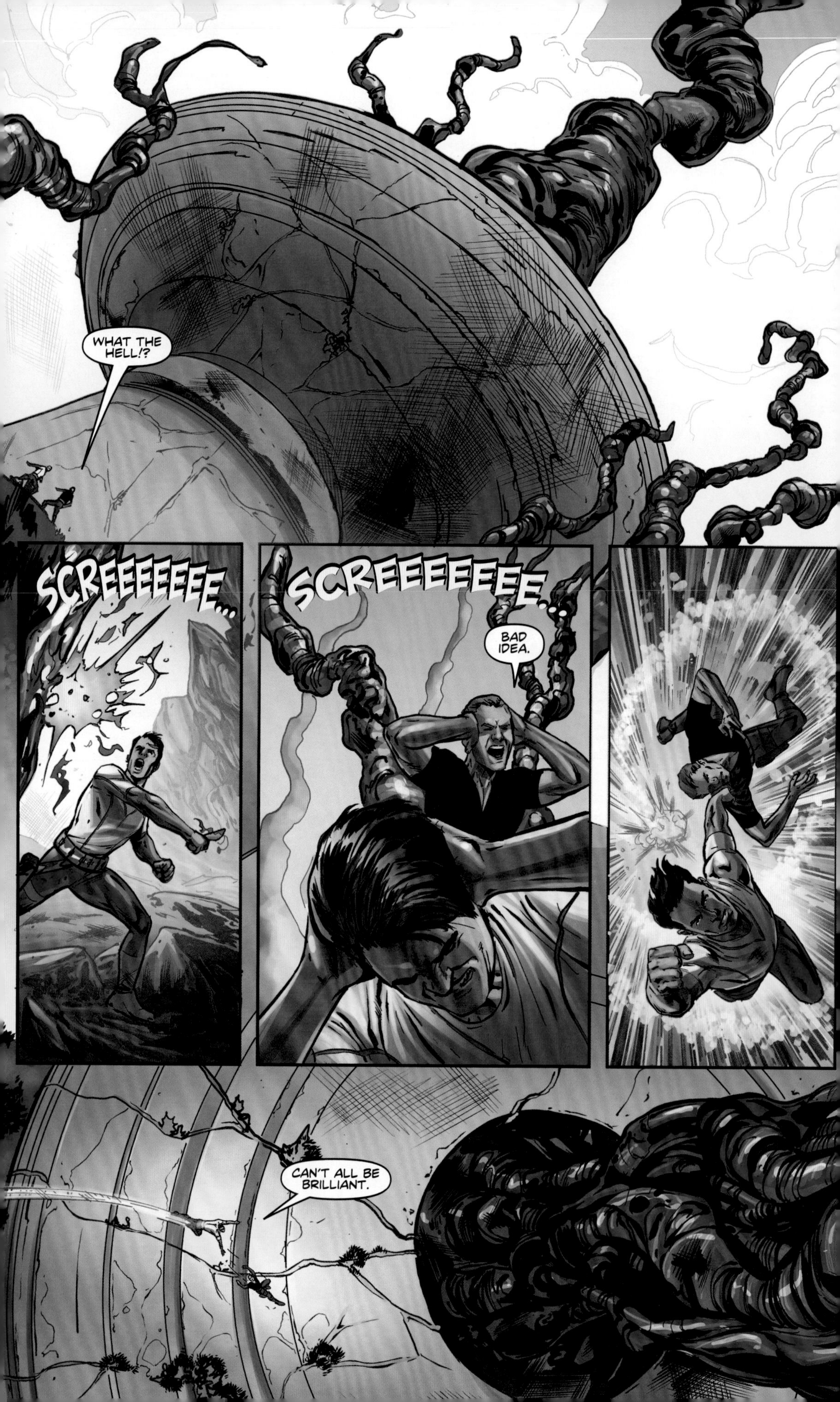
WHAT THE HELL!?
SCREEEEEEEE...
SCREEEEEEEEE...
BAD IDEA.
CAN'T ALL BE BRILLIANT.

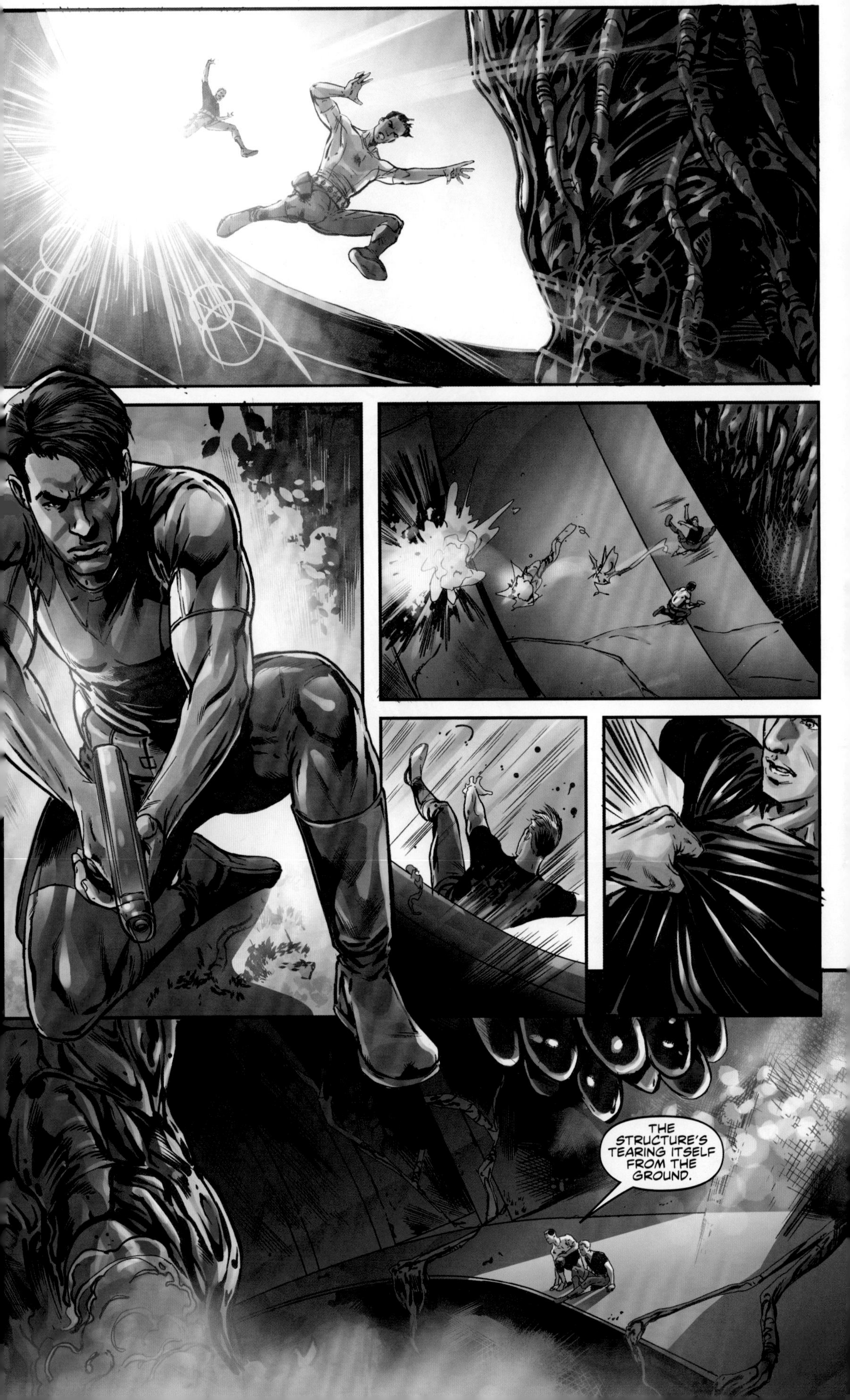
THE STRUCTURE'S TEARING ITSELF FROM THE GROUND.

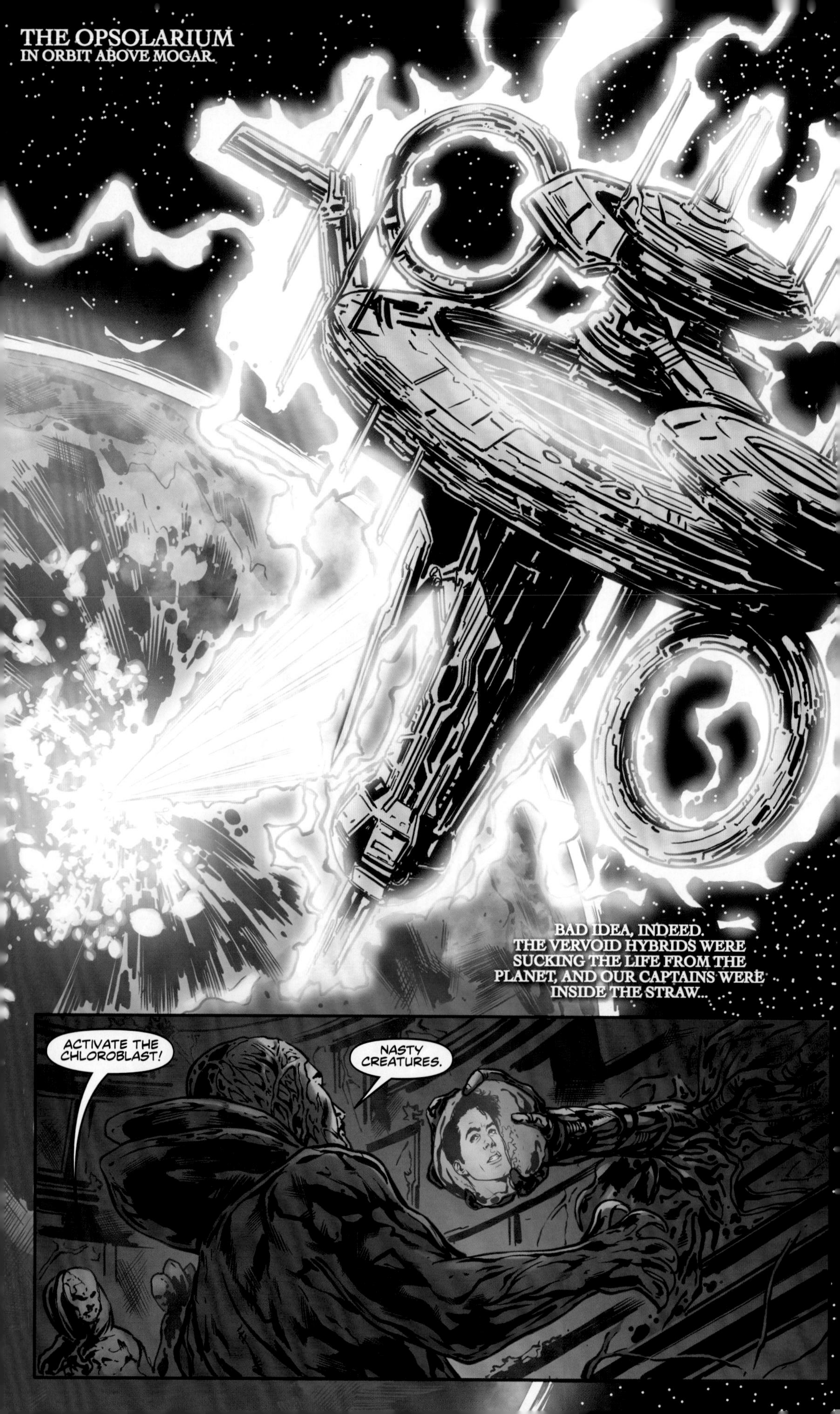
THE OPSOLARIUM
IN ORBIT ABOVE MOGAR.
BAD IDEA, INDEED. THE VERVOID HYBRIDS WERE SUCKING THE LIFE FROM THE PLANET, AND OUR CAPTAINS WERE INSIDE THE STRAW...
ACTIVATE THE CHLOROBLAST!
NASTY CREATURES.

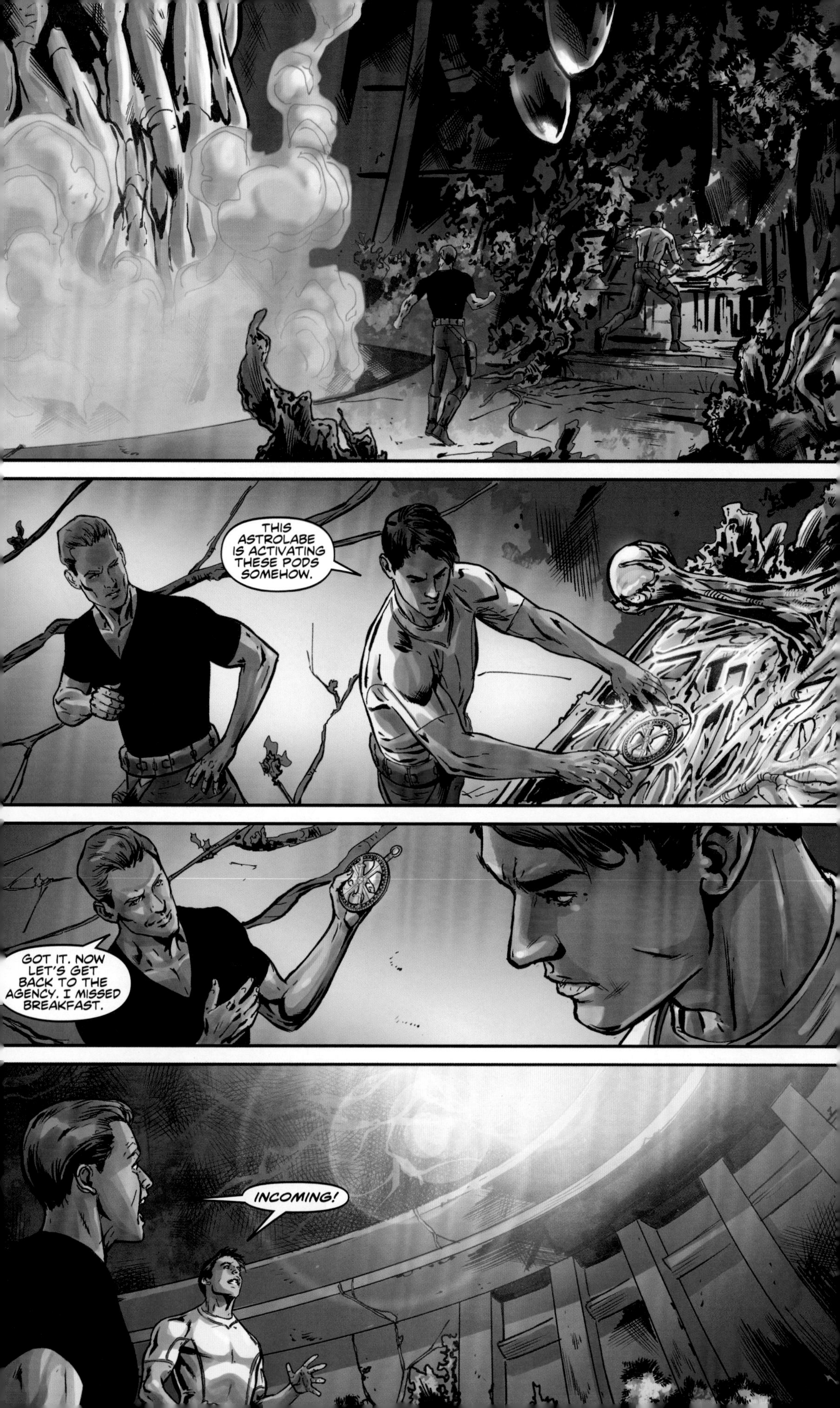
THIS ASTROLABE IS ACTIVATING THESE PODS SOMEHOW.
GOT IT. NOW LET'S GET BACK TO THE AGENCY. I MISSED BREAKFAST.
INCOMING!

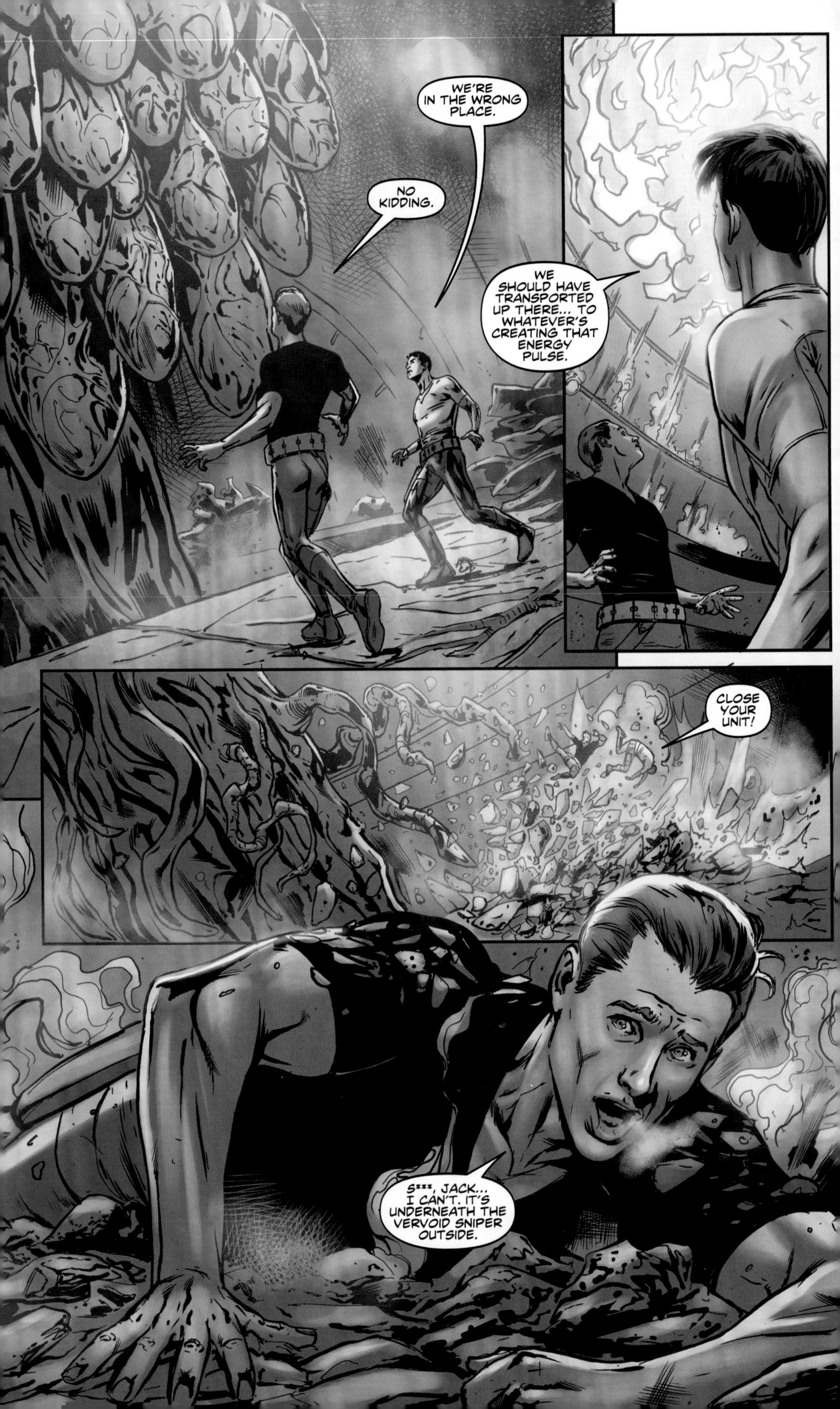
WE'RE IN THE WRONG PLACE.
NO KIDDING.
WE SHOULD HAVE TRANSPORTED UP THERE... TO WHATEVER'S CREATING THAT ENERGY PULSE.
CLOSE YOUR UNIT!
S***, JACK... I CAN'T. IT'S UNDERNEATH THE VERVOID SNIPER OUTSIDE.

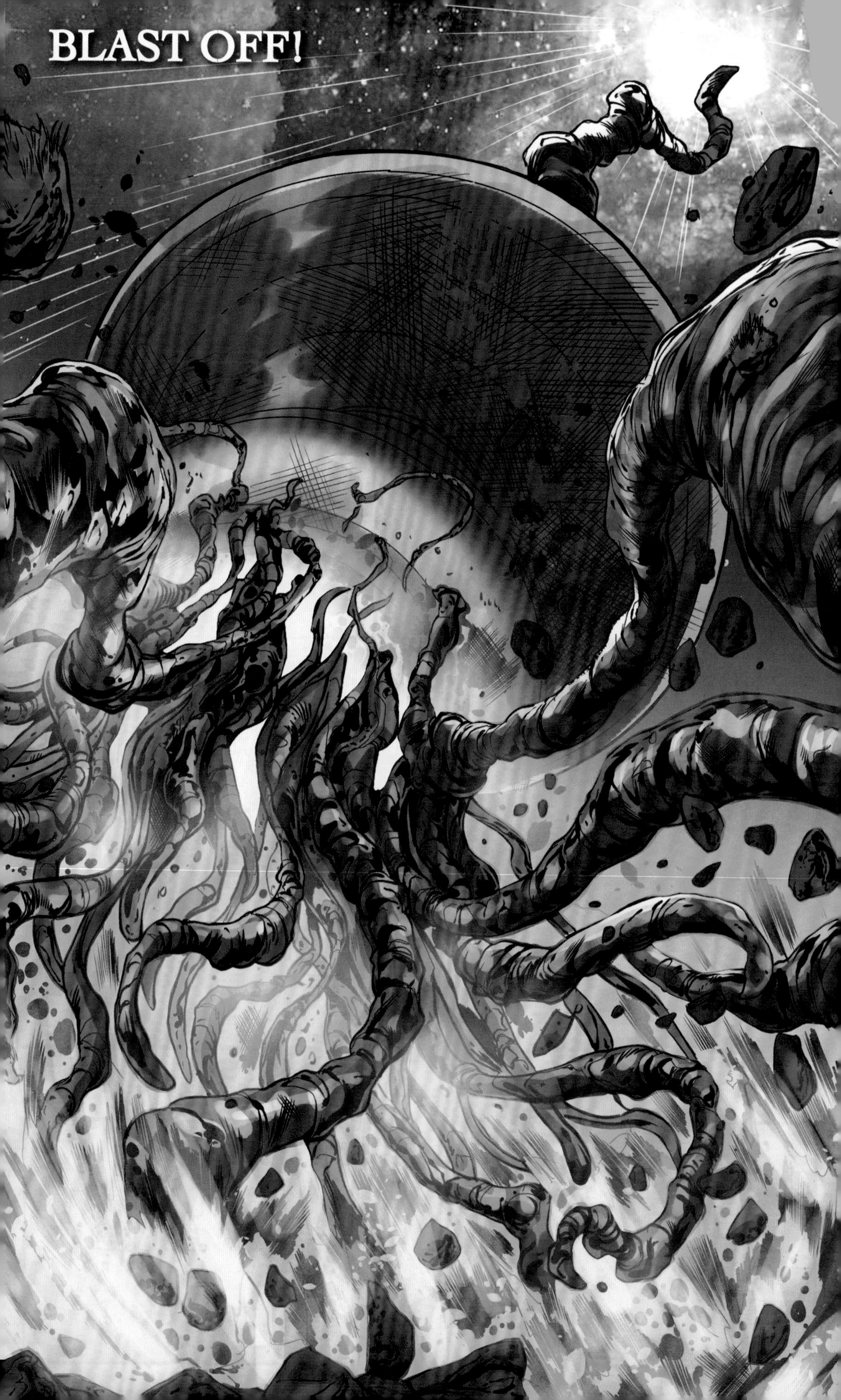
BLAST OFF!

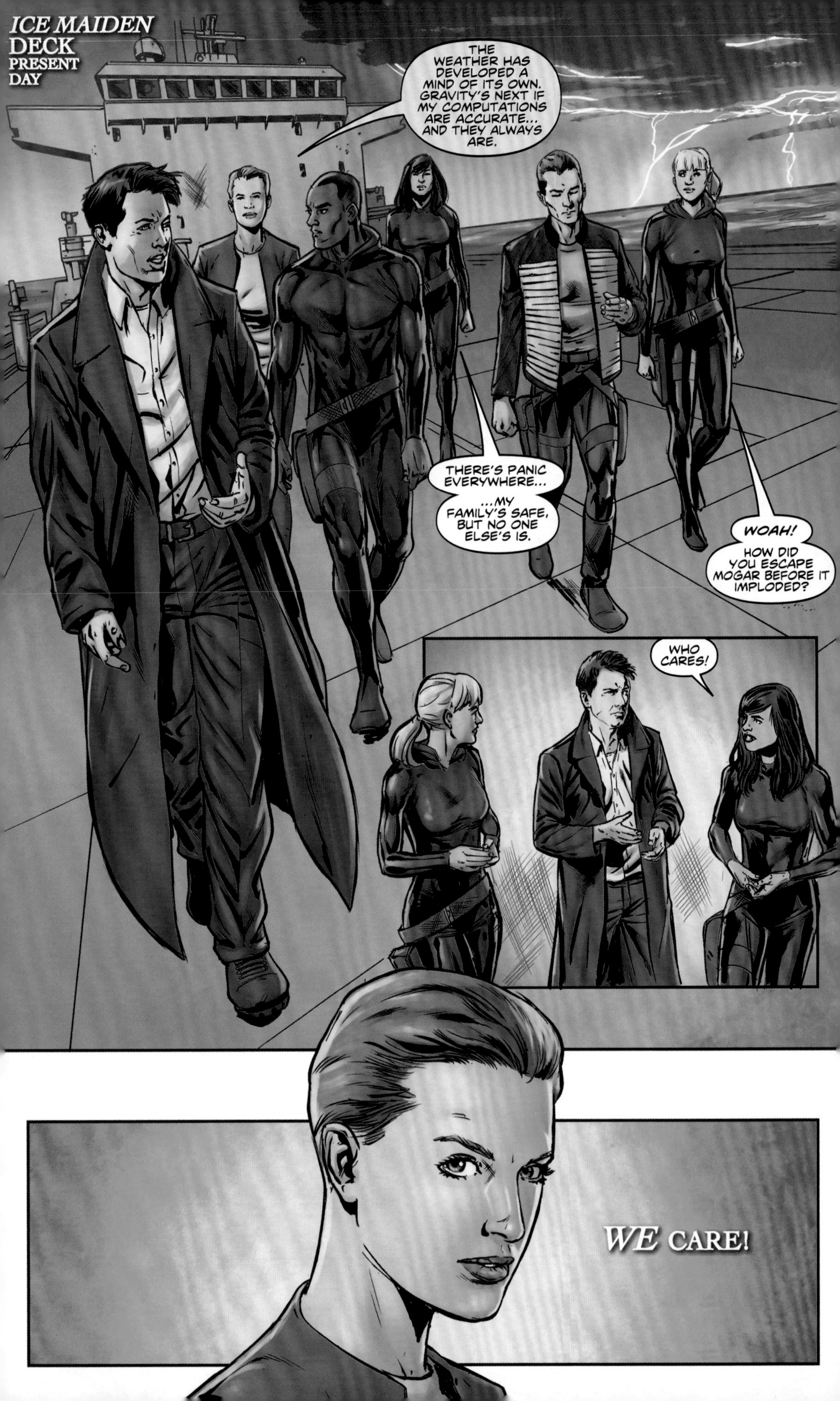
ICE MAIDEN DECK PRESENT DAY
THE WEATHER HAS DEVELOPED A MIND OF ITS OWN. GRAVITY'S NEXT IF MY COMPUTATIONS ARE ACCURATE... AND THEY ALWAYS ARE.
THERE'S PANIC EVERYWHERE...
...MY FAMILY'S SAFE, BUT NO ONE ELSE'S IS.
WOAH! HOW DID YOU ESCAPE MOGAR BEFORE IT IMPLODED?
WHO CARES!
WE CARE!

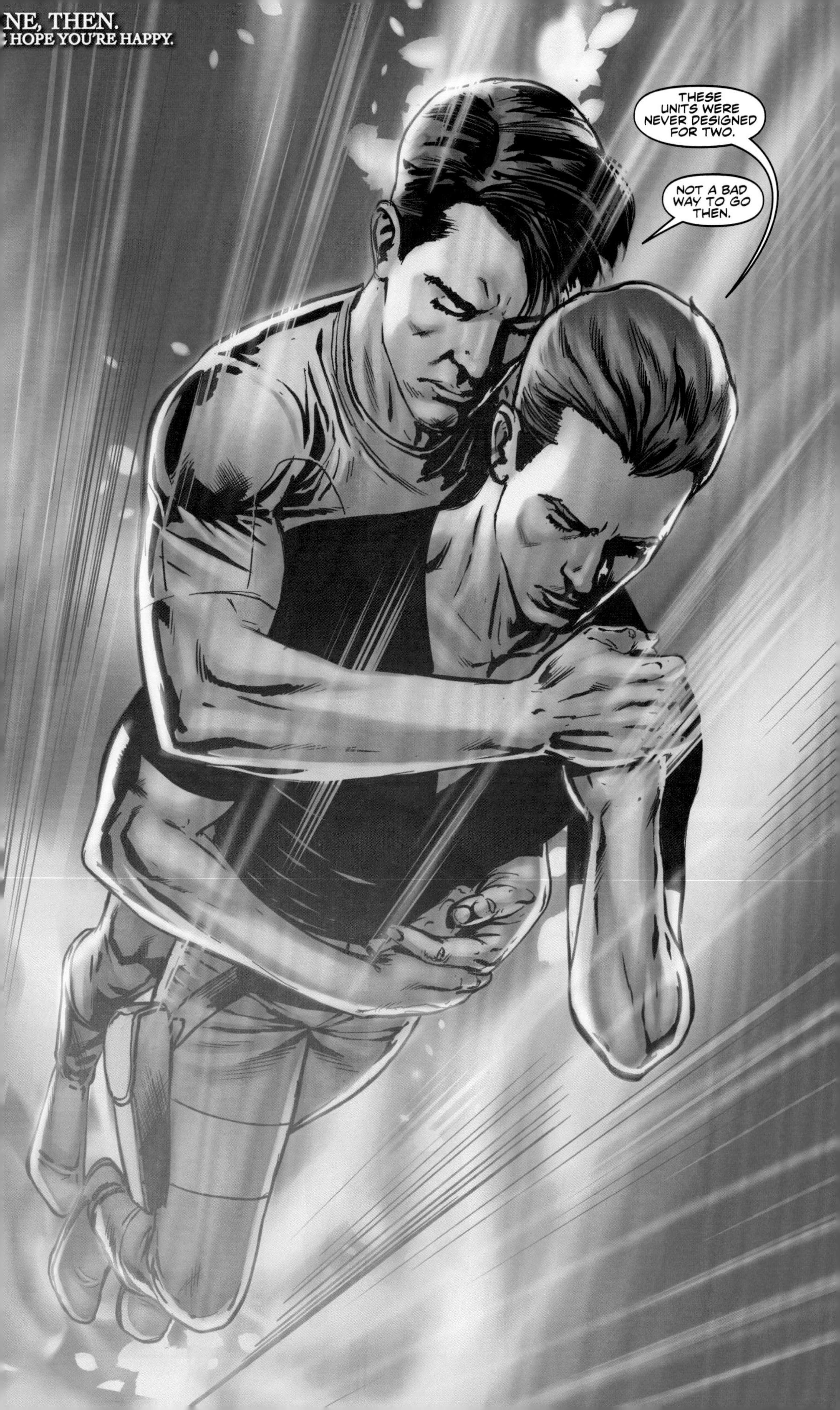
NE, THEN.
HOPE YOU'RE HAPPY.
THESE UNITS WERE NEVER DESIGNED FOR TWO.
NOT A BAD WAY TO GO THEN.

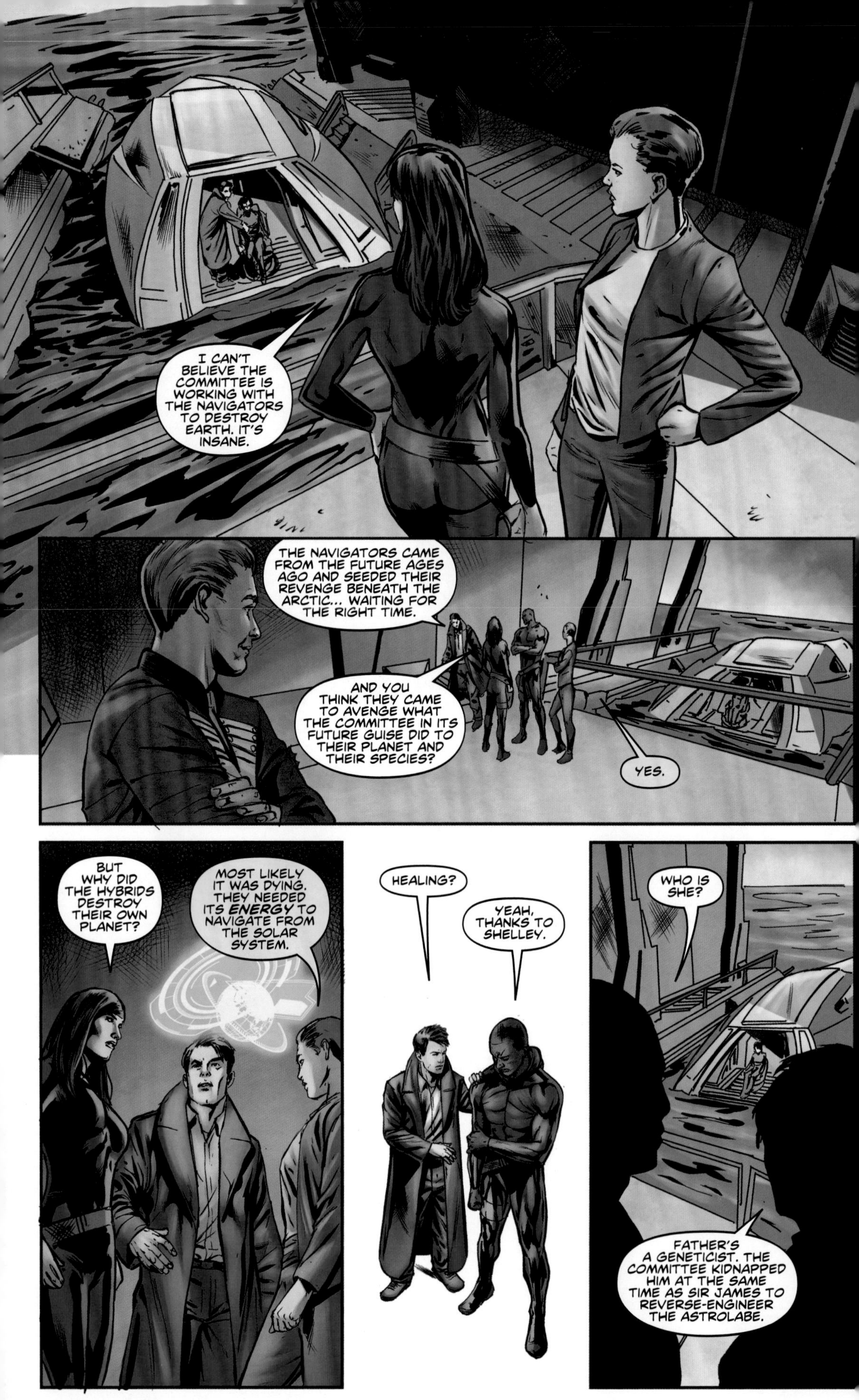
I CAN'T BELIEVE THE COMMITTEE IS WORKING WITH THE NAVIGATORS TO DESTROY EARTH. IT'S INSANE.
THE NAVIGATORS CAME FROM THE FUTURE AGES AGO AND SEEDED THEIR REVENGE BENEATH THE ARCTIC... WAITING FOR THE RIGHT TIME.
AND YOU THINK THEY CAME TO AVENGE WHAT THE COMMITTEE IN ITS FUTURE GUISE DID TO THEIR PLANET AND THEIR SPECIES?
YES.
BUT WHY DID THE HYBRIDS DESTROY THEIR OWN PLANET?
MOST LIKELY IT WAS DYING. THEY NEEDED ITS ENERGY TO NAVIGATE FROM THE SOLAR SYSTEM.
HEALING?
YEAH, THANKS TO SHELLEY.
WHO IS SHE?
FATHER'S A GENETICIST. THE COMMITTEE KIDNAPPED HIM AT THE SAME TIME AS SIR JAMES TO REVERSE-ENGINEER THE ASTROLABE.

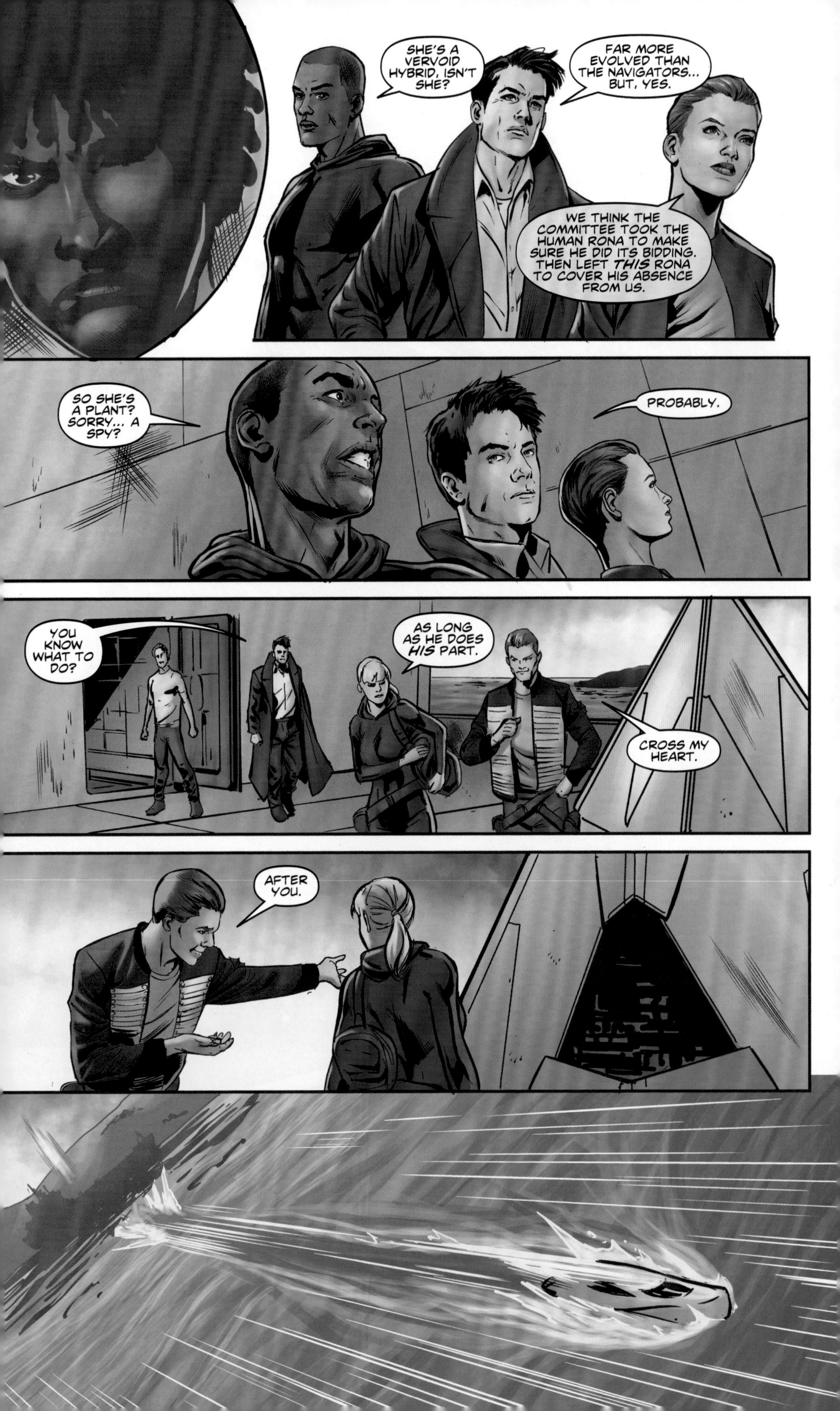
SHE'S A VERVOID HYBRID, ISN'T SHE?
FAR MORE EVOLVED THAN THE NAVIGATORS... BUT, YES.
WE THINK THE COMMITTEE TOOK THE HUMAN RONA TO MAKE SURE HE DID ITS BIDDING. THEN LEFT *THIS* RONA TO COVER HIS ABSENCE FROM US.
SO SHE'S A PLANT? SORRY... A SPY?
PROBABLY.
YOU KNOW WHAT TO DO?
AS LONG AS HE DOES *HIS* PART.
CROSS MY HEART.
AFTER YOU.

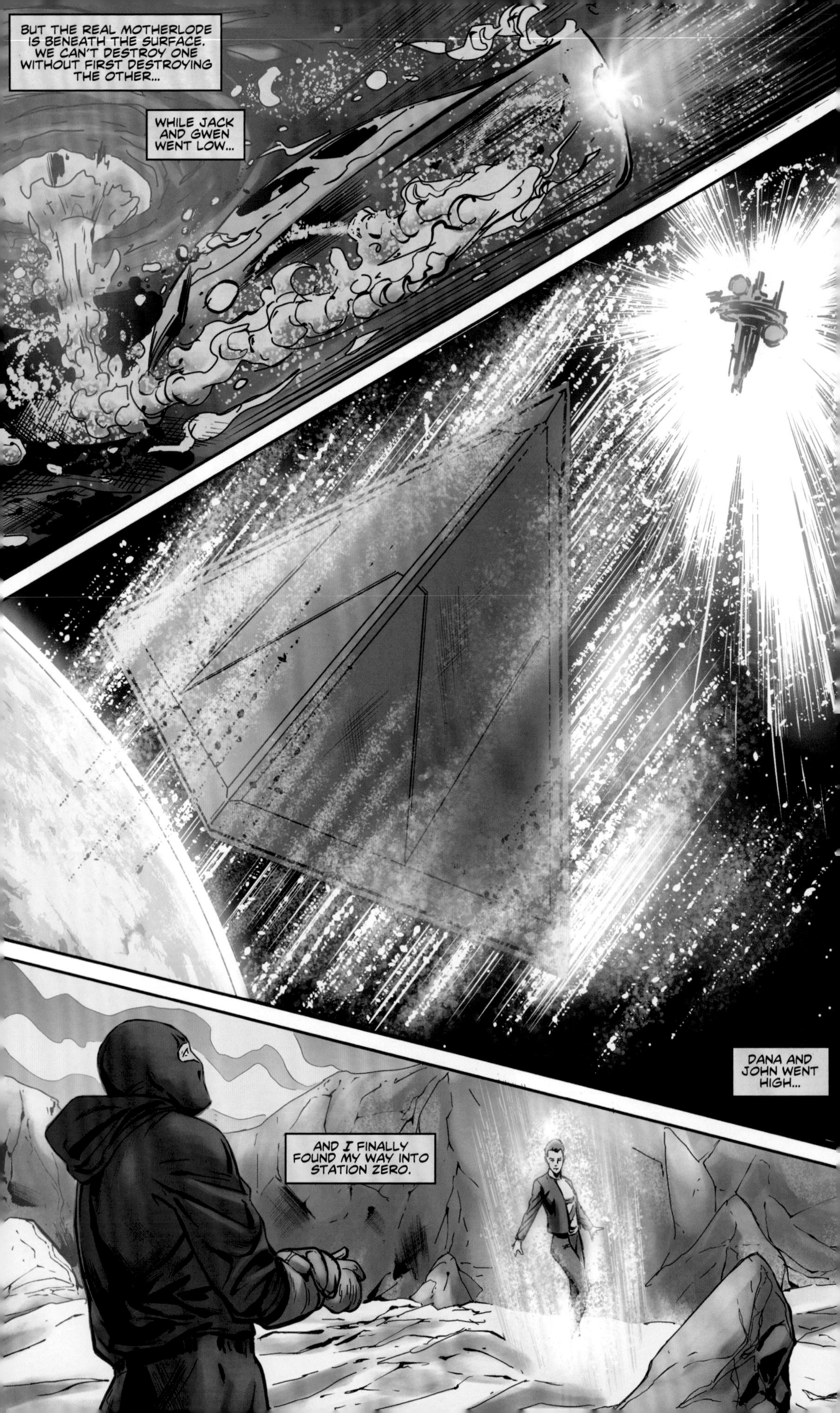
BUT THE REAL MOTHERLODE IS BENEATH THE SURFACE. WE CAN'T DESTROY ONE WITHOUT FIRST DESTROYING THE OTHER...
WHILE JACK AND GWEN WENT LOW...
DANA AND JOHN WENT HIGH...
AND I FINALLY FOUND MY WAY INTO STATION ZERO.

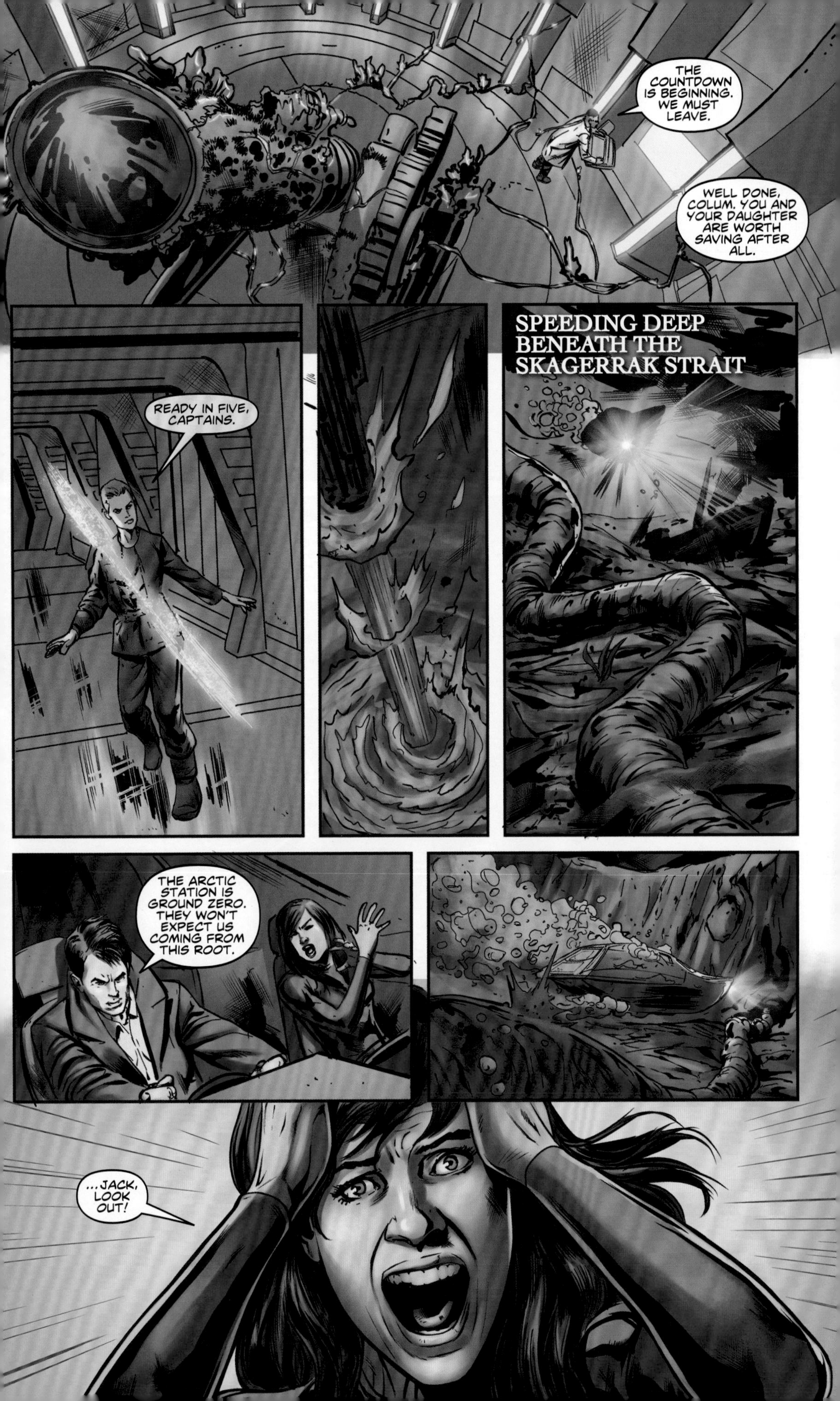

THE COUNTDOWN IS BEGINNING. WE MUST LEAVE.
WELL DONE, COLUM. YOU AND YOUR DAUGHTER ARE WORTH SAVING AFTER ALL.
READY IN FIVE, CAPTAINS.
SPEEDING DEEP BENEATH THE SKAGERRAK STRAIT
THE ARCTIC STATION IS GROUND ZERO. THEY WON'T EXPECT US COMING FROM THIS ROOT.
...JACK, LOOK OUT!

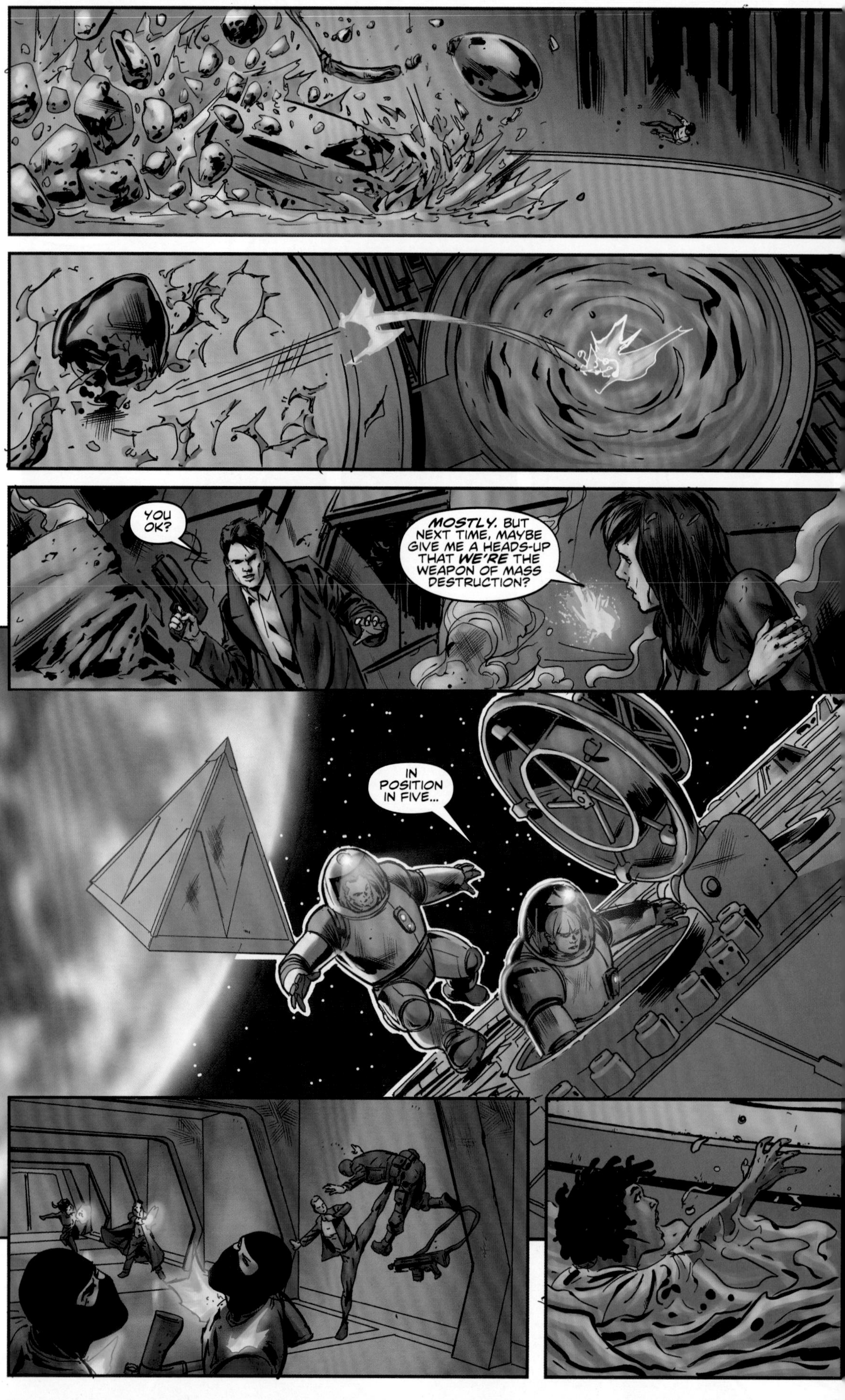
YOU OK?
MOSTLY. BUT NEXT TIME, MAYBE GIVE ME A HEADS-UP THAT WE'RE THE WEAPON OF MASS DESTRUCTION?
IN POSITION IN FIVE...

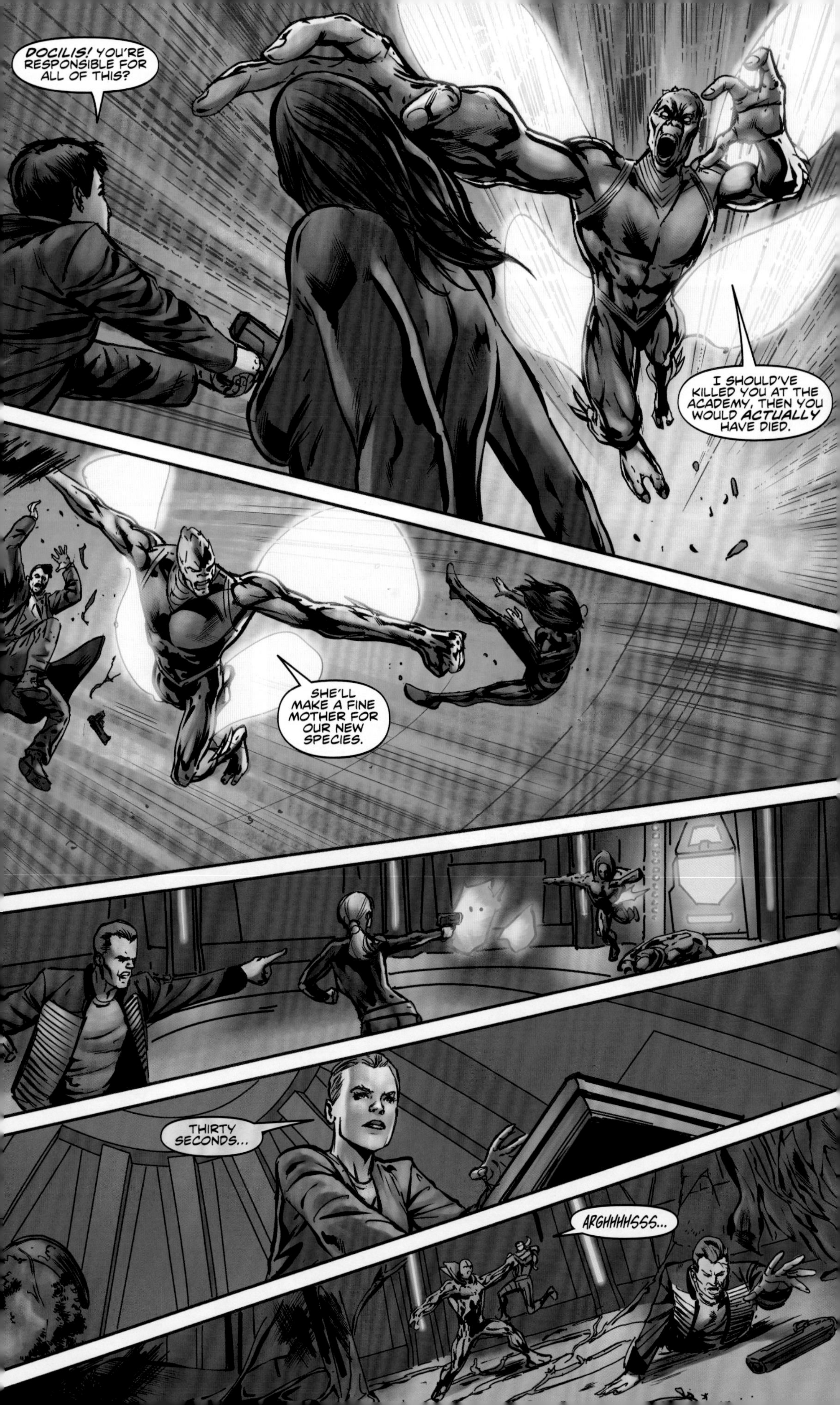
DOCILIS! YOU'RE RESPONSIBLE FOR ALL OF THIS?
I SHOULD'VE KILLED YOU AT THE ACADEMY, THEN YOU WOULD ACTUALLY HAVE DIED.
SHE'LL MAKE A FINE MOTHER FOR OUR NEW SPECIES.
THIRTY SECONDS...
ARGHHHHSSS...

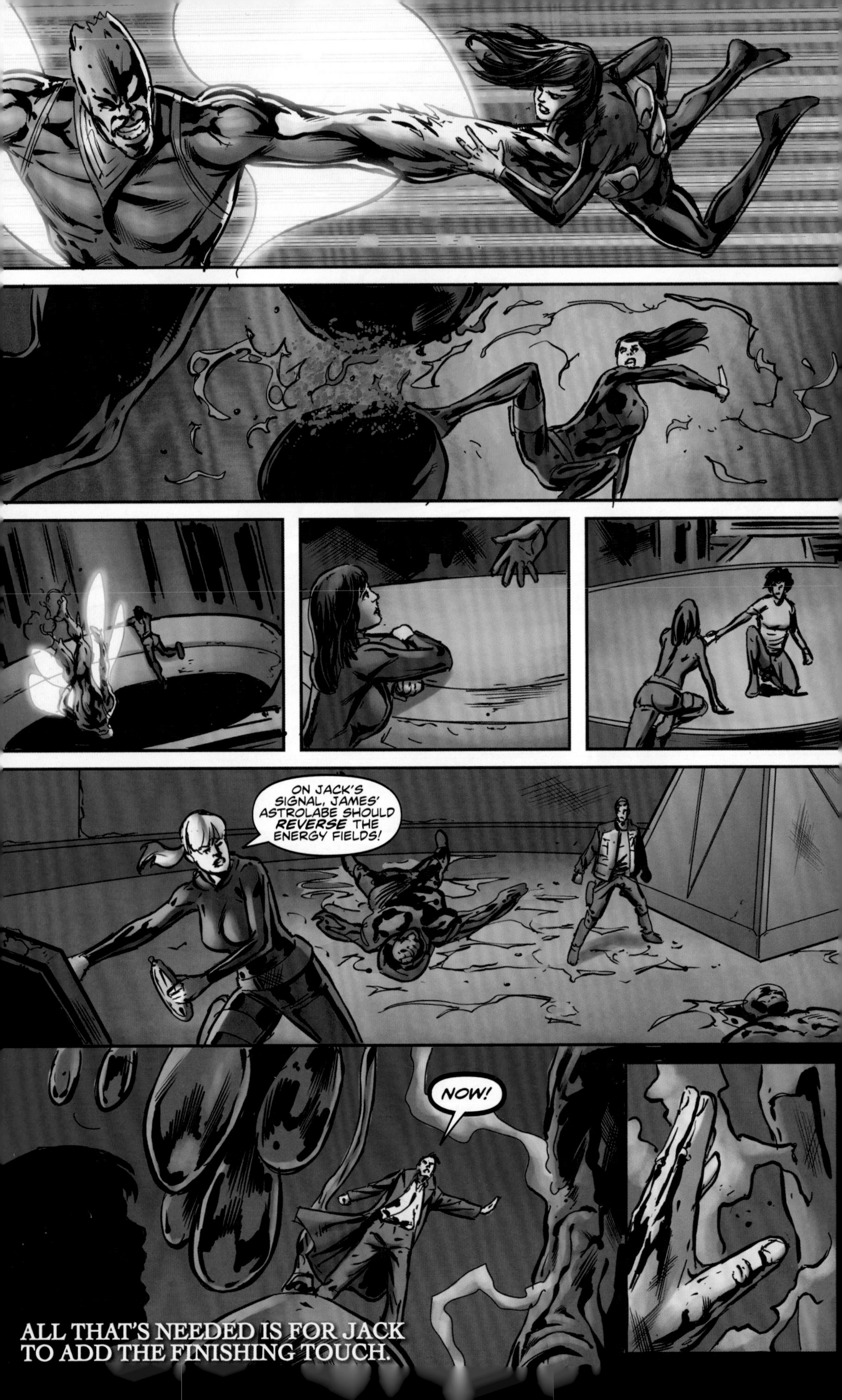
ON JACK'S SIGNAL, JAMES' ASTROLABE SHOULD REVERSE THE ENERGY FIELDS!
NOW!
ALL THAT'S NEEDED IS FOR JACK TO ADD THE FINISHING TOUCH.

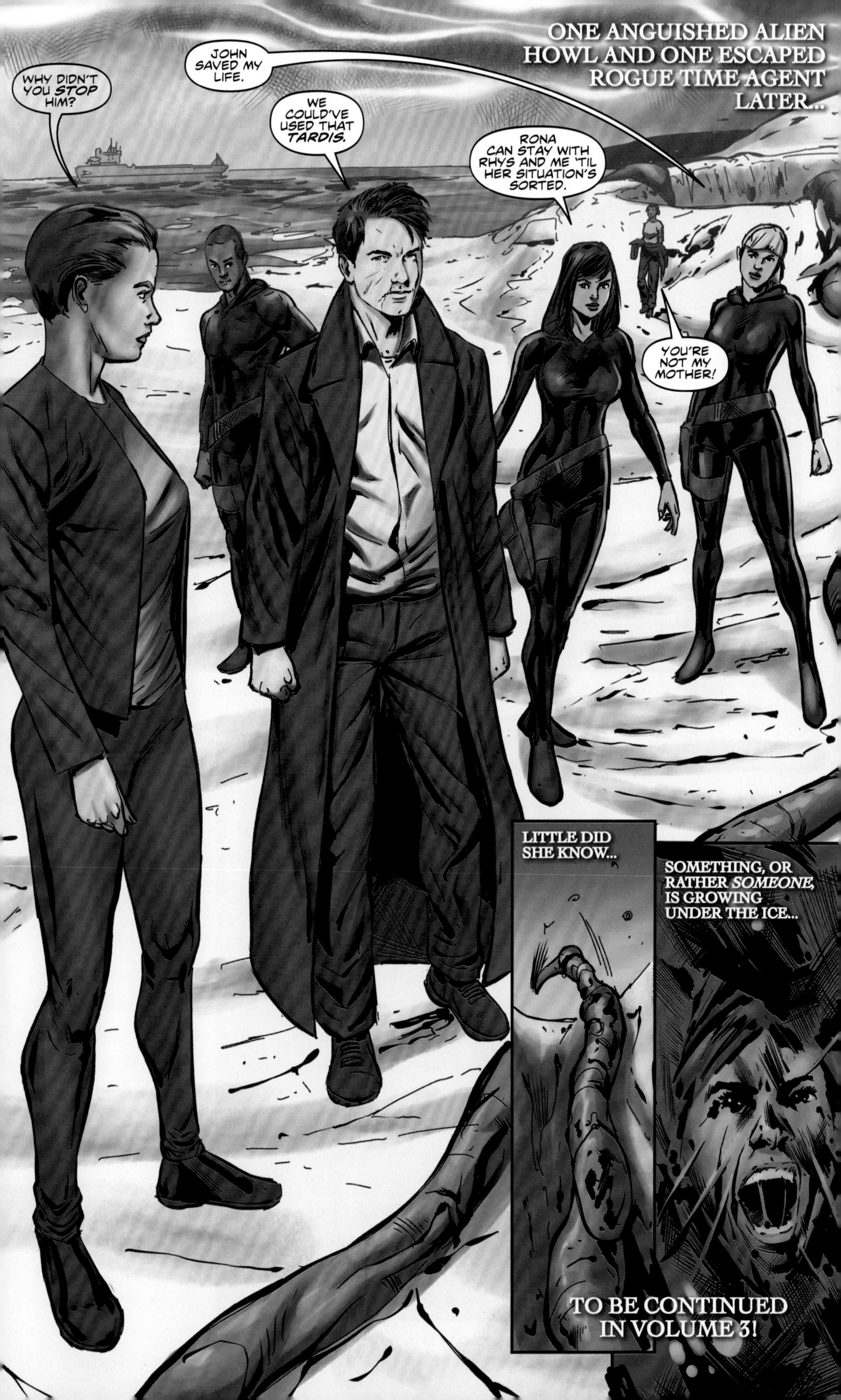
ONE ANGUISHED ALIEN HOWL AND ONE ESCAPED ROGUE TIME AGENT LATER...
WHY DIDN'T YOU STOP HIM?
JOHN SAVED MY LIFE.
WE COULD'VE USED THAT TARDIS.
RONA CAN STAY WITH RHYS AND ME 'TIL HER SITUATION'S SORTED.
YOU'RE NOT MY MOTHER!
LITTLE DID SHE KNOW...
SOMETHING, OR RATHER SOMEONE, IS GROWING UNDER THE ICE...
TO BE CONTINUED IN VOLUME 3!

COVER GALLERY

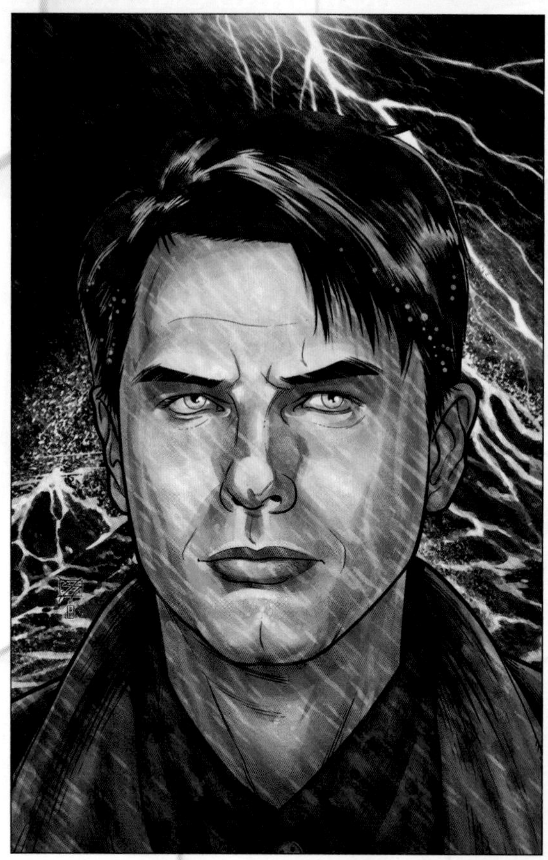

Issue 1 Cover A by BLAIR SHEDD

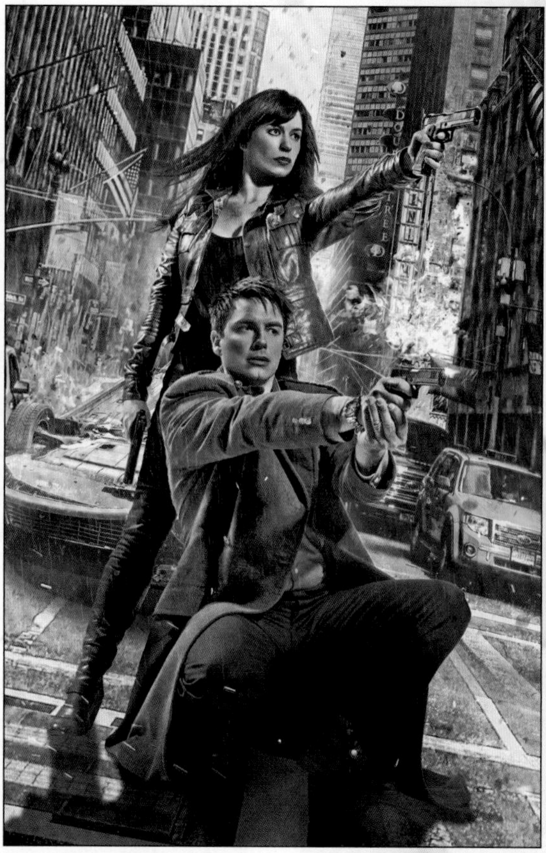

Issue 1 Cover B by WILL BROOKS

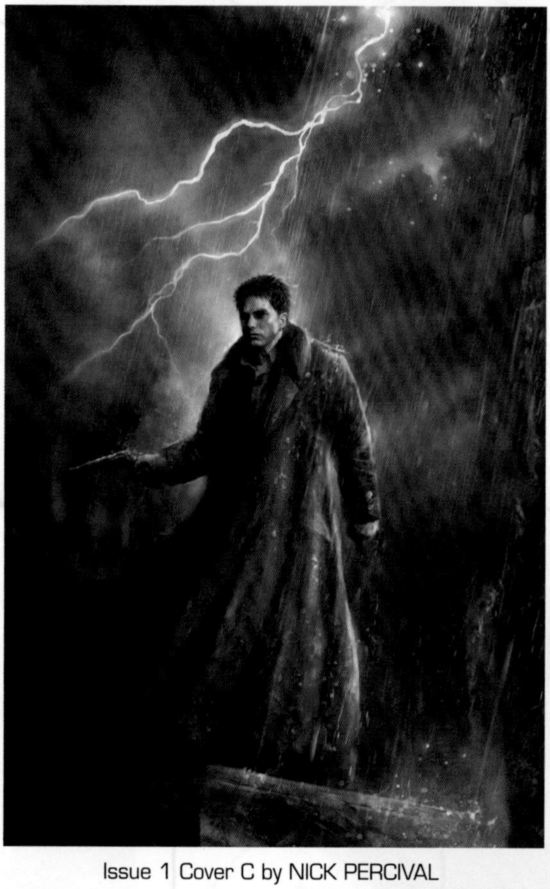

Issue 1 Cover C by NICK PERCIVAL

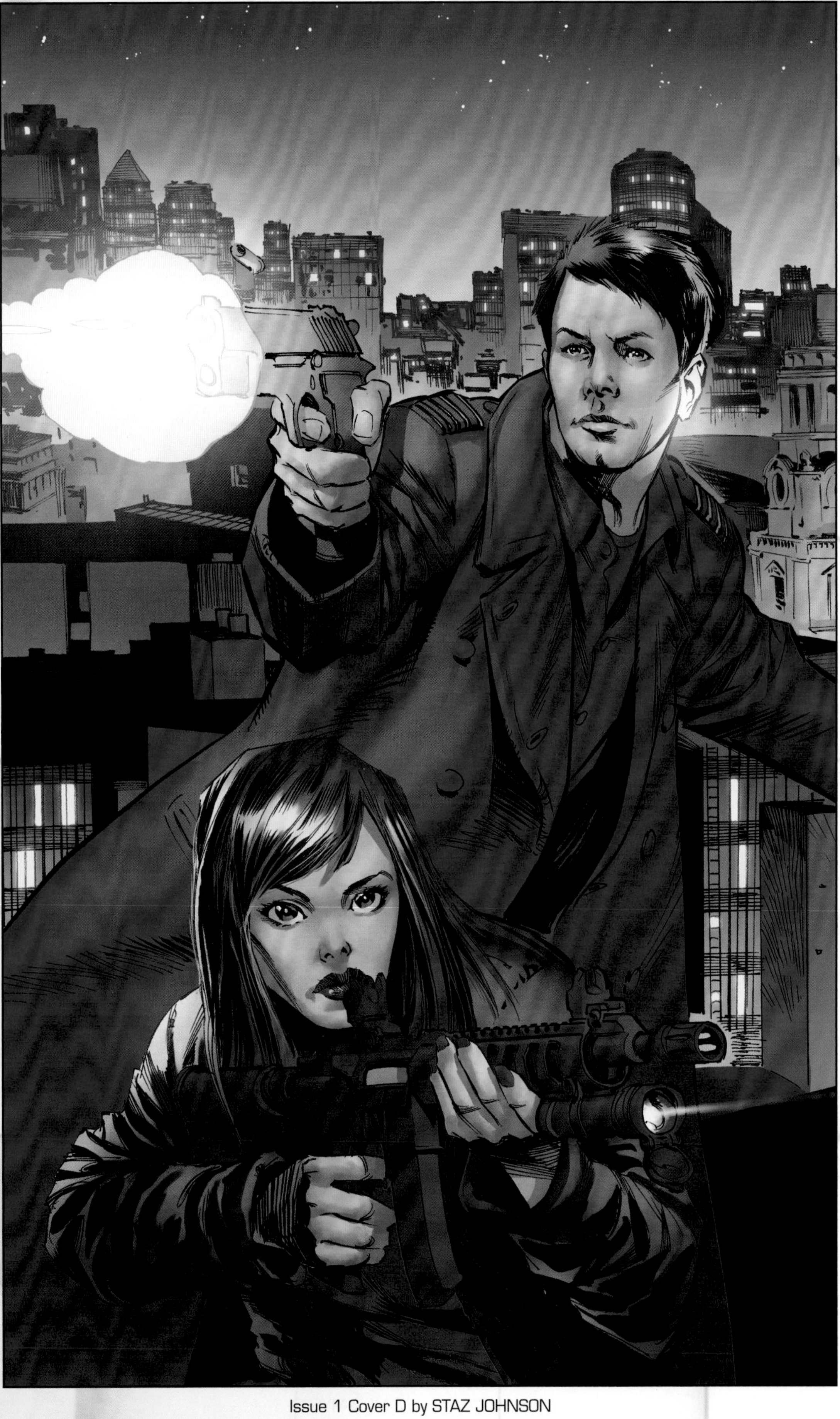

Issue 1 Cover D by STAZ JOHNSON

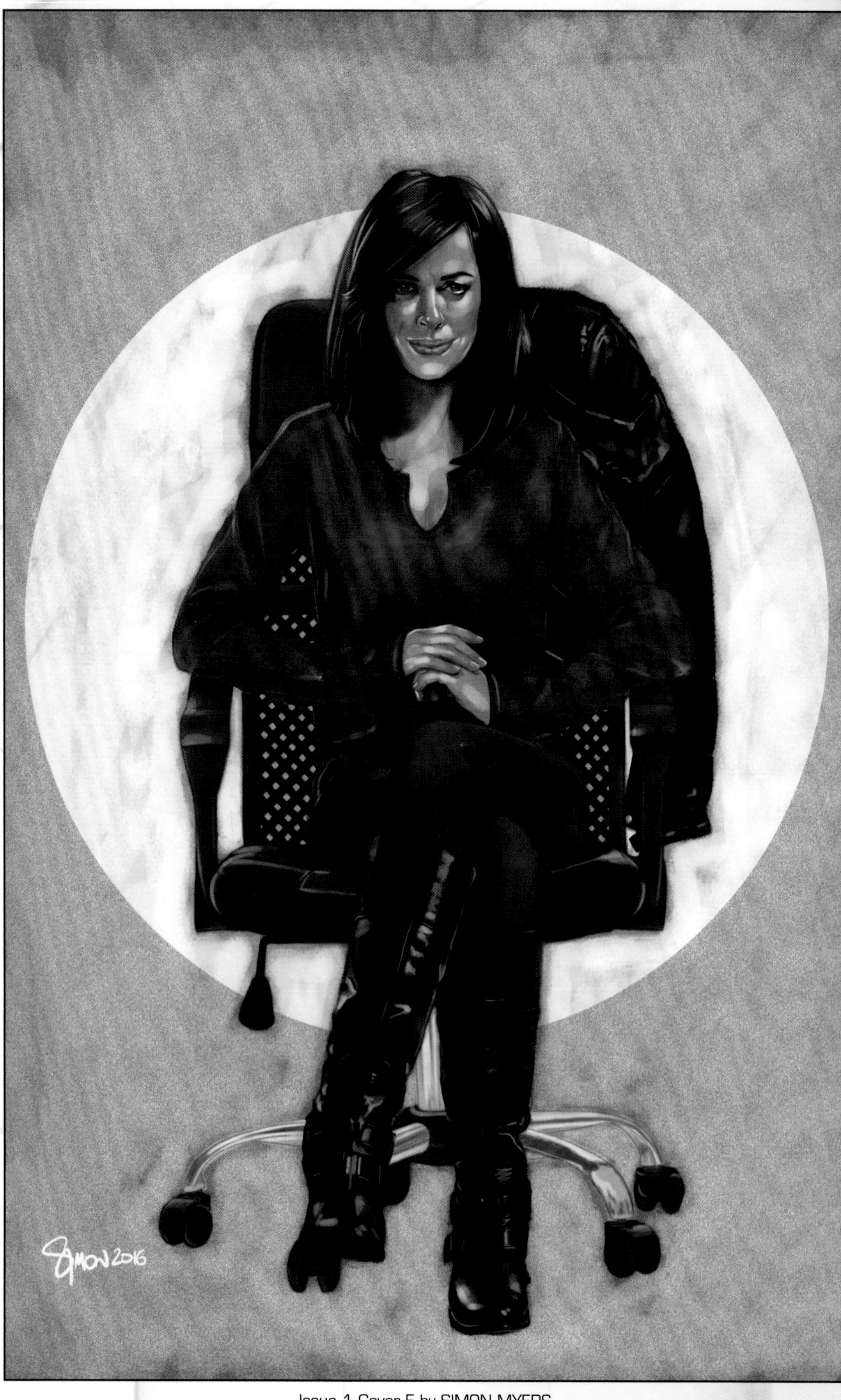
SIMON 2016

Issue 1 Cover E by SIMON MYERS

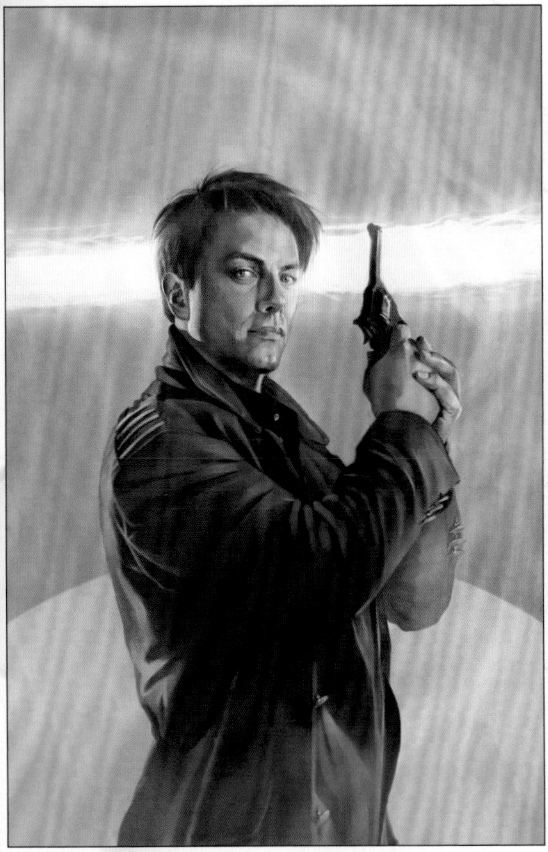

Issue 2 Cover A by CLAUDIA CARANFA

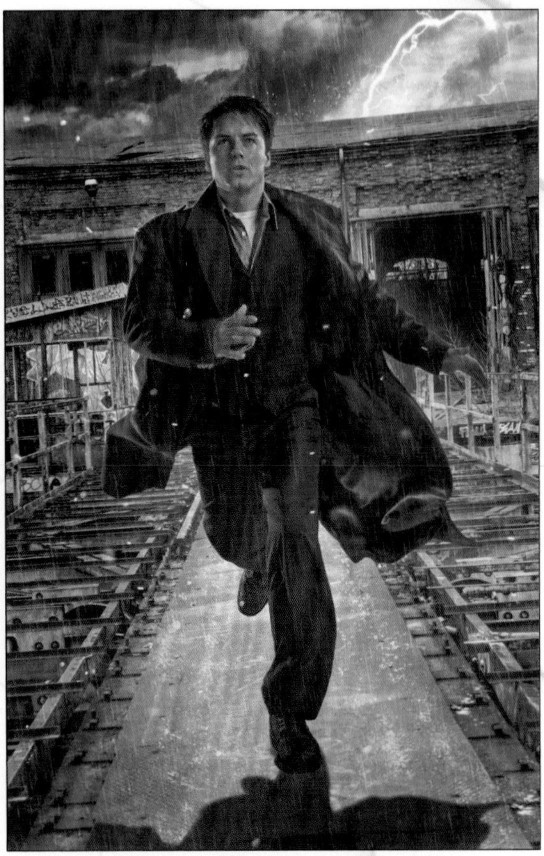

Issue 2 Cover B by WILL BROOKS

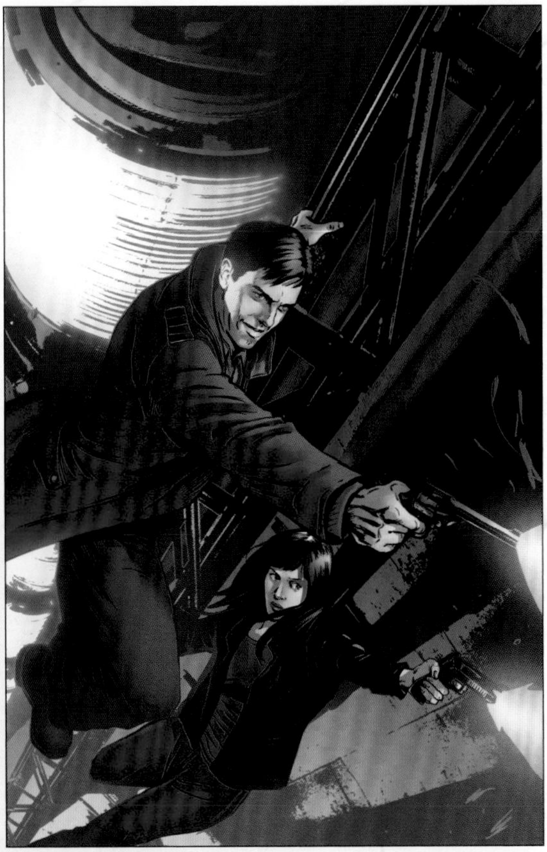

Issue 2 Cover C by BRIAN WILLIAMSON

Issue 2 Cover D by SIMON MYERS

Issue 3 Cover A by CLAUDIA CARANFA

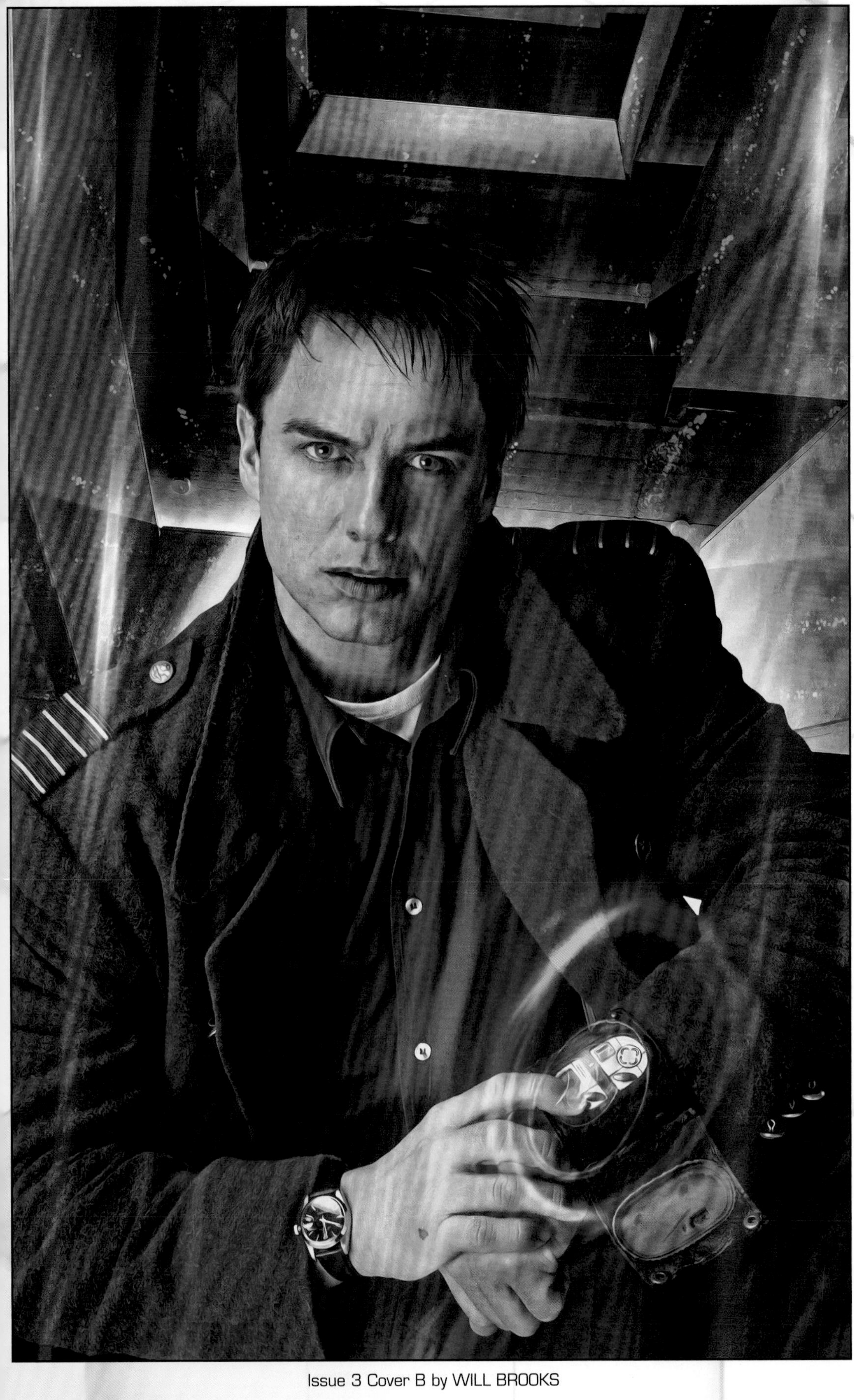

Issue 3 Cover B by WILL BROOKS

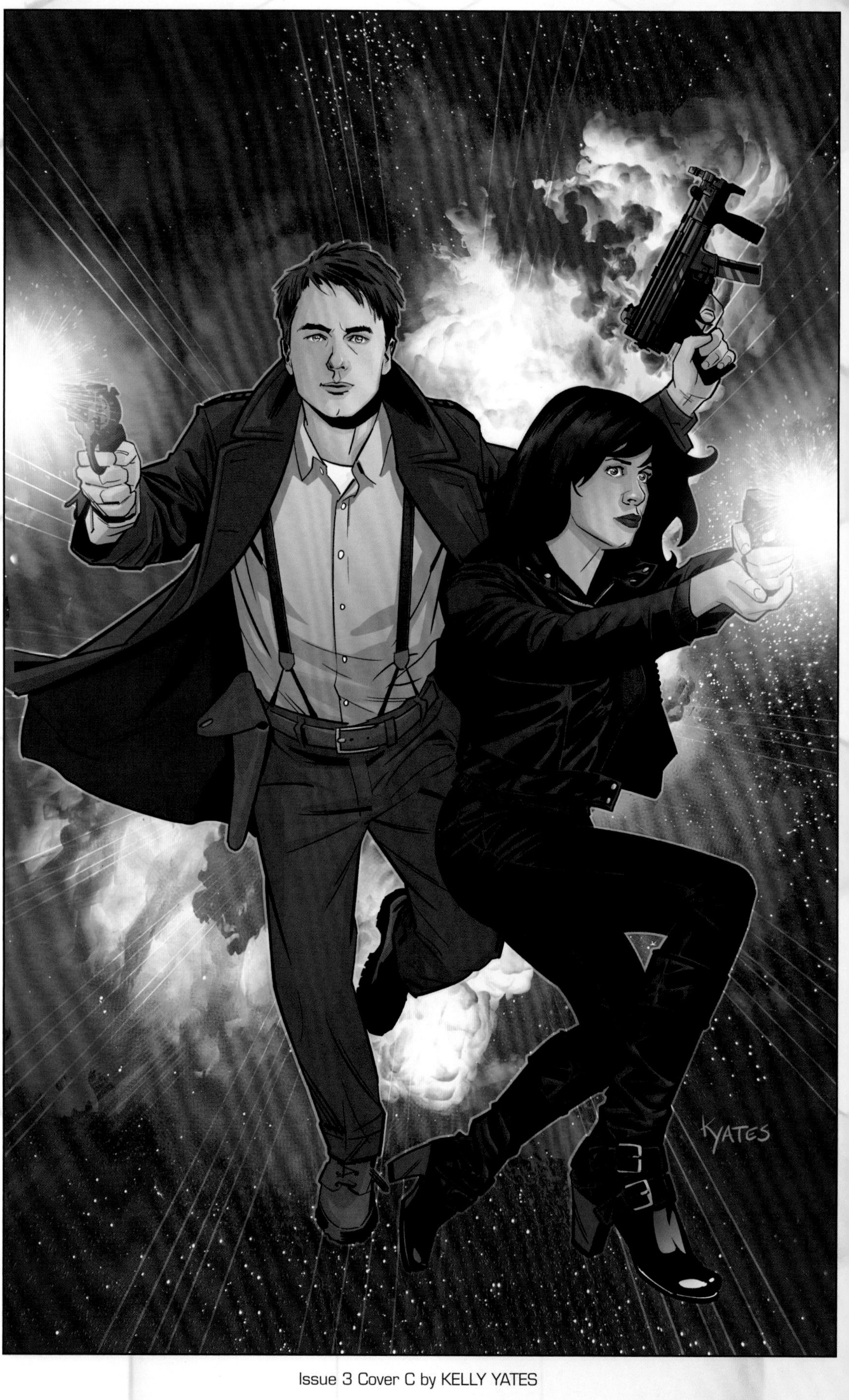
KYATES

Issue 3 Cover C by KELLY YATES

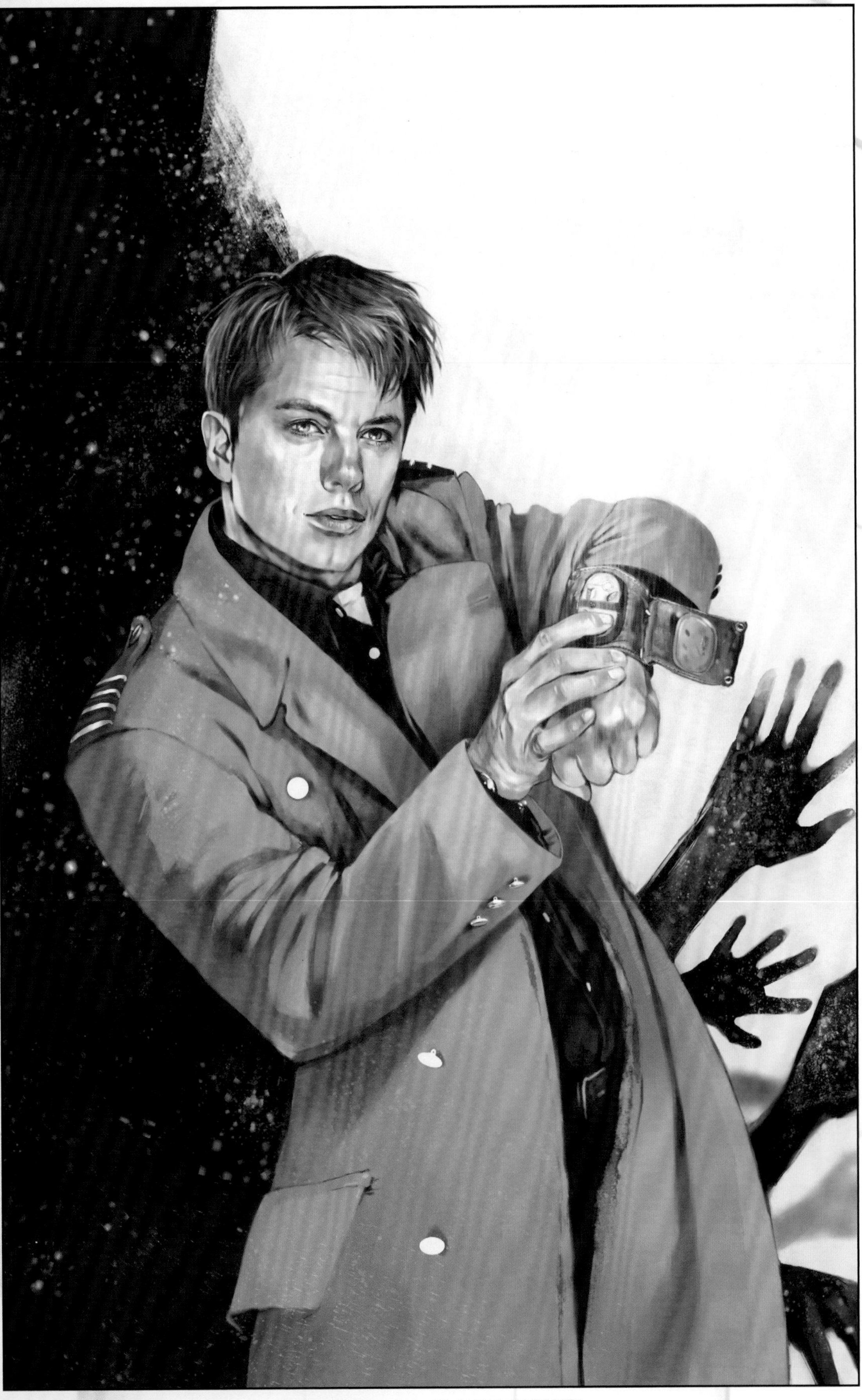

Issue 4 Cover A by CLAUDIA CARANFA

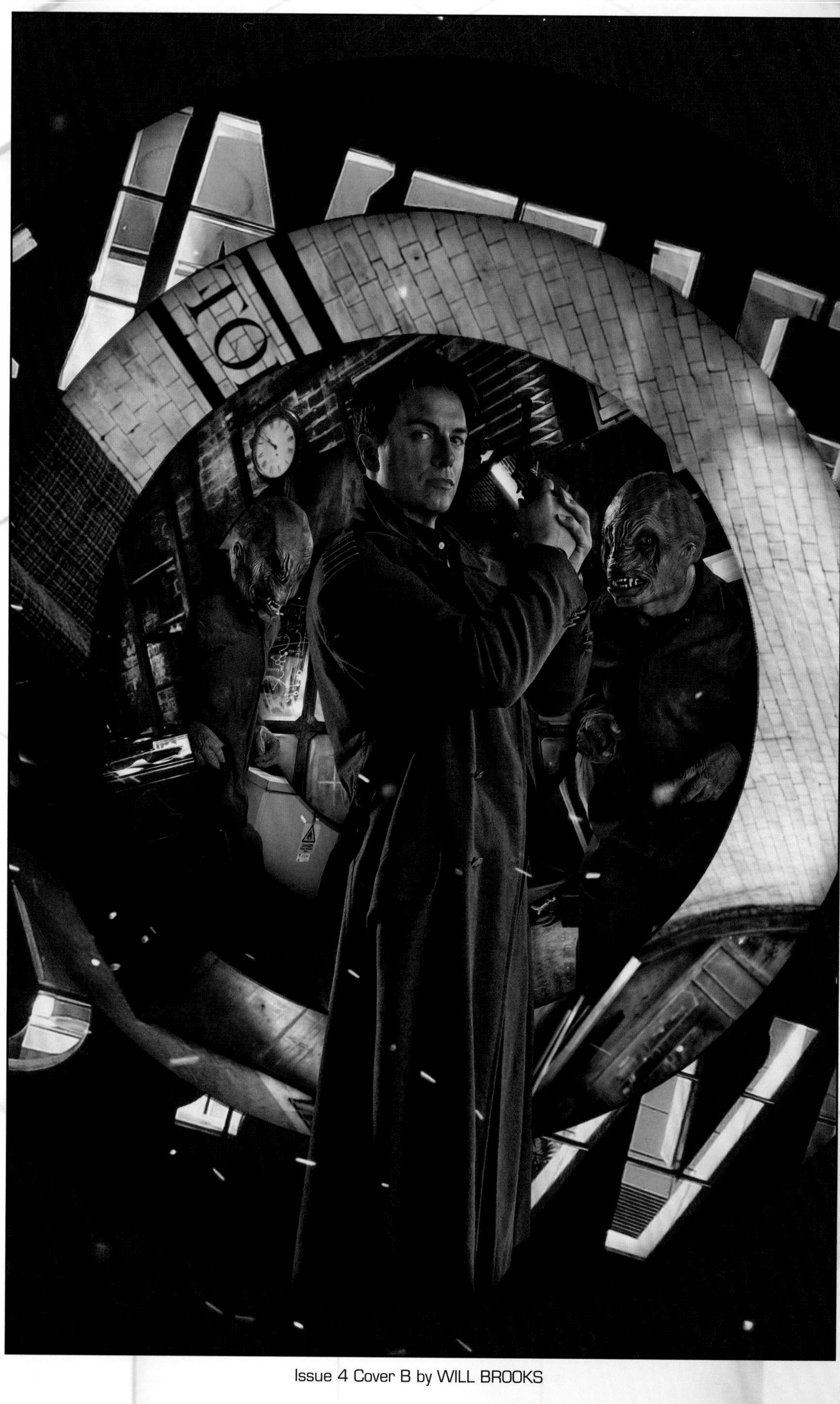
TO

Issue 4 Cover B by WILL BROOKS

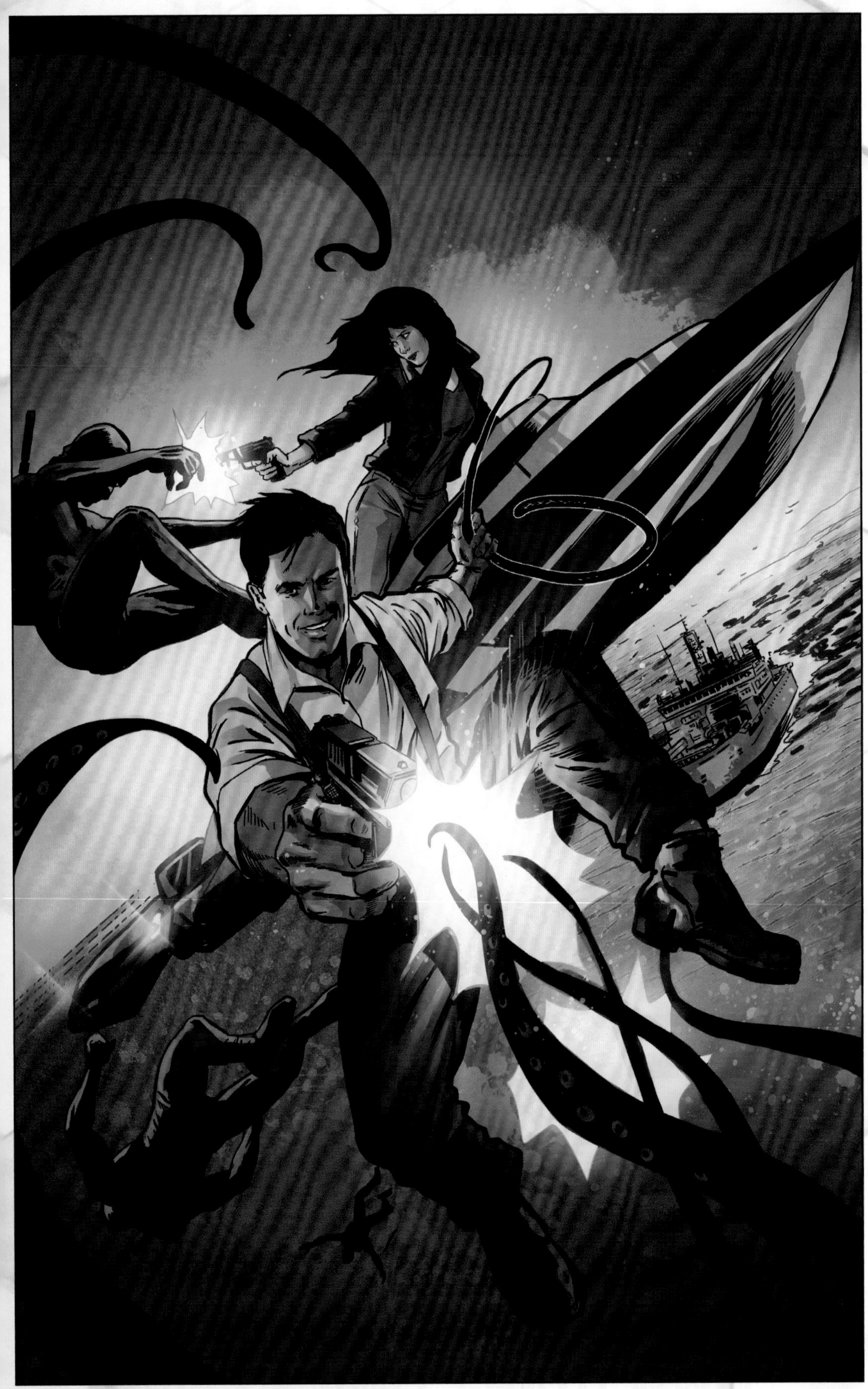

Issue 4 Cover C by BRIAN WILLIAMSON

COMING SOON!

AVAILABLE IN PRINT AND DIGITALLY
WWW.TITAN-COMICS.COM

JACK ATTACK!

As you'll have seen, this volume introduces a new artist to the *Torchwood* comic fold – Neil Edwards! Get an insight into what goes into the making of the art of the comic, with these character sketches of Jack himself!

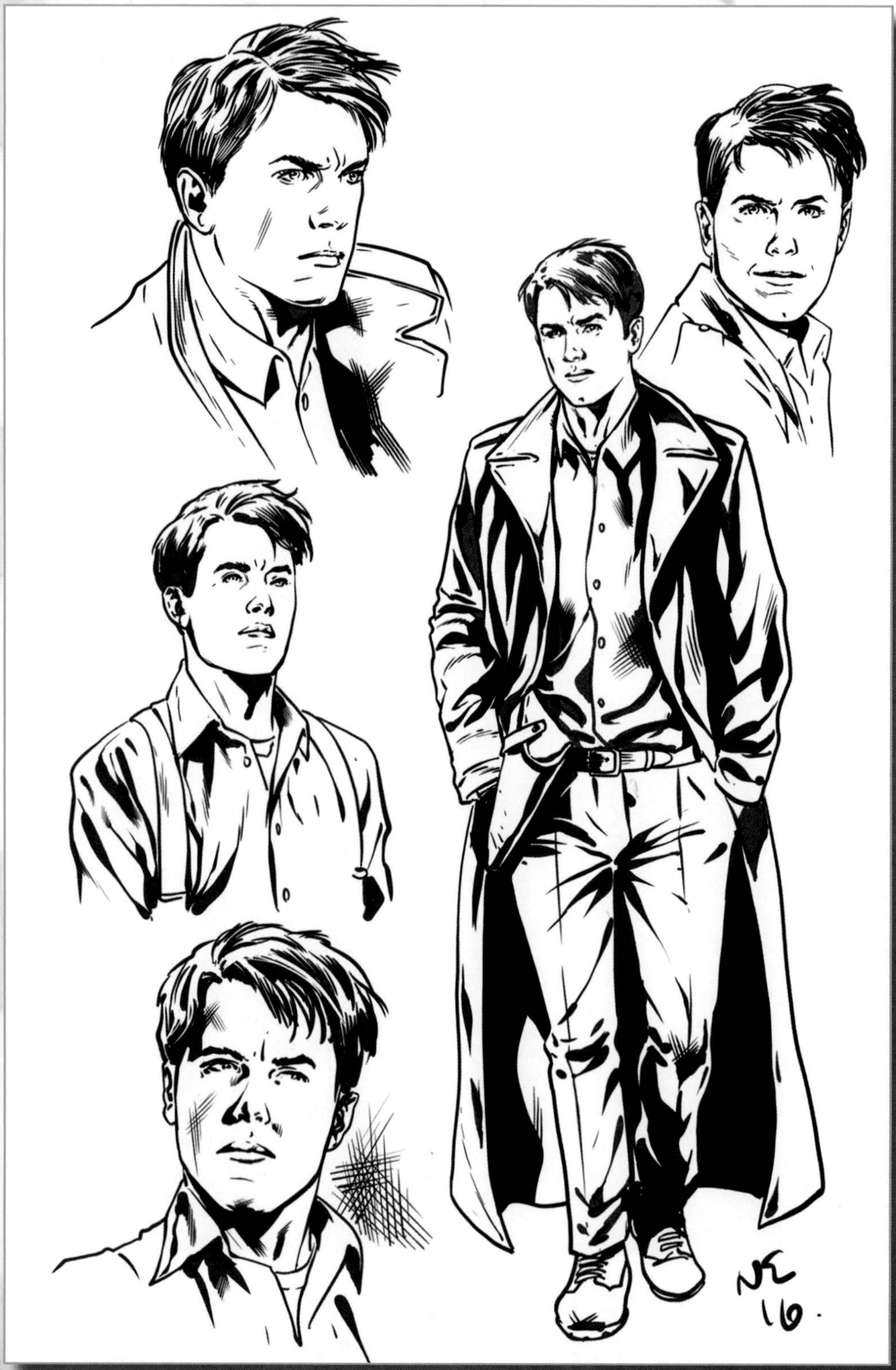

NE
16.

BIOS

JOHN AND CAROLE BARROWMAN

Siblings Carole and John Barrowman were born and raised in Glasgow, Scotland, emigrating to the US with their family in the late 1970s.

Carole and John have collaborated on a number of writing projects, including their latest novel, *Conjuror*; John's autobiographies, the first of which, *Anything Goes*, was a *Sunday Times* bestseller; a fantasy series *Hollow Earth*; and *Exodus Code*, a *Torchwood* novel.

John is a unique entertainer with a career that includes theater, television, music and film. He is currently starring as Malcolm Merlyn in *Arrow* and *Legends Of Tomorrow*, and is acclaimed for his portrayal of Captain Jack in both *Torchwood* and *Doctor Who*.

Carole is an English professor and Director of Creative Studies in Writing at Alverno College in Milwaukee, WI, writes a column for the *Milwaukee Journal Sentinel*, and reviews for the *Minneapolis Star Tribune*.

For more on their collaborations go to **www.barrowmanbooks.com**

NEIL EDWARDS

Neil Edwards is a comic book artist best known for his work on *Spider-Man, Dark Avengers, Fantastic Four and Herc* for Marvel Comics, *Justice League, Green Lanterns, Justice League United* and *Forever Evil: A.R.G.U.S.* for DC Comics and *Doctor Who* and *Assassin's Creed* for Titan Comics. He lives and works in North Wales.

NICOLA RIGHI

Born in Bolzano, Italy, Nicola Righi graduated from the International School of Comics in Florence in 2006 and began to work as a colorist in France and Italy for publishers such as Clair de Lune, Les Humanoïdes Associés and Panini.

In 2016, Righi began to work with Titan Comics on *Doctor Who* and *Torchwood*. At the moment he works regularly with Titan Comics, Sergio Bonelli Editore and Soleil Editions.